WILDFOWL
of the BRITISH ISLES
and NORTH-WEST EUROPE

WILDFOWL
of the BRITISH ISLES
and NORTH-WEST EUROPE

Brian P. Martin

Paintings by Alastair Proud

David & Charles

DEDICATED TO W. H. HUDSON

Frontispiece: eider ducks (see caption on page 126)

A DAVID & CHARLES BOOK

© Brian P. Martin, 1993
First published 1993

Brian P. Martin has asserted his right to be
identified as author of this work in accordance
with the Copyright, Designs and Patents Act
1988.

A catalogue record for this book is available
from the British Library.

ISBN 0 7153 9996 9

Typeset by ABM Typographics Ltd., Hull
and printed in Scotland by Bath Press Colourbooks
for David & Charles
Brunel House Newton Abbot Devon

CONTENTS

INTRODUCTION

THE aggressive, hybrid duck taking stale crusts on the town pond and the over-weight domestic goose waddling down the lane are sad reflections of the birds' ancestry. They are the products of man's close association with wildfowl stretching back many thousands of years. Yet, to the surprise of many people, the wildness of wildfowl lives on. Even in overcrowded Britain these often ridiculed birds continue their ancient ways, from the northern loch where the bugle cry of the migrant whooper swan heralds winter, to the bleak east coast where legions of grey geese battle against autumn gales, and secret, southern flightponds where the aerial mastery of teal puts the seal on any sunset.

In Britain the birds popularly known as wildfowl comprise the ducks, geese and swans, which are scientifically grouped together in the family *Anatidae* within the order *Anseriformes*. In the past, the name wildfowl often also included waders and other edible species, more in keeping with the popular North American term waterfowl.

The world has about 140 species of ducks, geese and swans and this book describes in detail the history and natural history of the 38 which currently regularly breed and/or overwinter in north-west Europe. In addition there are notes on species which have been introduced or are very rare visitors — the 'accidentals' or 'vagrants'.

These birds vary widely in many aspects, not least in size and colour, but they also share characters which usually make members of the group instantly recognisable. Probably the most familiar is the generally broad and flattened bill, which is adapted to water feeding and most marked in surface plankton feeders. Then there are those characteristic calls — especially the basic quacking of ducks and honking of geese, the webbed toes, relatively short legs, awkward waddle and dense, soft plumage best known through eiderdown.

Such characteristics have done much to promote the birds' popularity. For most of the twentieth century children have grown up with the cute, but often laughable image provided by fictional characters such as Donald Duck and Jemima Puddle-Duck. On the other hand, wildfowl are also strongly associated with grace and beauty, the ballet of Swan Lake being foremost in widespread artistic involvement.

Yet this image is mostly modern as man's ancient interest in wildfowl is primarily founded on food. Originally, most species were hunted and eaten by people whose chief concern was a full stomach. Even the mute swan became the focus of medieval banquets. But later, as alternative foods became available and tastes changed, man became more fussy and concentrated on culling those species which were more palatable.

Unfortunately for wildfowl, widespread drainage of their habitat, chiefly from the seventeenth century on, coincided with the arrival of reliable guns. Furthermore, although hunting for food really started to decline in the nineteenth century, the concept of hunting for sport was already well established. The net result was that the populations of many species started to decline alarmingly and with the birth of the conservation concept the wildfowler came under attack as one pressure too many.

Stimulating the interest of schoolchildren will improve long-term prospects for wildfowl. Photo: B. Martin

This century has seen bitter conflict as wildfowlers have tried to defend their ancient 'rights' against the tide of popular conservation. Fortunately, common sense appears to have prevailed and we now have a scientific rather than emotive approach which accommodates most interests. Accordingly, species which need it are protected by law and modern wildfowlers are among the greatest champions of their quarry, having already done much to preserve and create suitable habitat. Although theirs is undoubtedly a sport in the sense that they do not *need* to hunt for food, we have seen fresh revival of the belief that nothing should be shot unless it is eaten. Furthermore, there is a strong movement against the taking of large bags and limits are often voluntarily imposed.

Unfortunately, although the sale of wild geese was outlawed long ago, the sale of goose shooting continues to threaten some populations through excessive disturbance and over-exploitation. An unscrupulous minority of landowners and their agents have also promoted for gain the licensed shooting of otherwise protected species, which is totally alien to the spirit of the law. It is also regrettable that many countries — even in north-west Europe — have a less well-developed custodial attitude towards wildfowl, so many protected birds continue to be shot while on migration.

After protracted argument, it now seems likely that lead shot will disappear — at least from wildfowl haunts — within a few years. Even if it is not entirely outlawed there is growing acceptance of the need to develop non-toxic alternatives. We already have strong precedents in the banning of lead shot in North America, where wildfowling is a major interest, and the recent phasing out of some anglers' lead weights in Britain.

Most importantly, both wildfowlers and conservationists are united in their efforts to save wildfowl habitat, which continues to be our chief concern. Creation of more refuges and the designation of further special protection areas (marine as well as coastal and inland) are essential to safeguard the future of many species. At the same time there must be constant scrutiny and control of agriculture and exploitation of land and sea to ensure that we avoid further environmental

*A rapid increase in the
number of bird-watchers
has led to improved
censusing. Photo:
B. Martin*

catastrophes. Wildfowl are especially vulnerable in that most species are highly gregarious and where they concentrate accidental mortality, such as through oil pollution or ingestion of agrochemicals, is always likely to be on a large scale.

Ironically, the attractiveness of wildfowl has brought them mixed blessings. In past centuries many exotic species were introduced to grace the lakes of great estates, and in the twentieth century many waterfowl collections have been formed, sometimes simply for sheer personal pleasure, but also for commercial gain or breeding and scientific research. Sadly, whatever the motives, the fact remains that many birds have escaped or been deliberately released to form feral populations, often resulting in unwanted pressure on native species or agricultural damage. As usual, legislation has attempted to close the stable door after the horse has bolted, but in some cases the situation seems irreversible.

These and many other threats, such as the rapid growth of water-sports, are discussed in the species accounts. These also give considerable historical background in an attempt to put current status in perspective. In this, it is important to note that population counts (in which Iberia is not included in north-west Europe) offer only a guide to trends rather than great accuracy. However, it is heartening to report that for wildfowl generally the tide has clearly turned and the majority of species appear to be in the ascendancy. It is up to all of us to maintain the momentum. But even then these birds will need the luck of the weather, so next time you snap the wishbone of your Christmas goose pray for the wild ones on their arctic breeding grounds.

BRIAN P. MARTIN
Brook, Surrey

MUTE SWAN
(Cygnus olor)

THIS largest of British birds is far from numerous, but its tameness and conspicuousness have made it familiar to everyone. In legend, literature and the arts it has long been regarded as the epitome of grace and beauty, an abiding symbol of rural tranquillity, yet for a thousand years its main attraction was on the dining table.

MUTE SWAN
Once known as wild swan, domestic swan and tame swan. Traditionally, the male is called a cob, the female a pen and young a cygnet

History and Conservation

In Britain, the mute swan's history does not appear to be anything like as long as that of the whooper and Bewick's swans. The earliest records are from the Bronze and Iron Ages, when it was found in East Anglia and Somerset. Presumably it does not occur alongside the migratory swans in glacial deposits because it is a bird of mainly temperate latitudes whereas they are more northerly breeders. However, it would be surprising if it were not in Britain during at least some of the warmer phases which occurred long before man made weapons to kill it.

Today, the tame birds which we encounter in much of western Europe and other parts of the world, where the species has been introduced, can seem a poor reflection of the wild, migratory populations, chiefly to the east. Man soon discovered that young swans were easy to tame so swan-keeping was seen as a source of ready meat. A large roast swan made a fitting centre-piece even for a medieval banquet, so from the tenth century the birds were status symbols and live ones gradually became 'owned' by holders of freehold land. Strays were deemed to be

In Victorian times wildfowlers shot almost anything, as can be seen in this engraving

9

MUTE SWAN

On discovering that his previous term — 'tame swan' — was inadequate, Pennant introduced 'mute swan' in 1785 — 'as this species emits no sound'. However, I cannot believe that he was ignorant of the bird's considerable vocabulary and can only imagine that he wanted to stress the lack of strong, musical calls possessed by other swans. Indeed, the word 'mute' seems even sillier when it is realised that the old Anglo-Saxon word 'swan' itself means 'sounder', which has the same base as the word sound. The Latin specific *olor* simply means swan because this was the *common* swan and the first to be scientifically described.

Even without the culinary interest, mute swans have remained popular as outdoor ornaments and are found in innumerable waterfowl collections. To quote Bewick, the swan 'throws himself into numberless graceful attitudes, as if desirous of attracting the admiration of the spectator'.

the property of the Crown and protected by law. This was no toothless legislation either: Henry VII imposed a sentence of imprisonment for a year and a day, plus a fine, simply for stealing a swan's egg! In due course swans were only assigned to others by royal licence and marked accordingly by unique cuts on their foot-webs or bills. Their value was further enhanced by their place in superstition and ceremony. Edward I had a swan as his badge and when he knighted his son two swans were brought to Westminster, 'gorgeously caparisoned, their beaks gilt', and upon these the King took an oath against the Scots.

Swan-keeping became so widespread — during the reign of Queen Elizabeth I there were over 900 recognised swan marks! — that the histories of the wild and tame birds are not easy to separate. However, we do know that the practice declined rapidly in the eighteenth century through increasing expense and competition with foods such as the domesticated goose and turkey (introduced in the sixteenth century), which were easier to manage and increasingly cheap. In 1801, Thomas Bewick wrote: 'Swans are not nearly so common now as they were formerly, being by most people accounted a coarse kind of food . . . but the cygnets are still fattened for the table, and are sold very high, commonly for a guinea each . . .'

Even when traditional swan-keeping died out, the Crown retained the right to the swans on the Thames between London Bridge and Henley-on-Thames, which it now shares with the Dyers Company and the Vintners Company, who have held traditional swan feasts for over 400 years. To prepare for such meals, succulent cygnets were put in special fenced pits containing a pond (or 'stew') to be fattened on grain.

On the Thames young birds still have their bills marked according to ownership during the annual 'swan-upping', but they have not been pinioned since 1978. They are rounded up and counted in July, when the adults are in wing-moult and the cygnets not yet fledged.

As Bewick said, '. . . this species cannot properly be called domesticated; they are only partly reclaimed from a state of nature'. They were not usually confined and, even though hampered by pinioning, most could choose their own mates. Thus, despite their tameness, British swans generally retain most of their original vigour and flock only in winter or as non-breeders, unlike truly domesticated animals, which are easily herded throughout the year. It is true that the monks at Abbotsbury managed to repress some of the male's territoriality, but only through the persistent selection of less aggressive males for breeding and supplying plenty of food to minimise competition.

The first systematic survey of the British mute swan population, in 1955–6, was stimulated by farmers' complaints of greatly increased crop damage and fishermen's worries about the impact of swans on fish reproduction. It revealed a population of 19,900–21,600, figures confirmed by another survey in 1961. But a third survey in 1967 revealed 25 per cent decline 1961–5. Collision with overhead wires accounted for 44 per cent of deaths *reported*, but in considering *overall* mortality the exceptionally cold winters of 1961–2 and 1962–3 were probably more significant.

Total numbers then remained fairly constant, but only because success in some areas masked sinister decrease elsewhere. Eventually, accelerating decline (estimated at 8–15 per cent 1955–81) prompted thorough investigation, especially in the English Midlands and along the Thames, where the fall had been greatest. It was discovered that every year between 3,370 and 4,190 swans were

dying unnecessarily as a result of ingesting anglers' split shot or leger weights. The birds appear to take the shot in mistake for plant seed or grit, which they need to break down food for digestion. Sudden increase in mortality was accounted for by the great increase in numbers of anglers and their willingness to accept the loss of ever cheaper tackle. Accumulations of lead shotgun pellets appear to have been far less of a problem for swans because they mostly sink out of sight whereas anglers' split shot is often visible on lost and discarded line.

Not surprisingly, anglers and the angling trade were slow to accept the introduction of alternatives to lead, many still insisting that the decrease in numbers of swans was mainly due to habitat deterioration, pollution (partly through leaded petrol used by power-craft), loss of waterweed and greatly increased disturbance by leisure-craft. No doubt these factors have played their part but, from 1987, the Government banned the supply or import of lead weights of 0.6–56.7g (up to 2oz), which were found to be the biggest killers. Although they never outlawed the use or possession of weights which had already been stockpiled, legislation was strengthened by the later prohibition of lead by water companies and other coarse-fishery owners. Happily, the measures have already resulted in a significant reduction in the incidence of lead poisoning of mute swans. Recent population increases have been greatest in those areas where lead poisoning had been a problem. For example, numbers have doubled in Surrey and parts of the Midlands. However, there have also been increases in areas where lead has not been a problem, perhaps partly through a succession of mild winters.

Although the future now looks bright for the mute swan, some are still being poisoned by anglers' lead weights, which are easily made at home from scrap

11

The mute swan is widespread and resident throughout most of the British Isles, avoiding only areas above about 300m (985ft) or lacking any fertile fresh water, chiefly in parts of south-west England, Wales, the Highlands, western Scotland and higher parts of Ireland. Greatest numbers occur in lowland river basins. In Scotland, it is abundant in the Uists and Benbecula and thrives on Orkney. Distribution scarcely changes throughout the year.

In 1986 the total Irish population was estimated at over 7,000 birds and the British at 3,150 breeding pairs plus 12,600 non-breeders. In 1990 Britain had an estimated 25,000-plus birds, with a further 3,500 in Northern Ireland. Autumn and winter counts confirmed continuing increase 1990–91. No British resort attracted a flock of 1,800 for international importance, but Lough Neagh/Beg held 1,205, giving a five-year average maximum of 1,226. Other nationally important sites and average maxima 1986–91 were: The Fleet/Wey 906, Abberton Reservoir 540, Ouse Washes 489, Colne Estuary 386, Christchurch Harbour 365, Upper Lough Erne 332, Lough of Harray 329 (a spectacular flock of 1,205 in October 1990), Tweed Estuary 309, Stour Estuary 287, Somerset Levels 286, Loch Bee 281, Rutland Water 280, Loch Eye 261, Thames Estuary 235, Strangford Lough 190, River Welland: Spalding 189 and River Avon: Fordingbridge 189. Other sites holding over 180 in 1990–91 were: Loch of Skene with 275, Derwent Water 266 and Fairburn Ings 197.

metal. Furthermore, lead split-shot is still sold legally in Ireland, a favourite haunt of many British anglers. Fortunately, lead poisoning is not a major problem in Scotland, where fly-fishing predominates, but oil pollution is a substantial threat there. Among the most serious incidents was one on the Cromarty Firth in 1974, when many of the 126 swans oiled died or had to be destroyed, and about 70 died when 209 were badly affected on the Montrose Basin in 1980. Collision with overhead wires continues to kill many swans throughout north-west Europe, but it is hoped that, in Britain at least, the marking of wires at trouble spots will alleviate the problem.

Distribution, Habitat and Population

With so many introductions throughout western and central Europe from the sixteenth century on, it is not easy to distinguish between wild and semi-feral stocks. However, the species is certainly indigenous to many parts of Eurasia, where it is now patchily distributed through mainly temperate middle latitudes in both oceanic and continental climates. It has also been introduced to North America, Australia, New Zealand, South Africa and the Faeroes. Wild birds in eastern Europe avoid man and breed in widely scattered pairs on large, open lakes with extensive shallows and rich vegetation; also sluggish rivers, river deltas, brackish lagoons, saltwater creeks and quiet coasts. In contrast, west European birds have become accustomed to the proximity of man and thrive on almost any natural or artificial water where there is sufficient food, often depending on hand-outs. However, deep waters lacking vegetation are avoided. In some areas it is wholly migratory, in others sedentary or partly migratory.

Since the 1950s there has been a large increase in the breeding population throughout Europe, much of which has shared Britain's run of mild winters, strengthening of legislative protection and general improvement in habitat management. The trend continues despite occasional cold spells. In Denmark the species was virtually extinct in the 1920s, but now it has colonised all suitable areas. Norway has been colonised since the war and now has a thriving population in the south. Numbers throughout southern Sweden have expanded greatly since the 1950s. This has probably helped increase in south-east Finland, where breeding was first recorded in 1934 following introduction to the Aland Islands. Further expansion northwards in Scandinavia is unlikely because of the great mortality in severe winters. Spread throughout the whole of the Netherlands since 1947 largely derives from feral stock. There is a strong population in Germany, where there has been gastronomic interest since medieval times, and that in France has expanded considerably since the 1970s. With relatively little suitable habitat, Switzerland provides the exception, its population necessarily remaining small since first introduction in 1690. In 1986 the north-west European winter population was estimated at 120,000, but is now likely to be well over 150,000.

Field Characters

With its gracefully curved neck, frequently arched wings and red-orange bill, the mute swan is easily distinguished from the whooper and Bewick's swans, which have black-and-yellow bills, much straighter necks and wings and much quieter wing-beats. There are no seasonal plumage variations and the only difference between the sexes is that the male usually has a larger black bill knob, which becomes bigger at the start of the breeding season. The juvenile is mostly grey-brown above and whitish below, with some white on the face, wing coverts and lower back. Its feet are grey turning black and its bill (lacking the knob) is grey, becoming suffused with pink and later dull orange. The plumage becomes increasingly white during the first winter and spring, but some birds still have brownish upperparts in their second winter. The 'Polish swan' morph is all white from its first down. Many birds have stained plumage.

On land the mute swan moves slowly and clumsily with a waddle, but on water it is very graceful with curved neck, down-pointed bill and frequently raised wings. It swims well, even on rough coastal waters, but the adult rarely dives. Take-off is awkward from both land and water, needing a long run with heavy flapping and noisy pattering across the surface to get the heavy body airborne. In flight the neck is extended like other swans and the wing-beats are slow and regular, producing a musical throbbing sound which is peculiar to this species and heard over long distances. Parties usually fly in diagonal lines, wild birds often at considerable height but tame ones mostly much lower. Breeding pairs are often isolated, but in winter flocks of 100 or more are common. This is an aggressive species, even towards man in the breeding season.

As its name suggests, the mute swan is mostly silent at all times, but it does have a variety of hoarse snorting, snoring, grunting and hissing sounds, mostly used during the breeding season and audible only at fairly close quarters. The hiss (heard from about ten days old) is used readily when threatened. Perhaps the sound of the wings compensates for the lack of a true contact flight-call. Other calls include a hoarse, muted trumpeting, a crude whistle (recalling wigeon), piping and gurgling. Wilder birds in the east and north of the range are said to have a loud, resonant cry like that of the crane. The cygnets utter a soft, goose-like contact call in a short series; a louder, rising-and-falling greeting call; a soft, low, sighing trill; and a high-pitched, persistent, peeping distress call.

Breeding

The pair-bond is mostly long-term, monogamous and year-round, although one English study of birds over six years old found a divorce rate of 3 per cent among pairs which had already bred and 9 per cent of pairs which had failed or not yet begun to breed. Courtship consists mostly of mutual head-turning as the birds face each other with neck feathers fluffed, breasts almost touching and wing-feathers sometimes raised. As well as the courtship greeting and the triumph ceremony, copulatory behaviour is important in maintaining the pair-bond, most pairs mating over a longer period and more frequently than necessary to fertilise the eggs.

Only a minority breed colonially, defending only their nest-sites, which are as close together as 2m (6ft) in Denmark. In Britain most defend substantial territories from about February to October. Nests on rivers around Oxford averaged 2.4–3.2km (1.5–2 miles) apart, with a 90m (295ft) minimum, but on a shallow, weedy Hamburg lake defended areas averaged only 300 x 150m (984 x 492ft). The nest is usually well within 100m (328ft) of water on an island or bank among reeds or other aquatic vegetation, but sometimes more exposed on the shore of a sheltered sea inlet. Many are rebuilt in subsequent years. The male takes a close interest in nest construction, sometimes selecting the site and laying the foundations. Both sexes build the great mound of reeds, rushes and other vegetation,

MUTE SWAN

The average length is 145–160cm (57.1–63in) (of which the body is only half; the male is generally larger), wing-span 208–238cm (82–94in), and the adult (over three years) weight 9,200–14,300g (20.2–31.6lb) for the male, 7,600–10,800g (16.7–23.8lb) the female. There have been heavier, tame individuals, but they probably lost the power of flight.

The mute swan is commonly said to reach the age of at least 50 years but the maximum so far recorded in the wild is 22 years. This is not very different from some other wildfowl — eg mallard 21 years, pink-footed goose 22 years and eider 23 years.

MUTE SWAN

The single clutch (replaced after loss at 2–4 weeks) of 5–8 (1–11) pale-green (later stained) eggs, average size 113 × 74mm (4.45 × 2.92in) and rounded at both ends, is laid from mid-March in England, but mostly from the second week in April to mid-June, as throughout north-west Europe. The male will sit during laying (eggs arrive at 48-hour intervals) and while the female is feeding, but generally only the female undertakes the 35/41-day incubation, which begins with the last egg. However, there is at least one instance of a male incubating successfully after the death of his mate.

The mute swan (centre) is easily distinguished from the Bewick's swan (back) and the whooper swan (front) by its orange-red rather than yellow bill.

which has an average height of 60–80cm (23.5–31.5in) and base width of 1–2m (3–6.5ft) on land but up to 4m (13ft) over water. In the top there is a depression 5–15cm (2–6in) deep, formed by the female's breast, bill and feet. Construction takes about ten days and the female adds material within easy reach during incubation.

Hatching is synchronous, within 24–36 hours. Both sexes are aggressive in defence of their young, which often ride on their parents' backs while small. They also help the young to feed themselves through pulling up vegetation and disturbing insects. The cygnets fledge at 120–150 days. Some are driven out of the breeding territory as soon as their plumage is mostly white, but others accompany their parents to the winter quarters, where they generally join a large flock in which they remain when the parents leave to breed again. However, if the parents do not breed the young may remain with them in the territory or in a flock during the next summer. Age of first pairing is usually two years, sometimes one, but most birds have an engagement period of at least one year before laying. Thus first breeding of the male is most commonly at four years, sometimes three and rarely two, and that of the slightly more precocious female usually three years, sometimes two. With the nests so conspicuous, vandalism continues to be a significant cause of egg loss in some areas.

Diet and Feeding Behaviour

The diet is predominantly vegetarian, mainly the leaves, shoots and starchy roots of aquatic plants being taken through full up-ending or dipping the head and long neck in shallows. Also emergent plants and seeds are taken by dabbling and grazing at the water's edge, and herbs and grasses by grazing on land. Feeding is mostly by day, but often continues for a short time after dark. Plant foods from fresh, brackish and salt water include algae, water crowfoot, arrow-grass, plantain, marsh foxtail, creeping bent, milkwort, spurrey, milfoil, waterside willow leaves (mainly fallen), marsh yellow-cress, stonewort, club-rush, saltmarsh turf, sea-aster, wigeon grass and eelgrass. Animal foods taken regularly include insects and their larvae, other invertebrates, frogs, toads, tadpoles, molluscs and worms, but whole fish are taken only rarely. Young birds and small mammals are sometimes killed, but not often eaten. This is also a well-known opportunistic feeder which will graze pastures, sprouting cereals and amenity grassland (mostly adjacent to rivers), glean stubbles, readily take bread and titbits in parks and regularly gather at refuse and waste sources, from Thames rubbish barges to Scottish distillery outfalls. However, it is not usually a significant agricultural pest unless large flocks (generally moulting birds) walk onto fields to feed.

Movements

In the British Isles, France and the Low Countries there is little or no migration and not even much local movement, the great majority of birds never moving more than 50km (30 miles), usually along valleys and watercourses. Many breeding pairs remain on their territories all year but immatures and non-breeders travel short distances to join winter flocks at very traditional sites. Most longer-distance movement is associated with the moult, including from the Midlands to the Lancashire coast, and from Northumberland and Durham to Loch Leven, Kinross. Exceptionally, birds ringed at Dublin have been recovered in Wexford

(Cork) and Wales, while others ringed in Scotland (chiefly the Uists) have wintered on Ireland's north coast. There are also scattered records from as far afield as Fair Isle, the Isle of May and St Kilda, and at least one English bird has been recovered in Ireland.

In Scandinavia and north Germany colder weather forces most birds to winter south. North Europe also has a major moult migration of non-breeders to the Oresund area, now mainly on the Swedish side, where over 15,000 have been present July–September, probably including most pre-breeders of the Baltic countries and Denmark. Later they are joined by others from Denmark, Sweden and Germany, which are forced to leave frozen waters. If the cold intensifies many move further west into Denmark and Germany, sometimes reaching as far as the Netherlands, Belgium, north France and south-east England. Exceptionally, Polish and Lithuanian migrants have been recovered at the Bodensee, on the Swiss/German border, and in hard winters others moved over 1,700km (1,056 miles) to Scotland's Solway Firth, Belgium, north France and the Adriatic. Spring migration mostly depends on the thaw but some Polish birds return to their breeding grounds from January.

WHOOPER SWAN
(Cygnus cygnus)

Once known as hooper, whistling swan, wild swan, elerch and elk

The name 'whooper swan', formerly just 'hooper', is known from 1566 and refers to the bird's hooping call. In 1768 Pennant chose 'wild swan' as his standard term, but in 1785 altered this to 'whistling swan'. Thereafter all three names were widely used until Yarrell chose 'hooper' in 1843, the change to 'whooper' in the late nineteenth century more accurately reflecting the call.

WITH its bugle-like call, this migratory swan is one of the great heralds of winter in north-west Europe. Although it is now only a very rare, sporadic breeder within the British Isles, it still overwinters in internationally important numbers and there are hopes of recolonisation.

History and Conservation

The species has a long history in Britain, going back to the Ice Ages, from the Cromerian Interglacial of the Middle Pleistocene onwards. It occurred in both warmer and colder phases and no doubt bred widely at suitable times, perhaps still fairly commonly during the early part of the 'Little Ice Age' 1550–1850. As guns became more efficient it was widely hunted along with other wildfowl, but appears to have clung on as a regular British breeder until the eighteenth century. In 1801 Bewick wrote: 'When they again retire northward to the arctic regions to breed, a few, indeed, drop short, and perform that office by the way, for they are known to breed in some of the Hebrides, the Orkney, Shetland, and other solitary isles; but these are hardly worth notice'. He also noted that in Iceland the flightless, moulting birds were

taken advantage of by the natives, who kill them with clubs, shoot, and hunt them down with dogs, by which they are easily caught. The flesh is highly esteemed by them as a delicious food, as are also the eggs.

The Icelanders, Kamtschatdales, and other natives of the northern world, dress their skins with the down on, sew them together, and make them into garments of various kinds: the North American Indians do the same, and sometimes weave the down as barbers weave the cawls for wigs, and then

manufacture it into ornamental dresses for the women of rank, while the larger feathers are formed into caps and plumes to decorate the heads of the chiefs and their warriors. They also gather the feathers and down in large quantities, and barter or sell them to the inhabitants of more civilised nations.

This century there have been only a few British breeding records, some of which have involved feral birds or wounded ones which were unable to reach their regular haunts. Today the species is legally protected but lead poisoning through ingestion of shotgun pellets has become serious at several wintering sites. There have also been occasional incidents of mass mortality after the eating of grain still carrying toxic seed-dressings. Small numbers also die through collision with overhead wires.

Increasing disturbance is a major threat to Britain's small breeding population, as tourists and sportsmen visit remoter parts of Scotland in ever larger numbers. It is vital that possible breeding areas are kept secret and protected from disturbance as recolonisation seems likely with the recent trend for some northern species to establish themselves in Scotland. Furthermore, with better international protection and the trend towards cooler springs and summers in western Europe, this swan has already greatly extended its range in Fenno-Scandia.

The wintering population, too, is at risk through increasing human disturbance, as well as continuing land drainage. Nonetheless, numbers appear to be steadily building within the British Isles. In Ireland this has been the most numerous wintering wild swan since the 1950s, having suddenly appeared widely in the 1940s.

Distribution, Habitat and Population

The whooper breeds throughout northern Eurasia, in Iceland and parts of Scandinavia, then continuously through the former USSR to the Bering Sea, south to about 47°N in the eastern Palearctic. Some birds winter in west Iceland but in the western Palearctic most winter well to the south or south-west of their breeding range. About three-quarters of Icelandic breeders winter within the British Isles while birds wintering around the coast of southern Norway, the southern Baltic, Denmark, Germany, the Netherlands, Belgium and northern France are chiefly from Fenno-Scandia and the north-west of the former USSR. Most east Palearctic birds winter around coastal south-east Asia, especially in Japan and China.

Except in Iceland and parts of arctic Europe, breeding is mostly south of the tundra. The variety of habitats used is much wider than that entertained by Bewick's swan and at more varying altitude, ranging from large, shallow, reed-fringed lakes, swamps and small ponds on grasslands and heaths to wetlands surrounded by forests, rivers, estuaries and the shores of sea inlets. Feeding waters must be shallow enough to allow grazing of rich bottom vegetation and mostly free from emergent and floating plants. On migration and in winter quarters it readily uses marine as well as fresh water and farmland habitats, including intertidal mudflats.

Field Characters

This all-white bird is easily distinguished from the similar-sized mute swan by its black-and-yellow bill, flattened forehead and generally straighter and slimmer

In north-west Europe the main breeding centre is Iceland, where only the east-centre is unoccupied. Many Icelandic birds do not breed but the recently increasing percentage of young in flocks visiting the British Isles indicates ascendancy. Neither do the majority of Sweden's 500-plus birds breed, but there has been recent increase in Lapland and in the small, fragmented population in the south. Since the war there has been marked increase in Finland, with over 80 breeding pairs among about 500 birds. Small numbers have colonised the northern coast of Norway since about 1970.

In most years a few individuals or pairs summer in Scotland, but there were only about ten records of eggs or young 1900–80. Since then 1–5 pairs, some probably feral, have bred or attempted to breed in most years. In 1972 a male whooper mated with a mute swan on Lough Corrib, Ireland, and produced young. A similar mating occurred in Galway in 1976.

Of the 16,700 recorded wintering in the British Isles in 1986, 10,320 were in Ireland. A recent survey is expected to show substantial increase. The whooper is widespread on the UK mainland, mostly north of a line from the Humber to the Wirral, but also notably on Anglesey and the Ouse Washes.

WHOOPER SWAN

neck. In flight the wings produce a swishing sound whereas those of the mute swan generate a distinctive mechanical throbbing. At close quarters the whooper is separated from the smaller Bewick's swan by its larger yellow patch on the bill. In flight it is much harder to distinguish from Bewick's but characterised by the slightly flatter profile of the bill and forehead and its lower-pitched, bugle-like call. The sexes are alike and there is no seasonal plumage variation, though many individuals become stained rusty, especially on the head, neck and underparts which are constantly in water, and particularly the iron-rich streams of Iceland. The juvenile's head, neck and upperparts are usually grey-brown, with paler cheeks, throat and foreneck and white underparts with grey-brown flanks. Its dark-grey bill has a pinkish base, traces of yellow starting to appear in the first winter, when the grey feet become blacker and the plumage whiter. Adult plumage is acquired at 15–20 months. The juvenile Bewick's may be distinguished by its head shape and size, as in the adult. The juvenile mute swan is darker and browner above and its grey bill lacks the pink tinge.

Very gregarious outside the breeding season, the whooper often occurs in flocks of up to 100 or more. Young migrants can be naïve, but generally it is wary of man. Although it is usually less aggressive towards other species than the mute swan, it has been known to kill species as large as a crow in defence of its young. It runs and walks well, with the neck erect or arched back over the body and then straight up, and without the mute swan's awkward waddle. When it is swimming the neck is mostly held erect and seldom arched like that of the mute swan.

Take-off is laboured, but flight powerful, with the neck extended and regular wing-beats. In low flight, parties are often disordered, but when higher they mostly assume long, diagonal lines or V-formation to benefit from the slipstream of birds in front. In fact this is the highest-flying British bird. On 9 December 1967, about 30 whoopers were spotted by the pilot of a civilian transport aircraft over the Inner Hebrides at a height of just over 8,230m (27,000ft). They were flying south and the altitude was confirmed by a radar controller in Northern Ireland. He reported that they were moving at a ground speed of about 75 knots — 139kmh (86mph). It is thought that these birds took off from a coastal lagoon at sea level in Iceland, in a ridge of high pressure at dawn, for a ride on the strong winds of the jet stream of the lower stratosphere. The temperature at that altitude was later calculated at lower than –48°C (–54.4°F) and upper wind data suggested a flight time of seven hours.

The whooper swan also has probably the most far-carrying flight-call of any bird. The loud, deep, bugle-like note helps to keep the family parties together on their very long migrations with frequently poor visibility, both by day and night. It is this *whoop whoop* or *whoop-a, ahng-ha* which gave rise to the bird's name. This is the species which is believed to be behind the legend of the 'Swan-song', as prolonged exhalation of air from the trachea of a dying bird can produce a series of musical notes. The fact that the species' calls are deeper and stronger than those of Bewick's swan is probably related to the extra loop of trachea within the sternum.

Breeding

A long-term, monogamous pair-bond appears to be usual, but it is not known whether divorce ever occurs. Some courtship starts in winter flocks but most pairing takes place in non-breeding herds and engagement lasts at least until the following breeding season. In courtship the male and female face each other while

head-turning with the neck feathers erect. The main greeting involves head-bobbing, but on meeting a pair often use the triumph display, in which the neck is repeatedly bent and extended and the quivering, half-open wings are lifted while the birds call loudly.

Breeding territories are large, averaging about 100ha (247 acres) in the scrub zone of the taiga. The nest is usually close to water, on a bank, hummock or islet which is snow-free and dry at first, though after the thaw some are in shallow water. Both sexes build the large mound of sedges, reeds, moss and other vegetation, which is 1–2m, exceptionally 3m, (3–6ft, exceptionally 9ft) wide at the base and about 50–70cm (20–28in) high. The top depression is about 5–20cm (2–8in) deep, formed by pressing with the breast, bill and feet, and lined with fine grasses and a little down. Many nests are rebuilt in subsequent years.

Hatching is synchronous and the young are well cared for by both parents, which even display aggressively at mammals and low-flying aircraft. The cygnets feed themselves but, like other swans, also take plant food pulled up by the parents. They fledge at 78–96 days and stay with their parents through the first autumn and winter, starting the spring migration together but separating before reaching the breeding grounds. Although pairing takes place from the age of two, first breeding is usually at four years and sometimes not till six. Breeding success is very variable in Iceland, the proportion of young in flocks wintering in Britain ranging from under 10 per cent to over 40 per cent, according to spring/summer

The whooper swan uses a wide variety of habitats but is threatened by continuing land drainage. Photo: Dennis Green

The average length is 145–160cm (57.1–63in) (of which the body is only half; the male is generally larger), wing-span 218–243cm (86–95.5in), and the weight 8,500–14,000g (18.7–30.9lb) for the male, 7,400–10,300g (16.3–22.7lb) the female.

WHOOPER SWAN

The single clutch (replacements not known) averages 3–5 (3–8) in Britain and Iceland, 4–7 in Siberia and 4–5 (2–7) in Finland. The white or ochreous eggs, average size 113 × 73mm (4.45 × 2.88in) rounded at both ends, often get scratched and stained, and are laid at 48-hour intervals. In mild years they are laid from late April in Iceland, but mostly mid-May to the third week in June, as is the case in Fenno-Scandia and Siberia. The few British clutches are mostly laid in mid-May. The male occasionally relieves the female during her 31/42–day incubation, which starts with the last egg, but the clutch is mostly deeply covered while the female is feeding.

The move towards farmland feeding has brought problems. There can be 'puddling' of cereal fields where swans congregate in wet seasons and there have been instances where groups of birds have died after uprooting seedlings which still carried toxic seed dressings.

weather. Furthermore, recent research has shown that even within Iceland there is great variability, adult birds in the lowlands tending to be heavier and lay more eggs which produce larger and heavier cygnets than those in the uplands. This suggests higher quality habitat at the lowland sites, which contribute disproportionately to Iceland's productivity.

Diet and Feeding Behaviour

Predominantly vegetable food is taken, consisting chiefly of the leaves, stems, roots, seeds and berries of mainly aquatic plants in fresh and salt water. However, as the population has recovered and the availability of nutritious agricultural crops has increased, most winter feeding is on farmland in some areas, including parts of the British Isles. The main feeding methods are up-ending or simply immersing the head and neck, sometimes while foot-paddling to loosen underwater plants. Items taken include crowfoot, cotton-grass, algae, crowberry, eel-grass (*Zostera*), wigeon grass (*Ruppia*), pondweed, roots of dicotyledons, stonewort, marsh yellow-cress, horsetail, stubble grain, potatoes (important in parts of Ireland), sugar-beet, pasture and saltmarsh grasses, winter cereals and growing and cut turnips. More unusually it scavenges potatoes and other refuse on dumps and takes fallen acorns and fruit such as plums. Small aquatic invertebrates are mostly taken on the breeding grounds, where insects and their larvae abound.

Movements

The bulk of the Icelandic population is migratory, the proportion varying with the weather and local food supplies. They start to leave as their breeding waters freeze, non-migrants moving to brackish coastal lagoons, interior lakes kept open by hot springs, and larger rivers, chiefly in western and southern Iceland. The first whoopers arrive in Ireland and Scotland in early September, but the main influx is from late September to November, and there can be further emigration at any time during the winter if the cold intensifies. Indeed, even short-term movements are well worthwhile because it has been shown that the journey from Iceland to Scotland can take as little as seven hours. There are frequent winter movements either way between Ireland and Scotland and other parts of Britain according to weather and availability of food. Ringing has shown that such journeys are often made by individuals rather than groups and there is considerable interchange between flocks. None the less, there is marked site fidelity. Most birds start to return to Iceland in March and April, with stragglers into May.

Birds from Fenno-Scandia and the former USSR leave their breeding grounds at the start of the freeze, usually mid- to late-September in the east and north but as late as mid-October in the west. Many fly across the White Sea and eastern Baltic to winter in coastal Germany, southern Sweden and Denmark, mostly arriving in October and November. Smaller numbers winter on the coast of central and southern Norway. The number which continue south and west to the Netherlands, Belgium, northern France and (rarely) south-east England varies with the weather. The spring return begins mid-March and ends in early May.

Individuals and small parties occasionally summer around the British Isles and Baltic countries. There are also short-distance moult movements within Iceland. In cold weather small numbers venture beyond the main wintering areas, for example to Italy, the USA and Greenland.

BEWICK'S SWAN
(Cygnus columbianus bewickii)

THIS subspecies of the tundra swan is very faithful to certain wintering grounds and has become familiar to many British people through its allegiance to the Wildfowl and Wetlands Trust reserves at Slimbridge, Gloucestershire, and Welney in Norfolk. This has facilitated intensive study of the bird and provided good publicity for conservation.

History and Conservation

The earliest British record is from the Pastonian Glaciation of the Middle Pleistocene, and it was present later, in the Devensian Glaciation. It probably bred here during those colder times, when tundra was present, but it is more likely to have been only a winter visitor when it occurred in the Fens during the Neolithic/Bronze Age period.

When it was identified in the early nineteenth century, this swan appears to have been quite common in winter. Among others, Morris (1850) wrote of a flock of 29 at Crumpsall, near Manchester, in December 1829, another of 73 at the same place in February 1830, six near St Just, Cornwall, in January 1830 and 20 at Whittlesea Wash in March 1855. There were also many records from Ireland, from Belfast to Wexford, and throughout Scotland, especially in Tiree and the Uists.

Reserves such as Slimbridge, Welney and Caerlaverock have become major attractions not only for their safe haven, but also because the birds there are regularly fed (sometimes by floodlight to increase feeding time!) with grain and potatoes and have been provided with well-managed grazing habitat. It was at Slimbridge that the late Sir Peter Scott became the first person to realise that Bewick's swans had different, permanent face patterns, which meant that the birds could be studied without the need to ring them. His keen observations revealed that some swans have returned to the reserves for many years and have become popular attractions for visitors who are able to watch them closely from hides without causing undue disturbance. One bird, called Prongy, visited Slimbridge for 26 consecutive winters. X-rays taken of 40 Bewick's swans in 1988–9 showed that 42 per cent carried lead shot. The bird is fully protected in Britain but it is likely that some are shot by mistake in gloomy conditions and many more deliberately in less caring regions of continental Europe.

Distribution, Habitat and Population

The two subspecies of tundra swan share a circumpolar distribution. The whistling swan (*C. c. columbianus*) breeds and winters in North America while Bewick's swan breeds across northern Eurasia from the White Sea to the Bering Strait, above 65°N. Birds wintering in north-west Europe — principally Denmark, the Netherlands, England and Ireland, but also Germany, Scotland and northern France — are from the single wholly migratory population breeding east to Taymyr in northern Siberia.

Once known as wild swan and tame swan

This swan was separated from the very similar whooper by Yarrell in the 1820s. When it was scientifically described in 1830 he proposed naming it after the famous wood engraver Thomas Bewick, who died in 1828 and did so much to engender interest in natural history, especially through his book *A History of British Birds*.

Bewick's swan continued to visit the British Isles in substantial, but varying, numbers, up to the 1930s, when there was sharp decrease in Scotland and increase in England. Influxes of several hundreds occurred in England during the winters of 1938–9 and 1955–6. Over the next 15 years English numbers increased to about 1,500 but fell to about half that in Ireland. Many marked regional fluctuations are accounted for by redistribution in response to changing weather, but overall increase appears to have been sustained through the 1980s. This has been concurrent with the swan's increasing tendency to feed on farmland and better protection provided by refuges.

While the future of Bewick's swans at the Ouse Washes, Slimbridge and Martin Mere seems assured, better protection is needed for other areas where significant numbers overwinter. Notification of further SSSIs would help, along with cessation of further drainage, which has been the main reason for sharp decline in Germany. Current de-intensification of agriculture and promotion of set-aside land should also help.

The breeding habitat is mainly low, marshy, grassy and fairly flat tundra, where there are many pools and lakes, but also along wide, sluggish rivers and back-waters, or on coasts and islands. More rarely it nests within the treeline. West European winter quarters have traditionally been on undisturbed, mainly shallow freshwater lakes, ponds and slow-moving rivers near grasslands liable to flooding, but also brackish lagoons and permanent pasture. Now there is an increasing tendency to accept the presence of man and to use farmland.

Field Characters

This smallest of the three European swans is easily separated from the mute swan by its yellow-and-black rather than red-orange bill and generally straighter neck. The whooper is harder to distinguish but has a greater amount of yellow on the bill and a flatter bill/head profile, while Bewick's is more goose-like, in flight, proportions and shape. The juvenile resembles that of the whooper and that too is best distinguished by shape and profile. The sexes are alike and there is no seasonal plumage variation. Individuals may be recognised by their bill patterns.

Outside the breeding season, Bewick's is even more gregarious than the whooper swan, often occurring in flocks of hundreds and sometimes thousands. It is less wary of man. Like the whooper it walks easily, usually with the neck erect, though this is sometimes curved when at rest. Flight is as powerful as that of the other swans, but the wing-beats are faster than those of the larger species. There is often no special flight formation at low altitude, but at greater heights diagonal lines or V-formation are common.

Flight-calls are far-carrying, but softer, lower-pitched and less trumpet-like than those of the whooper swan, chiefly a honking *bong*, recalling geese. However, it is often noisier than the whooper when on the ground or water, flocks sometimes babbling or barking when active, but uttering a gentle murmur at rest. Brief swishing of wings, chiefly at take-off and landing, is not thought to have any signal value.

Breeding

The pair-bond is monogamous and long-term and lost mates are usually replaced within months, though sometimes not for several years. As in the other swans, mutual head-turning is prominent in courtship, the male and female facing each other with the neck feathers erect. The triumph ceremony is used in greeting, loud calls being given while the wings quiver in a half-open and lifted position.

In Siberia nests are mostly widely dispersed, averaging one pair per 2,000ha (4,942 acres) of wet tundra, but may be as close as 200m (yards) at favoured sites, such as the mouth of the Pechora River, and even closer on islands. The nest is usually placed on a dry hummock or bank, but it may be in water after the thaw. Many are rebuilt in subsequent years. Both sexes build the large mound of grasses, sedges, moss and other vegetation, which has a base diameter of about 1m (3ft) and height of 50–60cm (20–24in). The slight depression in the top is lined with moss, soft grasses and down.

Hatching is synchronous and the young are well cared for by both parents. They feed themselves, but at first also take vegetation pulled up by their parents. Fledging is at 40–45 days, but the family remains intact through the first autumn and winter, the young dispersing on spring migration before reaching the breeding grounds. Some birds pair in their second winter, but most in their third, and first breeding is at three to four years, often later. Widely varying proportions of young — 7–44 per cent — in British winter flocks confirm highly variable brood size and breeding success. This is largely due to the condensed arctic breeding season, which forces birds to nest within a short period and thereby increases overall vulnerability to weather. Also, relative naïvety of first-winter birds means that they are more likely to be shot on migration.

Diet and Feeding Behaviour

The diet is predominantly vegetable, chiefly the leaves, shoots, roots, rhizomes, tubers and seeds of aquatic and waterside plants, but with an increasing tendency to take cultivated varieties on migration and in winter quarters. Feeding methods are up-ending, immersing the head and neck, grazing and digging with the bill and feet. Animal food is probably unimportant except when insects are abundant on the breeding grounds. Feeding is chiefly diurnal but in disturbed areas commonly continues for an hour or more into the night. Floodlit hand-feeding, chiefly with grain, has become usual at some reserves. Items regularly taken include rhizomes of pondweeds, leaves of hornwort, milfoil, stonewort, eel-grass, floating sweetgrass, creeping bent, marsh foxtail, roots of marsh yellow-cress, waste potatoes, sugar-beet, stubble grain, carrots, white clover, pasture grass and sprouting winter cereals.

BEWICK'S SWAN

The average length is 115–127cm (45.3–50in) (of which only half is body and the male averages larger), wing-span 180–211cm (70.9–83.1in), and weight 4,900–7,800g (10.8–17.2lb) for the male, 3,400–7,200g (7.5–15.8lb) the female.

The single clutch (replacements not recorded) of 3–5 (2–6) white or pale-yellow eggs, average size 103 × 67mm (4.06 × 2.64in) and rounded at both ends, is mostly laid from the third week in May to the third week in June. The female's solo 29/30-day incubation begins with the last egg. The male sometimes sits while she feeds, otherwise the eggs are covered with down and nest material.

In recent years some 16,000–16,500 have wintered regularly in north-west Europe. Although they are strongly attached to traditional sites, local numbers can vary considerably with breeding success and because many more birds push west in midwinter during very cold weather. In 1990–91 the peak UK count was almost 8,400 compared with almost 9,000 1989–90. By far the most important British resort is the Ouse Washes, with an average peak count of 4,974 over the five winters 1986–91. Other main resorts and their averages were: Nene Washes 865, Martin Mere/Ribble Estuary 662, Breydon Water 420, Severn Estuary 317, Lough Neagh/Beg 314, Walland Marsh 236, River Avon: Ringwood 188, Walmore Common 165 and St Benet's Levels 157. Most of the birds on the Ouse Washes occur on the Wildfowl and Wetland Trust's reserve at Welney.

A November 1990 count of 1,046 at Martin Mere/ Ribble Estuary emphasised the rapidly increasing importance of that reserve too. Other important sites 1990–91 were: Block Fen with 250, Lough Foyle 195 and Ludham How Hill 155. In Ireland, the Wexford flock built up from 1969–70 to some 700 in the mid-1970s, when the national population was estimated at 2,000–2,500. Since then many have moved from the Slobs to other Irish sites, the most important including the Shannon Valley, several turloughs in Galway and Roscommon, and the Lough Swilly area.

Movements

The birds which winter in north-west Europe leave their north-west Siberian tundra breeding grounds from early September to mid-October. They migrate on a narrow front around the coast to the White Sea, thence overland to the Gulf of Finland, the Baltic, Gotland and Southern Sweden to reach Denmark, Norway, north Germany, the Netherlands, Belgium, the British Isles and France. Arrivals can be as early as late September in the British Isles, but are mostly in October and November and continue throughout the winter as birds are pushed west by cold weather. Numbers usually peak in December in the Netherlands, but mostly January in the British Isles. Frequent midwinter movements between Britain, Ireland and the Netherlands are stimulated by varying food supplies and weather. In mild years the spring return may start in February, but March is more usual, the majority having left the British Isles by mid-March and the Netherlands by the end of March. Most birds arrive back on their breeding grounds from mid-May to early June.

In very cold weather birds occur outside their main wintering range, in southern and central Europe. A small number (7 accepted to end of 1990) from the North American race, known as the whistling swan, have been recorded in the British Isles, chiefly Ireland.

GREYLAG GOOSE

Once known as greylag, grey lag goose, grey laggoose, grey goose, wild goose, common wild goose, fen goose, marsh goose and stubble goose

GREYLAG GOOSE
(*Anser anser*)

THIS ancestor of most farmyard geese once bred widely in Britain, but now only a tiny fraction of the native stock remains. However, the country's winter population is now of international importance and there is a growing feral flock.

History and Conservation

The greylag occurs early in the British fossil record, in the warmer periods of the Pleistocene, from the Cromerian Interglacial onwards. Whereas the eastern greylag was already widely 'farmed' by man, the western race seems to have been domesticated during the Iron Age and no doubt bred widely in the extensive marshlands of the time. Geese were certainly kept during the Roman occupation, but apparently chiefly as watch-dogs rather than for food.

Despite widespread domestication from the Middle Ages on, the greylag continued to breed freely in the wild, but with the acceleration of land drainage and its persecution as a pest of greatly expanded agriculture, the British range shrank rapidly. In eighteenth-century England it was largely confined to eastern counties, and during the early nineteenth century it even disappeared from Norfolk and Lincolnshire. Last recorded wild breeding in England was in 1831. At the same time the Scottish range retreated northwards and by the twentieth century it was restricted to the north-west and the Hebrides. In the early 1950s there were under 200 pairs left, chiefly on relatively undisturbed islands. But with the introduction of legal protection the population started to build again, reaching some 500–700 pairs in the mid-1980s.

Feral populations were established in the 1930s and subsequently spread to many areas. Major increase took place largely through the interest of wildfowling clubs, which took the population from some 1,700 in the late 1960s to about 13,000–14,000 birds in the mid-1980s. The sharpest rise in population has been in southern and central England, where reclaimed gravel-pits have provided suitable habitat.

The wintering population has prospered too, helped by climatic amelioration 1900–1950 and extension of the cereal belt northwards. Furthermore, the species' willingness to use new reservoirs as roosts has enabled it to exploit more inland feeding grounds. However, the steady increase may now have halted. The species remains a much-valued legal quarry and it is essential to control disturbance at major roosts and feeding grounds. Commercially-stimulated over-shooting has been a major problem, especially in Scotland. Furthermore, breeding sites of native birds are far from secure, with increased disturbance and widespread afforestation of Cathness and Sutherland peatlands. The effects of these activities are especially devastating because the bird is so site-faithful, and so numbers in the national count dropped from 115,000 in 1990 to 87,000 in 1991.

Distribution, Habitat and Population

The greylag breeds chiefly on large, open fresh waters with thick emergent vegetation and easy access to feeding grounds on grazing pastures, meadows and wetlands. More occasional nesting habitats include steep, rocky slopes, tall heather and the Machair (herb-rich grassland) of the Outer Hebrides. It ranges through northern and central Eurasia, in boreal and temperate latitudes almost entirely south of the Arctic Circle, only sparingly using the tundra. The main breeding range is in a continuous, wide belt from the Sea of Okhotsk, west to the edge of the west Palearctic, where it has become very fragmented after widespread drainage. The geographical dividing line between the eastern race, *A. a. rubrirostris*, and the western race, *A. a. anser*, is obscure and there is a broad zone of intermediates in east-central Europe. In the former USSR the range is now split into many small areas through hunting and habitat destruction, with an estimated population of 50,000–60,000 pairs in 1967. Germany has about 2,000–3,000 pairs, Denmark 2,000 pairs, Norway thousands of pairs around the coast except in the far south, Sweden hundreds of pairs, Finland about 250 pairs, and Poland some 500 pairs.

The Icelandic breeding population increased steadily over recent decades, from 3,500 pairs and 30,000 birds in 1960 to at least 105,000 birds in 1987. Success there was largely due to the fact that some 80 per cent of Icelandic birds winter in Britain, mainly in Scotland and northern England, where they thrived in previous decades through improved protection and fortuitous cropping regimes.

The greylag tends to winter in milder climates than most geese, in temperate to warm temperate zones south of the breeding range, favouring estuaries, floodlands, lakes and reservoirs. The west European wintering population increased from 80,000–110,000 in the 1960s to 236,000 (including Denmark, Germany, the Netherlands, Belgium and Spain) in 1990.

Field Characters

This is the largest and heaviest of Europe's native geese, with a brownish-grey body, thick neck, stout bill and pink legs. The slightly larger and paler eastern race

GREYLAG GOOSE

There are many explanations for the origin of the current name, but simple 'gray lag' is first noticed in the work of Ray, in 1713, and 'grey lag goose' was introduced by Pennant in 1768. Lag is a name of great antiquity and said to have derived from the call *lag-lag-lag*, widely used in driving domesticated geese. Another explanation is that this was the goose that lagged or stayed behind when all the other grey geese went north. But equally plausible is the suggestion that this was the bird which commonly grazed the fields or leys (sometimes leas) — ley goose. The Latin *anser* simply means goose, this species having the same specific because it was regarded as the original wild goose.

In Britain the native population is estimated at 2,000–3,000 birds, about two-thirds of which are in Uist, Outer Hebrides. Caithness and Sutherland have some 300 pairs. The peak feral count was 15,300 in January 1991, although the estimate was over 22,000, chiefly in England and Wales, but also notably south-west Scotland. Many feral birds do not breed.

25

A greylag goose takes flight. Photo: A. Christiansen/FLPA

has a pink bill which is 15 per cent longer than the orange bill of the western race, which includes north-west European breeders. Some birds have white around the base of the upper bill. The sexes are alike, although the male is larger, and there is no seasonal variation. In flight it is distinguished from all other European geese by its very pale-grey forewing, which contrasts with the darker saddle and primaries. The thick-set silhouette is another good indicator. At close range note the barred back, that the folded wing does not reach beyond the end of the tail and that the underparts are often flecked with black, though almost always less than the barring of the smaller white-fronted goose. At close range the juvenile may be distinguished by having less distinct transverse lines on the back, a more broken white line along the edge of the folded wing, and paler legs and bill.

The average length is 75–90cm (29.5–35.5in), wingspan 147–180cm (57.9–70.9in) and weight 2,600–4,450g (5.7–9.8lb) for the male, 2,070–3,960g (4.6–8.7lb) the female.

The greylag is very gregarious, except when nesting, flocks sometimes numbering many thousands. It often mixes with other grey geese. On land it takes off quite easily, almost vertically when there is a good wind, but in calm conditions needs more of a run than the other grey geese. Launching from water is more difficult. Its flight is deceptively fast, with powerful, regular wingbeats alternating with gliding on outstretched wings or planing down on angled wings to land with a characteristic flutter. Sometimes flocks indulge in playful aerobatics with sud-

The greylag goose is the ancestor of most farmyard geese.

27

den banking and side-slipping. The species swims well, but dives only to avoid danger. On land it generally walks more slowly than other geese, with a pronounced nautical roll. This is often one of the tamest of geese, young birds being especially naïve, but where they are shot they soon become very wary and difficult to approach.

There is a wide range of calls, mostly used in flocks, whose excited clamouring carries a long way. Perhaps the most familiar is the sonorous, clanging *aahng-ung-ung*, which is more guttural than that of other grey geese and reminiscent of domesticated birds. Equally common is the gabbling *gaa-gaa*.

Breeding

The single clutch (replaced after loss) of 4–5 (3–12, but 13-plus with two or more females) of ovate, occasionally elongated, creamy-white (often subsequently stained) eggs, average size 85 × 58mm (3.35 × 2.28in), is laid from late March or early April in Britain, where the main laying period is mid-April. In Iceland laying begins at the end of April but the main period is in mid-May.

Fully wild greylags are almost always monogamous and pair for life, but a stable pair-bond is not usually formed until the third or fourth year. Both established and potential pairs frequently perform the highly ritualised triumph ceremony at all times of the year. Courtship includes extensive calling, horizontal and vertical stretching or retraction of the neck, and head dipping. Display diminishes with age and may even be omitted in long-standing pairs.

At favoured, relatively safe sites breeding is loosely colonial. Breeding density is highest among feral populations, some on wooded islands, such as in south-west Scotland, where nests are as little as 2m (6ft) apart. Sites are often traditional and generally only island nests are more than 10m (33ft) from water. The male helps in site selection and often stays close by while the female builds the ground nest among reeds or bushes, at the base of a tree (often in pollarded willows), or on a raft of vegetation. She uses material within easy reach to make a substantial foundation of twigs, grass, reeds, heather and other vegetation, with a small cup which is lined with grass and a little down. Some nests are raised substantially after laying has started.

The female's solo 27/28-day incubation starts with the last egg. Hatching is synchronous, the young feed themselves and are cared for by both parents. Families often group together while the goslings are still small. Fledging is at 50–60 days. The family remains together through the first autumn and winter and leave their winter quarters together, but the young disperse before reaching the breeding grounds. Single goslings tend to stay with their parents longer than larger broods.

Diet and Feeding Behaviour

Apart from the goslings' consumption of abundant protein-rich insects which accelerate early growth, the greylag's diet is almost entirely vegetarian. This varies according to location and season, but nowadays almost always contains a high proportion of cultivated crops, which brings the goose into conflict with man.

The powerful bill, which has tooth-like serrations along the upper mandible and horny lamellae, is adapted to breaking stems, stripping seeds and digging up the starchy roots and tubers of mostly marsh plants. Such underground storage organs are preferred in winter whereas the young green parts of plants are favoured in summer. Leaves, stems, flower-heads and fruits are clipped off with the side of the bill, but pieces of root and tuber are scraped off by the end nail on the upper mandible. Although most food is taken on land, the greylag also feeds on and around water, taking floating material, sometimes up-ending to pull up submerged material and tugging at stems to expose roots in soft mud.

Not so long ago, greylags concentrated in British estuaries, where they ate roots of rushes and sedges, as in other parts of their range, but in recent decades they have moved almost exclusively onto farmland. Here the species is very opportunistic so the feeding pattern varies considerably, but in Scotland a cycle of autumn stubble grain, followed by potatoes and grazing, is often followed. The tremendous increase in the acreage of cereals has been of particular benefit and, while stubbles are the main attraction, grain is also taken from standing stalks around field edges. On arrival in Britain, some 70 per cent of greylags feed on barley and oat stubbles and most of the remainder on grass. After the grain has been exhausted or the stubbles ploughed in, greylags turn more to grass and root crops. Some swedes, turnips (including some put out for cattle), carrots, sugar-beet and potatoes are taken, but many of them are waste after the harvest and have been softened by frost. Rape, kale and brassicae are more likely to be eaten in severe cold. The big change to winter cereals has been a great boon too, the young shoots mostly being taken in late spring. This can cause significant economic loss. The farmer also takes a dim view of the greylag's feeding on spring grass because the early growth is especially rich in protein and valuable to farm stock in improving milk yields and body condition.

Inland, greylags feed mostly by day, usually flighting to the feeding grounds at dawn or soon after and returning to roost at dusk. But there is much local variation according to the level of disturbance, and in tidal areas most feeding is nocturnal, starting a couple of hours before sunset and ending an hour or two after sunrise. Sometimes greylags will flight inland and feed all the while there is bright moonlight, presumably because there is sufficient light to spot predators by. After feeding, the geese commonly flight to the coast to take grit in the form of sand, to aid digestion.

Movements

Most greylag populations winter well to south of their breeding range, but some move little and a few not at all. Most breeders of Norway, Sweden, Denmark and Germany migrate from late September, through the Netherlands (where some overwinter) and France, to Spain (a few to Portugal), but a small number visit the British Isles, where they are joined by the entire Icelandic population. Most of these arrive in Scotland in late October, with the tail end in early November, many passing on or going straight to northern England or Ireland. Icelandic birds drift north in late winter before they leave Britain for their breeding grounds in March and April, occasionally May. Native British breeders are mostly resident but a few move to other parts of Scotland or Ireland. Feral flocks make mostly only very local movements at any time, although some birds disperse widely. Birds resembling the Siberian race are occasionally reported in western Europe, but may be from feral stock.

Winter movements are mostly determined by the availability of food. Only the most severe weather will lead to mid-season long-distance movements as the species is quite happy to 'sit out' cold snaps. There is no clear moult migration of Icelandic birds, but some moulting non-breeders gather there. Elsewhere, moult gatherings are variable but appear to be increasing as the west Palearctic population builds, with notable assemblies in some years at Limfjorden and Sjaelland in Denmark, IJsselmeer and Haringvliet in the Netherlands, Gotland in Sweden and the Vega and Vikna Islands off west Norway. Most assemble in late May.

Numbers visiting the British Isles are of major international importance. In 1990–91 Great Britain's peak count of almost 115,000 Icelandic birds (November) was considered to be an under-estimate. Northern Ireland's peak count of 1,113 was in March, with no separation between wild and feral, the latter being predominant. Britain has many sites which regularly achieve the 1,000–bird level for international importance. The distribution is constantly changing but overall the concentration is on the Scottish lochs and firths, and in parts of northern England and Ireland. Greatest numbers are in agricultural areas of eastern and central Scotland. Over the five winters 1986–91 19 resorts attracted an average peak count of over 2,000, the most important being Dinnet Loch/River Dee 13,760, Inner Moray Firth 12,023, Loch Eye/Cromarty Firth 11,572, Loch of Skene 11,071, Loch Spynie 7,640, Loch of Strathbeg 6,165, Haddo House Lough 4,684, Tay/Isla Valley 4,580 and Drummond Pond 4,357. Other sites, too, sometimes receive well over 2,000 birds. After steep decline, from about 6,000 birds early this century to less than 200 in the early 1950s, numbers of wild birds wintering in Ireland have been picking up, to over 3,000 in recent years

BEAN GOOSE

(*Anser fabalis*)

THIS Old World species has suffered severe decline since the nineteenth century. Only very small numbers now visit the British Isles but the winter population of north-west Europe as a whole is of international importance.

History and Conservation

Once known as corn goose, wild goose, grey goose and small grey goose

When Pennant introduced the Lincolnshire name 'bean goose' in 1768 there was a suggestion that it derived from the similarity of the nail of the bill to a horsebean. But there is no doubt that the name's true origin lies in the bird's diet. The current scientific name, too, was given in the eighteenth century, *fabilis* deriving from the Latin *faba* for bean. In those days field beans were grown much more extensively than now and it is said that the bean goose was the first British species to exploit farm crops in a big way.

The earliest British record of the goose comes from South Wales, in the last inter-glacial, the Ipswichian, but there are few other fossil remains. The three sub-species now found in the west Palearctic have adapted to wide-ranging habitats, even (uniquely among indigenous geese) nesting within dense coniferous forest or birch scrub, so it it likely that the species was much more numerous and wide-spread until modern times. Indeed, the early literature confirms this, not-withstanding confusion with the pink-footed goose, which was not separated from the bean goose until 1833.

There is no doubt that it was still a very common winter visitor to north-west Europe, including the northern British Isles, in the eighteenth and nineteenth centuries, when it probably bred more widely. Bewick (1801) claimed that it bred 'in great numbers in the Isle of Lewis', but then he was not aware of the pink-footed goose, which Morris (1850) reported as another Hebridean breeder. The latter writer also claimed that the bean goose bred in the Faeroes and Iceland, but again there could have been confusion with the pink-footed.

Steep decline in the British winter population started in the 1860s and con-tinued into the twentieth century, through a combination of agricultural change, drainage and over-shooting. New techniques such as direct drilling of beans put much food out of the bird's reach and changed cropping regimes did away with autumn stubbles where the geese once gleaned. Overseas, the pressures have often been greater and some have continued until quite recently. For example, during the 1950s and probably later the people of northern Russia still commonly exploited the species through shooting, egg collecting and rounding up during the flightless period. Similar persecution has brought about a sharp decline in numbers of Scandinavian breeders, and despite increased protection many are still shot in parts of Continental Europe, where there is continued confusion with the pink-footed goose. In Britain it is protected under the Wildlife and Country-side Act 1981.

The bean goose (centre front) was not scientifically separated from the pink-footed goose (right) until the nineteenth century.

Unfortunately, in Britain and the Netherlands the bean goose is very site-faith-ful, but until very recently the few remaining good sites enjoyed little protection. For example, much of the once-favoured Dee Valley (where there were some two hundred bean geese in the 1950s) has been converted to barley or re-seeded, and in Norfolk's Yare Valley, where the geese spend only part of their time on the SSSI notified for their protection, these factors plus drainage, introduction of sheep-grazing and competition with the increasing wigeon flock have caused many of the birds to move. However, the overall situation improved greatly in 1992 with the Royal Society for the Protection of Birds' purchase of the important Buckenham and Cantley Marshes, raising their total land holdings in the Yare Valley to 1,600 acres. Recent research has shown that the maintenance of unimproved cattle-grazed marshes and minimisation of disturbance are critical in the management of this species.

West Palearctic wintering sites are scattered through eastern and southern Europe, and in the southern Baltic and the Low Countries, notably southern Sweden and eastern Germany. Birds which winter in Britain are almost entirely of the nominate race *fabalis* and come from the taiga of northern Europe, from Scandinavia east to the Urals, while south Baltic and Low Countries visitors originate from both taiga and tundra zones. In 1986 the population of *A. f. fabalis* was estimated at less than 100,000 and in recent years only a few hundred of these have regularly visited Britain, the concentration having shifted from the north to eastern England. Now east Norfolk is the only regular British wintering locality. In January 1991 a record number (since counts started in 1940) of 485 were in the Yare Valley, considerably more than in recent years. That month a further 24 were noted at numerous other localities, but the only other site with more than 10 came from Loch Ken.

The length averages 66–84cm (26–33.1in), wingspan 142–175cm (55.9–68.9in), and weight (*fabalis*) 2,690–4,060g (5.9–8.9lb) for the male, 2,220–3,470g (4.9–7.6lb) the female.

Distribution, Habitat and Population

The breeding range is continuous throughout northern Eurasia from Scandinavia to the Bering Sea, mostly above 60°N but south to 50° in much of the east. The entire population is migratory, wintering chiefly in south-east Asia and western Europe, though little is known about the origins of each group. Those of the Siberian tundra are smaller and thick-billed while those of the taiga (pine forest) are larger and longer-necked, and most authorities now recognise an eastern and western race of each of these two ecological types. The taiga race of Scandinavia and western Siberia is known as the western bean (*A. f. fabalis*) and its bill is shorter and more orange than the eastern taiga bean *A. f. middendorfi*. The tundra races have a deeper, heavier bill, the western Russian bean (*A. f. rossicus*) being smaller than the thick-billed bean (*A. f. serrirostris*). There is continuous variation latitudinally as well as longitudinally, so intermediates are common and races overlap in most characteristics. Bill length increases from west to east. A fifth race, *A. f. johanseni*, is sometimes recognised, being an intermediate between *fabalis* and *middendorfi*.

Little is known about breeding numbers but the species is numerous in the former USSR and the bulk of birds are outside the west Palearctic. The species breeds throughout northern Finland, where it has declined substantially over the last fifty years, mainly through killing of moulting birds. Persecution has also contributed to the decline in Sweden, where changes in forest habitat now restrict the bird to a narrow strip running from north-west Finland to the central-western border with Norway, where there has also been decline. An isolated population exists in central-southern Sweden.

Field Characters

The dark-brown head and neck of this generally brown, rather long-necked and long-billed goose are obvious even in flight. The sexes are alike and there is no seasonal variation. Field separation of the three west Palearctic races is difficult (see Distribution section above), but currently only *fabalis* is known to visit Britain. Its upperparts are dull, rather uniform brown with pale feather tips creating a transverse pattern. The chest is very pale brown weakly banded with darker brown and, in contrast, the upper- and under-tail coverts and tail edge are white. There is also a clear white line along the upper edge of the flanks and some orange-billed birds have white feathering around the base of the upper bill. In poor light or at long range separation from other grey geese is difficult, but good pointers are the erect stance, conspicuously long, dark head and neck, and uniform upperwing in flight. It is distinguished from the pink-footed goose by its orange legs and orange and black bill (colours varying in proportion), larger head and brown rather than grey body. Its head and neck are more slender than those of the stockier greylag, which has flesh-coloured legs. The white-fronted goose lacks the bean's distinct pale edgings to the wing-coverts and generally has noticeable black barring on the underparts. Up to winter, juveniles can be distinguished by relative dullness, marbling rather than streaking on the wing-coverts, mottled underparts, lack of white edging to flanks and duller bill and legs.

Although gregarious outside the breeding season, the bean usually occurs in smaller flocks than most other geese, even where it is numerous. It swims well but is less aquatic than other grey geese, walking more easily but with more of a roll

than the greylag. It mixes freely with other geese but is shyer and feeds more slowly than the pink-footed and is more likely to roost on or near the feeding grounds. Take-off is easier than that of the greylag and in flight it is as powerful and fast, lacking the latter's hint of labouring. The neck is always extended and its regular wing-beats alternate with gliding on outstretched wings. It planes in to land on angled wings, alighting with a characteristic flutter.

The bean goose has suffered greatly through exceptional site-fidelity. Photo: Dennis Green

This is the least vocal of the grey geese, with far-carrying, cackling, bassoon-like calls similar to but lower than those of the pink-footed. Flock flight-calls are given as *ung-ank* and a steady *bow-wow*, whereas single birds utter *ow ow-ow ow* or *gock.*

Breeding

The monogamous pair-bond is lifelong. In courtship there is much neck posturing and the male cackles while approaching the female with head lifted and wings spread.

Nests are mostly well dispersed but there may be loose colonies and the male is strong in defence of the female. The ground site is mostly very close to water but may be up to 1km (about half a mile) away, on a low hummock or bank where it is free from post-thaw flooding on the open tundra, or among scrub or trees in the marshy taiga. The female does most of the building, using vegetation such as grass, leaves and moss within easy reach to create a low mound with a shallow cup lined with down. Old nests may be re-used, but are given a new lining.

The female's solo incubation (28–29 days in taiga races but from 25 days in smallest tundra forms) starts with the last egg. Hatching is synchronous, the young feed themselves and are cared for by both parents until fledging from about 40 days. The family remains united until the following spring, but the young leave before they reach the breeding grounds. First breeding is usually at three years but a few birds probably pair in their second spring.

The single clutch of 3–8 (averaging 3–5 in tundra geese, 4–6 in taiga forms) rough-textured, oval, straw-coloured eggs, average size 84 × 56mm (3.31 × 2.2in), is mostly laid from mid-May to mid-June in the west Palearctic, but is often delayed by cold weather. Tundra birds often do not start laying until early June.

Diet and Feeding Behaviour

Nowadays, in autumn, winter and early spring the bean goose feeds almost entirely on agricultural land. The predominantly vegetarian diet varies regionally

There is evidence that the Yare population originates from an isolated Scandinavian breeding population. Of 36 geese fitted with collars at Vaesterbotten, northern Sweden, in 1987, no fewer than 22 wintered in the Yare Valley in 1987–88 and all but one of these returned in the following winter. Most of the other collared geese went to Jutland, Denmark, but none went to the main *fabalis* wintering ground in the Netherlands. This also emphasises the cold-weather link between England and Denmark. Among other British sites which have held significant numbers in recent decades are the Carron Valley, west Stirling, and Slammanan in the Avon Valley. Very few birds occur in south-west England and Wales, but in some years small numbers turn up in the Severn Valley, Gloucestershire. Ireland does not have records in every year and the 8 which visited in 1981–2 were described as 'a major influx'.

with the cropping season, local abundance and ease of access but there is overall concentration on grasses and the leaves, seeds, roots and tubers of cereals and other farm crops, including barley, wheat, rye, maize, oats, clover, Brussels sprouts, weed seeds and potatoes. Britain's Yare Valley flock selects cattle-grazed swards, the main food plant being the grass *Poa pratensis/trivialis*. Recently improved swards are largely ignored. Elsewhere in Britain the species concentrates on fairly poor-quality grassland and grazing marshes. On migration and on the breeding grounds both goslings and adults also eat water and land insects, molluscs, crustaceans and even fish roe as well as the leaves, buds, flowers and berries of arctic plants. Flights to feeding grounds are relatively short, flocks generally arriving at roosts after sunset and leaving before dawn.

Movements

It is not yet known precisely where most birds overwinter, but there is considerable overlap between the races. However, we do know that very few *rossicus* birds visit Britain and recent ringing (see *Distribution* above) has confirmed that the main British (Norfolk) population of *fabalis* has recently come from one just one population in northern Sweden. Birds usually start arriving in Britain in October but do not build to a peak until January, suggesting secondary movement from Denmark, where birds from the same Swedish population have been recovered. In 1991 there were no British records in March, suggesting an interrupted spring return, perhaps via Denmark. Large numbers of Fenno-Scandian and north Russian birds of both taiga and tundra races visit Scania, southern Sweden, before hard weather drives them south and west, chiefly to eastern Germany (mainly *rossicus*), Denmark and the Netherlands (mainly *fabalis*).

Throughout the range non-breeders and immatures make a northward moult migration. For example, large concentrations in southern Novaya Zemlya originate in western Siberia. These birds are flightless in complete moult for about one month, July–August.

PINK-FOOTED GOOSE
(*Anser brachyrhynchus*)

Once known as grey goose and long-billed goose

When Bartlett identified the species and devised its current English name in 1839 he was unaware that in 1833 Baillon had already declared it to be scientifically distinct from the bean goose. Furthermore, Temminck asserted that it had been recognised in Holland in 1829–30.

THE pink-footed goose was not distinguished from the bean goose until the early nineteenth century. Since then numbers have grown spectacularly and in winter Britain now holds about 80 per cent of the world population.

History and Conservation

Little is known about the early history of this species, but it may well have nested in Britain during the colder phases of the Pleistocene. The earliest records are from the Pin Hole Cave, Derbyshire, in the last glaciation, and from Jersey.

It is not clear why this species was apparently quite so scarce in Britain for much of the nineteenth century. Persecution does not appear to have been significant at the time, notwithstanding the Icelanders' rounding up of moulting birds (now stopped), so it is likely that subsequent increase was the result of major redistribution. This was made possible chiefly by the pink-foot's exploitation of changing agriculture. Not only did foods such as waste potatoes and sprouting winter wheat prove more nutritious than plants of estuarine saltmarshes, but also the cereal belt steadily extended northwards with climatic amelioration 1850–1950. Generally, there was greater continuity of food supplies and the geese were able to exploit them through using new inland roosts, especially reservoirs and, more recently, new refuges. This has been especially important as coastal disturbance has increased.

Along with the greylag, the pink-foot remains one of Britain's two main quarry geese, but with continuing population increase the *total* annual cull is apparently very reasonable. Fortunately, the pink-foot's enterprising mobility reduces its vulnerability. However, there has been local exploitation encouraged by commercialisation of sport, adding to the wider problem of disturbance at established wintering areas, principally roosts. In addition, the Wildlife and Countryside Act 1981 allows the pink-foot to be shot under licence during the close season for the purposes of crop protection. Equally worrying is possible flooding and development for hydroelectricity of main central Icelandic breeding grounds.

Distribution, Habitat and Population

The species' breeding range is very restricted, being confined to just three arctic areas: the central-east coast of Greenland, central Iceland and chiefly western coasts of the Svalbard archipelago. In Iceland favoured nest-sites are in inaccessible river gorges, where safety from predators seems to be most important. In the mid-1980s Iceland's principal breeding colony of Thjorsarver held over 10,000 pairs and east Greenland about 1,000 pairs, but since then there has been a sharp increase.

Apart from a few which visit Ireland, the entire Icelandic population, which is joined by birds from Greenland, winters in Scotland and England. The Svalbard population winters almost entirely in Denmark, the Netherlands and Belgium, numbers having grown from an estimated 7,000–10,000 in the late 1950s to over 30,000 in the mid-1980s.

Field Characters

The sexes of this grey goose are alike, although the male is slightly larger, and there is no seasonal plumage variation. The best field mark is the contrast between the dark-brown head and neck and the pale-grey body. In flight its pale-grey forewing contrasts with the dark flight feathers, but not so noticeably as that of the larger and heavier greylag. The folded wings extend slightly beyond the end of the tail, unlike those of the greylag. No other grey goose has pink bill *and* (variably) pink legs. The bean goose has orange legs, longer and shallower part-orange bill, and a darker back and forewing. Some birds have white around the bill base. Early-winter juveniles are generally duller than the adult, darker and browner above (with less distinct pale feather edges) and somewhat mottled below, with less rounded outline.

The pink-foot gets airborne a little more easily than the greylag and flies in similar direct lines with even, powerful wing-beats, though somewhat faster than the larger species. It is also more inclined towards aerobatics, frequently indulging in a 'whiffling' spiral descent from considerable height. In 'V' flight-formation flocks

The Latin specific *brachyrhynchus* derives from the Greek *brakhus* for short and *rhunkhos* for beak, making the point that it is shorter-beaked than the bean goose with which it had been confused.

Helped by better legal protection, including the banning of the sale of dead wild geese from 1968, the British wintering population grew from about 30,000 in 1950 to over 100,000 in 1983 and nearly 170,000 in 1988. Even so, the distribution of this very mobile goose still changes frequently with varying food supplies.

The average length is 60–75cm (23.6–29.5in), wing-span 135–170cm (53.2–66.9in), and weight 1,900–3,350g (4.2–7.4lb) for the male, 1,790–3,150g (3.9–6.9lb) the female.

The single clutch (no replacements recorded) of 3–5 (1–9) white or buff (often stained), rough-textured, oval eggs, average size 78 × 52mm (3.07 × 2.05in) is mostly laid from early May to early June in Iceland, but generally two or three weeks later in Svalbard and Greenland.

Great Britain's 1991 count produced a staggering record peak of nearly 230,000 birds. Distribution changes significantly from year to year so the five-year average counts are particularly useful in giving an overall picture. In some years about three-quarters of the wintering population occurs in Scotland, chiefly in areas of lowland farmland, where suitable roosts occur within commuting distance of feeding grounds. From the 1970s there has been major decline in numbers (previously 50 per cent or more of the entire population) in east-central Scotland in favour of more northerly and southerly haunts. In recent years up to 30 per cent of the population has roosted regularly in north-east Scotland, at Loch of Strathbeg and Meikle Loch. In England numbers in coastal Lancashire have increased dramatically since the 1960s and the Wash population has multiplied five times over the same period. In southern England and Wales the species is only a straggler. Sites which regularly hold over 2,000 and their average maxima 1986–91 are: Loch of Strathbeg 30,030, Westwater Reservoir 29,592, south-west Lancashire 28,563, Dupplin Loch 26,550, ▶

are mostly very evenly spaced. The pink-foot walks easily for a large goose and swims well, but dives only in response to danger.

This noisy bird has a shrill medley of calls which are lighter and higher-pitched than the bean's, lower than the distinctive 'laugh' of the white-front and not so deep as the greylag's. *Wink-wink* or *wink-wink-wink* and *ung-ung* or *ung-unk* are among the most common renderings.

Breeding

The monogamous pair-bond is lifelong and new pairs are often formed after the loss of a mate. Courtship is apparently very similar to that of other grey geese, especially the bean.

Nesting is mainly loosely colonial, in groups of up to 10, sometimes only a few metres (yards) apart. The male is strong in defence of his mate, nest and brood, though his interest wanes a little during incubation. Nest-sites are often re-used, some in central Iceland being at least 45 years old, in which case they develop a substantial rim. Most are on low, tundra hummocks and banks which are above post-thaw floods and snow-free at the time of building. Others are on rocky tundra outcrops or on ledges and pinnacles in river-gorges. Sometimes the male helps his mate to build the low mound of sedges, grasses and other vegetation, using nearby material, before the shallow cup is liberally lined with down — both during and after laying. Droppings and moss may be added too.

The female's 26/27–day incubation starts on completion of the clutch and hatching is synchronous. The young feed themselves and are well cared for by both parents. They fledge at about 56 days and leave the family group during the spring migration to the breeding grounds. Age of first breeding is usually three years, sometimes two.

Diet and Feeding Behaviour

Some insects are taken in summer, being especially valuable to the goslings as a protein source to facilitate rapid growth. The young also take parts of plants around the nest, but at 21–28 days their diet resembles the adult's, which is over-whelmingly vegetarian and in summer and early autumn includes the roots, shoots, leaves, buds, berries and seeds of tundra plants such as alpine bistort, horsetail and cotton-grass, chiefly on land. The pink-foot feeds like the greylag but with a smaller bill and gizzard has to concentrate on softer material.

As the population has grown, away from the breeding grounds the bird has become increasingly dependent on farming, especially in Britain. Here it feeds very opportunistically so there is considerable seasonal and local diet variation as well as annual change according to which crops are currently favoured. Autumn cereal stubbles (mainly barley) are a great attraction because spilt corn is easier to gather than wild seeds and predators are relatively easy to detect on increasingly large fields. As winter progresses, grass becomes increasingly important, especially *Puccinellia* and short herb swards on saltmarshes (mostly grazed), pastures and meadows. Ever-earlier (sometimes before the geese arrive) ploughing-in of stubbles has not been too serious because it is generally followed by early sowing of winter corn, whose tender shoots are eagerly grazed by the geese. Where main crops are not undersown, these highly mobile birds soon find alternatives. Occasionally important foods include potatoes (chiefly waste softened by frost),

carrots (notably on the Lancashire mosses), brassicae, sugar-beet and spring-sown cereals. Grass and growing cereals are most important in spring.

Unless they are heavily persecuted, pink-feet feed by day inland, flighting in at dawn or soon after and returning to roost at dusk unless disturbed. They also commonly feed by night when there is sufficient moonlight to see predators by. Sand and grit are taken to aid digestion. Until recently, significant numbers of pink-feet were killed by seed dressings, but now most of the offending chemicals have been outlawed.

Movements

The entire population is migratory. The Icelandic stock, and Greenland birds which travel via Iceland, mostly arrive in Scotland from late August (as early as the second week of July exceptional), but the main influx is usually in the first half of October. As winter progresses the flocks become more fragmented, their subsequent dispersal within the British Isles depending largely on the current availability of farm crops and to a lesser extent on severe weather. However, intense cold will increase the small number of immigrants from Svalbard, which are driven further west from their regular wintering grounds in Denmark, Germany and the Low Countries. Some of these may also reach Belgium and north France. The return to Svalbard starts in late February and in some years about three-quarters of the population will gather in Denmark before moving out in May. They arrive back on the breeding grounds from mid-May to early June. Icelandic birds start to return in April, after gathering in northern Britain, peak passage being at the end of the month and the end in mid-May.

There is no record of any moult migration of Svalbard birds, but in early June thousands of non-breeders move from Iceland to east Greenland. Their exceptional recovery in mainland Europe is usually related to unusual weather.

Pink-footed geese at dusk – one of the great spectacles of nature. Photo: R. Glover

▶ Montrose Basin 19,320, Slains Loch/Ythan Estuary 19,156, Solway Estuary 13,685, Loch Leven 13,280, Hule Moss 11,618, Carsebreck/Rhynd Loch 10,626, the Wash 10,510, Fylde/Morecambe Bay 9,357, Scolt Head 9,176, Aberlady Bay 8,880, Fala Flow 7,626, Wigtown Bay 7,539, Cameron Reservoir 6,764, Castle Loch 6,083, Findhorn Bay 5,762, Loch of Kinnordy 5,443, Loch Eye/Cromarty Firth 4,833, Loch Mahaick 4,324, Lour 4,180, Crombie Loch 3,927, Kinmount Ponds 3,853, Gladhouse Reservoir 3,600, Beauly Firth/Munlochy 3,398, Loch Tullybelton 3,300, Lake of Menteith 2,916 and Cowgill Reservoir 2,675. Ireland's most regular resort is the Wexford Slobs, but even there only 5–9 birds winter each year.

WHITE-FRONTED GOOSE
(Anser albifrons)

THE British Isles lie at a crossroads for this arctic breeder. Southern England and Wales are but two of many countries which the relatively abundant European or Russian race (*A. a. albifrons*) visits, but the threatened Greenland race (*A. a. flavirostris*) winters almost entirely in Ireland, Scotland and Wales.

History and Conservation

The earliest British record is from the Middle Pleistocene Wolstonian Glaciation. There is little subsequent information until modern times, but the species may have bred here in earlier cold phases. During the early nineteenth century it was said to breed in northern Sweden and Iceland, its range subsequently retreating with climatic amelioration from 1850.

The white-front is mentioned in Welsh chronicles as early as the twelfth century and it is likely that numbers wintering within north-west Europe were substantially higher before extensive drainage from the seventeenth century and the great increase in shooting in the nineteenth century. Furthermore, substantial numbers of flightless moulting birds used to be rounded up for food. The Greenland race was still widespread and numerous throughout the boglands and marshes of Ireland in the early nineteenth century, but numbers started to decline rapidly as serious drainage got underway from about 1850. Fortunately, reclamation of the Wexford Slobs from Wexford Harbour started at the same time and the geese started to use them regularly by 1900, numbers increasing rapidly to 4,000–6,000 in the 1940s. They have been the main Irish resort ever since.

Winter habitat loss continues to be a major problem and, along with persistent scaring, is driving the burgeoning population into an ever smaller number of suitable areas. Ironically, aggrieved farmers are shooting themselves in the foot because the concentrated flocks are more likely to cause significant local damage. Under normal circumstances the species is much less dependent on farmland than the other grey geese. On the Islay stronghold there have been many complaints of crop damage and licences to shoot unlimited numbers of geese have been granted despite strong protests from conservationists. Furthermore, some of these geese have been shot by paying sportsmen, which is totally contrary to the spirit of the law. The species remains on the open-season quarry list in England and Wales, but fortunately most of the birds which occur there are of the much more numerous European race. There is negligible overlap between the two sub-species. None the less, some English/Welsh wildfowlers and clubs commendably have their own voluntary local bans, especially in those few western areas where Greenland birds occasionally occur.

As Greenland white-fronts are sensitive to disturbance at wintering areas to which they are very faithful, the creation of refuges — especially on the Islay stronghold — is essential. Maintenance of the traditional system of low-intensity agriculture (such as promoted by the ESA scheme) and saving the peatlands are also important. In 1992 the species became the subject of an unique international management plan, in which all range states — Greenland, Iceland, Ireland and the UK — were involved. Such an approach to the conservation of migratory

The white-fronted goose (left) occurs in Britain in internationally important numbers, but the lesser white-fronted goose (right) is a rare visitor here.

WHITE-FRONTED GOOSE

By far Britain's most important site for Greenland white-fronts is the island of Islay, Argyll, with a five-year average of 7,930 peaking at 8,857 in March 1991. Other British sites with 1986–91 averages passing the 220 level for international importance were Machrihanish 962, Rhunahaorine 875, Tiree 835, Stranraer Loch 611, Coll 583, Loch Ken 374 and Endrick Mouth 284. Ten further sites had averages about the 100 level for national importance, plus a further four in 1990–91 alone. In Wales, Anglesey and Tregaron have been most important in recent years, with numbers generally below 100.

The 1990–91 British peak count for European white-fronts was only 4,025, almost 1,800 down on the previous winter as the range appears to be shifting eastwards. The main resorts and their five-year averages to 1990–91 were: Severn Estuary 3,534, Swale Estuary 1,892, Thames Estuary 281, River Avon/Sopley 269, North Norfolk Marshes 256, Middle Yare Marshes 136, Minsmere 122, River Tywi/Dryslwyn 107 and Alde Complex 61. As recently as the 1960s, the most westerly flock, on the wet pastures of the Tywi, had comprised 3,000 birds. Only a few ever reach Ireland, the most recorded together being 6 on the North Slob, Wexford in 1983.

birds was relatively new in western Europe and would form a key basis for the forthcoming Western Palearctic Waterfowl Agreement under the Bonn Convention. In 1991 Greenland followed Ireland and Scotland's 1981 lead in affording the species legal protection, which has done much to boost numbers. Now Greenland must also give careful consideration to the proposed reintroduction of the musk ox to the important white-front breeding ground at Naternaq.

Distribution, Habitat and Population

There are four or five subspecies (according to accepted taxonomy) of white-front within a north Holarctic breeding range. In North America it occurs from Alaska to Hudson Bay and is the only 'real' grey goose. There the combined population of the two or three races may have declined substantially since the 1976 estimate of 350,000. Western North American birds winter mainly in the Central Valley of California, some south to Mexico, whereas eastern birds winter in the Gulf states, mainly Texas and Louisiana, some reaching Mexico. The 'Russian' or European race, *A. a. albifrons*, breeds right across the top of Eurasia from the Kanin Peninsula eastwards to the Bering Strait, taking in southern Novaya Zemlya, and winters in north-west Europe, the Mediterranean, the Caspian Sea, the Persian Gulf, eastern China and Japan. *Flavirostris* breeds only in central-west Greenland and usually winters only in western Scotland, Ireland and Wales, a few birds sometimes straggling into England. Little is known about the size of the breeding population of the nominate race but it could be double the North American total.

With a much smaller range, *flavirostris* is easier to monitor, but even so numbers are mainly estimated from winter counts. From a low point of some 16,000 in the 1970s, the British Isles wintering population rose steadily to a peak count of 29,388 in 1990–91. About half of these occur in Ireland, where the dominant resort is the Wexford Slobs, which attract some 7,000–10,000. Elsewhere in Ireland the largest flocks are found at the Midland lakes, the Little Brosna, the Suck, Lough Gara, Lough Sheskinmore, Lough Foyle and Lough Swilly, but all have contained fewer than 350 birds in recent years.

Some 240,000 *albifrons* white-fronts, mainly from the north-west Russian breeding range, winter in the Baltic-North Sea region. The number wintering in southern Britain has declined recently despite steep ascendancy of the Siberian breeding population. This is because many birds have been 'short-stopping' in the Netherlands and the Nord-Rhein Westfalia region of Germany, where there have been significant improvements in feeding and protection.

Field Characters

This medium-sized, grey-brown goose is best distinguished by its white forehead and black-barred underparts, which are variable but generally show up well in flight and at rest. There is also a noticeable white line along the folded wing and white under-tail coverts. The sexes are alike, though the male is slightly larger, and there is no seasonal plumage variation. The European race *albifrons* is paler and slightly smaller than the Greenland race *flavirostris*. Both races have orange legs but only the Greenland has a predominantly orange-yellow bill, that of the European being shorter and pink (some show orange tinge near nail), usually with more white at the base. The juvenile lacks the barring underneath (some develop a few flecks in spring) until the second summer and the white at the base of the bill does not appear until the end of the first winter. The adult is darker than the larger and noticeably greyer greylag and pink-footed geese, the latter having a distinctive dark head and neck. The white-front's head is much smaller than that of the greylag and bean goose and its body slimmer and more angular than the other grey geese. The lesser white-front is almost always smaller and has more white on the forehead.

The white-front is gregarious except when nesting, but flocks vary greatly in size from a few birds to thousands, often mixed with greylag and pink-footed geese. *Albifrons* is much more sociable than *flavirostris*. This is the most agile of the grey geese. It can take off almost vertically with a sudden spring and flight is direct and powerful, but lighter than the greylag's and more often in tight bunches or V-formation. Of all the grey geese the white-front is most likely to make a sudden spiralling descent from considerable height with the wings half-folded. More wary than the greylag and pink-footed, it is capable of abrupt aerial turns. It walks and swims well.

The species' old name 'laughing goose' refers to the gabbling, almost merry *kow-yow* or *kow-lyow* flight calls, which are louder, higher-pitched and more musical than those of the pink-footed. The chorus of a flock has been likened to bells.

WHITE-FRONTED GOOSE

The average length is 65–78cm (25.6–30.7in) and wing-span 130–165cm (51.2–65in). The average weights of *albifrons* are 1,440–3,340g (3.2–7.3lb) for the male, 1,150–3,120g (2.5–6.9lb) the female; and for *flavirostris* 1,615–3,230g (3.5–7.1lb) for the male, 1,445–3,290g (3.2–7.2lb) the female.

Breeding

The monogamous pair-bond is of lifelong duration and lost mates are often rapidly replaced. Courtship is similar to that of the greylag, including the triumph ceremony, and pair-bonds are repeatedly reinforced.

Nests are widely dispersed over most of the range, but the white-front is some-times loosely colonial. Exceptionally high density (nearly 1,000 geese on less than 40sq km (15.4sq miles) during the favourable summer of 1991) occurs at the Ramsar site of Naternaq in central-west Greenland, on a vast, low, flat plain of maritime sediments recently uplifted from the sea-bed and now dotted with hundreds of small lakes and marshes with meandering streams. Tundra nest-sites are usually very near water, but carefully placed on hummocks and banks which are snow-free at the time of building and avoid submersion after the thaw. Many old nests are re-used, especially where they have a commanding view. It is mostly the female which gathers nearby vegetation to make a shallow depression lined with lichen, grass and a lot of down.

The female's solo 27/28-day incubation starts with the last egg. Hatching is syn-chronous, the young feed themselves and are cared for by both parents. They fledge at 40–43 days but do not leave the family group until the following spring, somewhere *en route* from winter quarters to the breeding grounds. Although nesting attempts and temporary pairing are known in the second year, successful wild breeding is not known before the age of three. Productivity varies consider-ably with the weather at the time of laying and hatching, the recent run of warm, dry seasons contributing significantly to the marked recovery of the Greenland race.

The single clutch (replacements not recorded) of 5–6 (3–7) smooth, oval, buff-white eggs, average size 79 × 53mm (3.11 × 2.09in), is mostly laid in early June in Greenland and throughout June in Siberia.

Diet and Feeding Behaviour

Apart from insects taken on the breeding grounds (chiefly by goslings), a few snails and other animal foods taken accidentally, the diet is overwhelmingly

The white-fronted goose is distinguished by white feathers on the face and black-barred underparts. Photo: Dennis Green

vegetarian. The white-front is still less dependent on agriculture than the other grey geese, taking the leaves, stems, stolons, tubers, rhizomes and seeds of many wild as well as cultivated plants, from saltmarsh and inland sites. This very active feeder may walk along pecking up to 130 times a minute, severing stalks with the side of the bill while jerking the head back. Sometimes it probes with the bill. Unless persecuted it feeds mostly by day inland, flighting in at daybreak or soon after and not leaving before dusk unless disturbed. In quiet areas it even roosts on the feeding grounds and sometimes feeds under the moon. As with other geese, it must take grit to aid digestion, often flighting to the shore specially to take sand.

The diet varies considerably with season and location. On the breeding grounds it includes sedges, grasses and horsetail, plus a few berries at the end of summer. In winter it can be surprisingly selective, the Greenland race favouring the plants of peatlands and freshwater marshes as well as relatively impoverished old pastures, whereas *albifrons* seems to prefer flat grazing land and often heavily fertilised new seed mixtures. Saltmarsh plants are commonly grazed and flooded fields are favourite feeding grounds. In autumn stubble grain is widely taken, later followed by frosted waste potatoes, sugar-beet, newly sown grain, sprouting winter cereals and nutritious spring grass shoots.

Movements

As their arctic breeding grounds are frozen in winter, all white-front populations are migratory. In the west Palearctic there are at least six fairly well separated main wintering groups, but it is not clear where most of the birds originate from. However, the movements of Greenland birds (*flavirostris*), which routinely winter only within the British Isles, have been well studied. After a flightless moulting period of about 25 days from late July, they start to move south and their main exodus is in September, tailing off in early October. Some travel south down the west coast of Greenland before flying direct to Ireland and Scotland, or even Wales. Most, however, appear to fly east over the Greenland ice-cap and then on to the west and south coasts of Iceland, where they may remain until late October before flying on to the British Isles. The Greenland race is only a vagrant to England and continental Europe.

In late winter there is gradual northward drift within the British Isles before birds start to leave in mid-April. Only a few stragglers remain in May, the latest sighting being on 19 May. Most return via Iceland, where they are seen throughout May, and arrive back on their west Greenland breeding grounds from the second week of May to early June. In 1969 there was an exceptional series of July records from Ireland.

Albifrons white-fronts from Novaya Zemlya and north-western mainland areas of the former USSR start to arrive in England and Wales in October, but relatively few come before December and they may not peak until February, as they are driven further west by colder weather. Most return in March and early April. Much larger numbers routinely winter in northern Germany, the Netherlands and Belgium, spreading into France according to severity of weather. There is little interchange between the North Sea and south-east Europe winter groups.

Earliest recorded arrival of Greenland birds in Scotland is 12 September, but the main British influx occurs in late October and early November, the latter month usually producing the peak national count. White-fronts show great site fidelity so winter counts are usually fairly constant at most places, but ringing has confirmed that there is some interchange between Scotland (Islay) and Ireland (Wexford and smaller resorts) and a little wandering between other neighbouring sites.

LESSER WHITE-FRONTED GOOSE
(Anser erythropus)

B EING so similar to the slightly larger white-fronted goose, this species has probably been significantly under-recorded until recently. Its main migration routes are east of western Europe, but small numbers appear to get mixed up with flocks of white-fronted and bean geese moving west and regularly turn up in North Sea countries.

History and Conservation

Very little is known of the species' early history. There are no certain fossil records and we do not know if its breeding range was ever more westerly or southerly, but it was probably more widespread in Europe during the 'Little Ice Age' 1550–1850. This century there has been marked decline and contraction at the western end of its breeding range, in northern Scandinavia. There has also been decrease in numbers wintering in south-east Europe. Apparent increase in the number of vagrants to North Sea countries is almost certainly the result of an upsurge of interest in bird-watching. Indeed, there is clear correlation between 'hot spots' and concentrations of bird-watchers.

Factors causing decline in the west, where this goose was never known to be numerous, are not clear. The breeding habitat appears to be fairly secure. Perhaps range contraction through climatic change has been accelerated by winter habitat loss and excessive hunting on migration and at the wintering grounds. The species is fully protected in the British Isles.

The common name simply reflects the fact that this is a small version of the white-fronted goose, recognised since 1758. The Latin specific *erythropus* derives from the Greek *eruthros* for red and refers to the bright-pink bill.

The species is accidental in the British Isles (123 accepted records to the end of 1990), France, Belgium, the Netherlands, Denmark, Germany, Austria, Czechoslovakia, Switzerland, Turkey and Egypt. Most of the small number which occur in most years in the British Isles are seen in southern England, often with European white-fronted geese at Slimbridge, and some are escapes. It has occurred only irregularly in Scotland since the first record in 1953. Ireland's first record was from the North Slob, Wexford, on 23 and 30 March 1969.

The average length is 53–66cm, (20.9–26in), wing-span 120–135cm (47.2–53.2in), and weight 1,800–2,000g (3.9–4.4lb) for the male, 1,400–1,843g (3.1–4lb) the female.

Distribution, Habitat and Population

This grey goose breeds in a narrow, almost exclusively inland band across northern Eurasia, from central-northern Norway, Sweden and Finland to the Anadyr Basin in eastern Siberia, mainly north of the Arctic Circle. There has been abrupt decline in Scandinavia since the 1950s, when Sweden and Norway probably had fewer than Finland's estimated 200 pairs. Unlike the white-fronted goose, the lesser is rarely associated with islands, coasts, estuaries, shorelines and low-lying tundras. Favoured nesting areas are on the fringes of wooded tundra or forest edge, craggy fells and foothills, and slopes by streams. Therefore its breeding zone falls between that of the high arctic and that of the low tundra.

Winter quarters are mostly within the continental climatic zone, in open, tree-less areas, from meadows and pastures to semi-arid salt steppes, lakes and rivers, rarely in marine waters. Western birds migrate through central Europe to partly unknown wintering grounds, probably chiefly in the eastern Mediterranean. In recent decades up to 5,000 birds have been seen in Hungary, but far fewer than there used to be and less than numbers now wintering on the southern Caspian in the former USSR, Iran and Iraq. Birds from eastern Siberia, probably in smaller numbers, winter in eastern China, Korea and Japan.

Field Characters

In a flock of white-fronted geese this species is best distinguished by its relatively small size, shorter neck, smaller head and more rapid movements. At close quarters further good pointers are the yellow eye-ring, and wings extending beyond the end of the tail (the larger bird's do not). The greater area of white on the forehead alone is not a safe indicator as some individuals of the larger species have this. The uniformly pink bill will distinguish from Greenland white-fronts. As in the white-fronted goose, the juvenile lacks the forehead white in early winter and the black barring on the belly, but at close quarters may be distinguished by the developing yellow eye-ring.

This very aerial bird is even faster and more agile than the larger white-fronted goose, its flying skills being clearly demonstrated in warding off predators. It also walks faster, sometimes breaking into a run.

The calls are similar to those of the white-fronted goose, but clearly faster and higher-pitched — almost squeaky. They do not carry so far as those of the larger geese. The male's main call has been given as *kyu-yu* or *kyu-yu-yu* and the female's as *kow-yow*.

Breeding

The single clutch (no information on replacements) of 4–6 (2–8) smooth, oval, yellowish-white eggs, average size 76 × 49mm (3 × 1.93in), is mostly laid in June in the west Palearctic.

The monogamous pair-bond is lifelong. Display is similar to that of other geese, concentrating on neck posturing, but movements are quicker.

Nests are mostly well dispersed (often 0.5–1km (525–1,100 yards) apart along rivers) and the male is strong in defence of his mate and eggs. The site is usually close to water, but may be up to some 150m (yards) away, mostly open on a snow-free hummock or rocky outcrop, but sometimes in dense birch scrub. Many sites are traditional, old nests being lined with fresh grass. The slight, flattened mound of vegetation is probably built by the female alone and the cup is liberally lined with down.

The female's solo 25/28-day incubation starts with the last egg and hatching is synchronous. The young feed themselves, fledge at 35–40 days and remain with their parents through the first autumn and winter, leaving the family at some point on the spring migration. Age of first breeding is usually at three years, sometimes two. The lesser white-front's stay on the breeding grounds is unusually long for an arctic breeder, apparently up to 120 days even though the breeding cycle may be completed in less than 80 days.

Diet and Feeding Behaviour

Very little is known about the diet. Only plant food is recorded, but it would be surprising if no insects were taken, especially by the goslings on the breeding grounds. Main items are the shoots, leaves and stems of grasses, herbs and other plants, varying with season and location. These include the least willow in Lapland and the white beak-sedge in Wales. Wild seeds and cereal grains are also taken. Most feeding is by day. The bill has only 18–23 'teeth' compared with 25–29 in the white-fronted goose.

Movements

North Scandinavian and arctic Russian breeding grounds are vacated in late August and early September, the main migration routes being from Fenno-Scandia through the Baltic states and south to south-east across the western part of the former USSR. Major wintering grounds, such as around the southern Caspian Sea, are reached from mid-October. Birds start to leave the Caspian area in February and most are gone by the end of March, passing through the Sea of Azov in early April. Most return to the breeding grounds in May. Birds which turn up in the British Isles and the Low Countries are usually in flocks of white-fronted and bean geese.

Long moult migrations are not known but non-breeders form substantial moulting flocks and, in Scandinavia at least, move upwards in the alpine zone.

The bold eye-ring of the lesser white-front helps to distinguish the species from the white-fronted goose. Photo: E. A. Janes/ ZAP

CANADA GOOSE
(*Branta canadensis*)

CANADA GOOSE
Once known as cravat goose and Canada swan

Both Latin and English names (the latter coined by Ray in 1678) indicate the bird's North American origin. The old name cravat goose derives from the species' white chin-strap.

The population growth has been remarkable since the first national census, in 1953, when there were an estimated 2,600–3,600 birds in Britain. The Wildfowl Trust survey of 1967–9 revealed 10,000–10,500 birds and the UK national wildfowl counts recorded 19,640 in 1981, rising to 39,000 in 1985. The upward trend is continuing and is causing problems not only for farmers but also for managers of amenity areas where the geese damage lawns, foul footpaths and destroy lakeside vegetation. There is also the worry of competition with native species such as the greylag (now also thriving ferally), whose vacant niche the Canada has partly filled. However, in some places greylags have increased despite the presence of Canadas. This has resulted in the regular occurrence of hybrids, but these are thought to be infertile as *Anser/Branta* crosses are thought to be genetically incapable of producing second-generation crosses.

'Black' geese: brent (left), Canada (centre), barnacle (right).

ORIGINALLY introduced from North America to grace wildfowl collections, this bird has escaped to form thriving feral populations in Britain and other parts of Europe. Unfortunately it has become a significant agricultural pest and many of the wildfowlers who encouraged its spread have been disappointed by the bird's sporting potential.

History and Conservation

The Canada goose was first imported into Britain in about 1665, when King Charles acquired it for his waterfowl collection. Following further introductions and escapes, the bird was breeding freely on the estates of wealthy landowners by the late eighteenth century. By the 1840s flocks wandered at will in England and in the 1890s it was breeding ferally in scattered groups as far north as Westmorland. In the 1930s there were over 2,000 on Scottish estates, but during World War II winter feeding had to be discontinued and by 1953 there were only about 150 north of the border.

The first complaints about damage to cereals and puddling of fields came in the early 1950s, when wildfowlers were sometimes called in to shoot the birds, though egg destruction was also tried. However, sportsmen were also keen to introduce the geese to other waters, so from the 1950s they started to round the birds up during their flightless period in areas where they were not wanted and take them to places where they would add variety to the bag. They were especially welcome at many of the new flooded gravel pits and reservoirs. This led to major increases in the 1960s and 1970s and the temporarily depleted colonies soon recovered as non-breeders found room to establish territories. Introduction or deliberate re-lease into the wild became illegal through the Wildlife and Countryside Act 1981, but the seeds of major expansion were already sown. It made little difference that many shooters had already lost interest in the sport they provided.

In Britain it is the relative tameness of the generally low-flying Canada goose which has put many sportsmen off shooting it, but there are those who say that the species quickly changes its habits where hunted regularly. Meanwhile the ascendancy continues and it has been estimated that at least another 2,000 would have to be killed every season merely to keep the goose at its 1980 level. This is most unlikely at a time when quarry shooters are being urged to concentrate on quality rather than quantity. Many British Canadas do not even flight to feed. Control is particularly difficult in parklands, where the geese often thrive and shooting is not possible or desirable. Rounding-up and destroying birds during their flightless moulting period would invite widespread criticism, especially among the majority of public who know no other wild goose. Licences for the pricking of eggs can be obtained but the goose is long-lived so this needs to be carried out very efficiently over at least several years to bring about a real decline. It is now considered that more effective control through egg removal occurs when dummy eggs are placed in the nests of early layers, as few geese nesting later will re-lay and incubate their second clutch. Licences to shoot the bird during the close season can be obtained under the Wildlife and Countryside Act 1981.

CANADA GOOSE

Yet there is hope that this very palatable goose will become more attractive to sportsmen as its behaviour changes. Indeed, part of the large Yorkshire population has already developed the migratory habit which is strong among most races in the native range. The species continues to be a major and much-valued quarry in North America, where vast numbers still occur. Ironically, it was the English who were at the forefront of developing sport there through early reliance on meat. For example, in the eighteenth century settlers at Hudson's Bay depended greatly on the geese, in favourable years killing three or four thousand, which they salted down in barrels. Pennant wrote: 'Their arrival is impatiently attended; it is the harbinger of the spring, and the month named by the Indians the Goose Moon.'

The Canada goose has been introduced to many countries, including New Zealand, where it has become a significant pest. Although it was not taken to Sweden until 1929, the population there is increasing more rapidly and is already greater than that in Britain. Finland already has a thriving migratory population although breeding was not recorded there before 1966. With free-flying birds also present in other European countries, and much apparently suitable habitat still unoccupied, the species seems set for further major expansion.

Distribution, Habitat and Population

The number of subspecies is still disputed but there appear to be at least twelve, breeding altogether being over most of Canada and the northern USA. In winter most of this vast range is too cold so birds move south and west, but in north-west Europe introduced birds of the *Canadensis* race are resident where the climate permits.

Sweden's feral population is concentrated in the south and had reached 50,000 in the early 1980s, with 5,000 breeding pairs. If it has continued to exceed the British rate of increase of some 8 per cent per annum it may now have passed 100,000. Finland has over 3,000 birds and Norway's population has expanded considerably since introduction to Oslo in 1936 and Trondelag in 1958.

Migratory Canada geese from the native range occasionally turn up in north-west Europe, especially in Ireland and western Scotland. (See *Movements*)

Field Characters

The sexes are alike and there are no seasonal plumage differences, but there is considerable variation in size and colour between the races. British geese are similar to the *Canadensis* race but in size they approach the *moffitti* ('giant' Canada goose) so there has almost certainly been some mixing of introduced birds. This long-necked (hence 'swan goose') species is easy to identify, being far larger than Europe's two other 'black' geese, the barnacle and brent, which have a black rather than pale breast. The Canada's best field mark is the white chin-strap, which contrasts strongly with the black head and neck and mainly grey-brown body. The juvenile has a greyer chin-strap but by its first winter is virtually indistinguishable from the adult in the field.

This goose is gregarious for much of the year, flocks composed of family parties often numbering thousands outside the breeding season. It walks easily, though sedately, and swims well and frequently. In Europe it is very tolerant of man, even tame in many situations, but soon puts a safe distance between itself and per-

Within the species worldwide, the length is 56–110cm (22–43.3in) and wing-span 122–183cm (48–72in), but in European feral populations alone the average length is 90–100cm (35.5–39.4in), wing-span 160–175cm (63–68.9in) and weight 4,170–5,410g (9.2–11.9lb) for the male, 3,670–4,950g (8.1–10.9lb) for the generally smaller and much lighter female.

Not everyone has welcomed this introduced species' ascendancy. Photo: B. Martin

sistent persecution. Flight is deceptively fast, with deep, regular wing-beats, often low in single file or loose flocks over short distances but generally much higher and in V-formation or diagonals on migration.

Unlike the wild flocks in America, European birds are not very noisy when settled but do have a low-pitched, gabbling ground conversation. The most common flight call is a distinctive and far-carrying *aa-honk*. A swan-like hiss warns off intruders or competitors.

Breeding

The monogamous pair-bond is lifelong and lost mates are replaced. As in the greylag, the cornerstone of courtship is the triumph ceremony, which is also used throughout the year but diminishes with age. In this there is much trumpeting and the pair often run together. There is also lots of posturing with the head and neck held parallel to the ground.

Nests may be isolated, but where prime sites are scarce or relatively secure on islands, nesting is usually loosely colonial. In England established pairs will use the same territory and nests each year, gradually re-establishing their rights in late winter and early spring, before the family group has disbanded, and usually including the adjacent mainland-bank grazing area. Territories are vigorously defended until the young start foraging. At high density colonial nesting often results in territories of minimum size and some birds unable to breed through lack of space. At relatively isolated sites in Britain the 'spare' birds are unlikely to colonise new waters without the aid of man because they are so sedentary.

The ground nest is usually less than 30m (yards) from water, often under a bush or tree but sometimes in the open, especially on preferred island sites. Where

The single clutch (replaced after early loss) of 5–6 (3–11) oval, dull white or creamy (often stained) eggs, average size 86 × 58mm (3.39 × 2.28in), is laid from mid-March in Britain, but mostly in the first half of April. In Sweden laying starts mid-April.

49

With an estimated 5 million birds in North America this is the most numerous goose in the world.

The 1990–91 count gave a British peak population of 37,994 in October (almost 4,000 up on 1989–90), with a further 252 in Northern Ireland, but it is known that many birds are missed because they often feed far from water. A 1991 survey indicates the population at well over 60,000 birds including non-breeders. The main resorts and average maxima 1986–91 were Kedleston Park Lake 1,348, Stratfield Saye 1,340, Bewl Water 1,059, Abberton Reservoir 935, Rutland Water 872, Dorchester gravel pit 670, Twyford gravel pit 661, Blithfield Reservoir 665, Drakelow gravel pit 608 and Harewood Lake 606. In the 1990–91 season alone other important sites and their maxima were: Fleet Pond 804, Bar Mere 800, King's Bromley gravel pit 714, Dinton Pastures 682, Tundry Pond 674, Capesthorne Hall 653, Eversley Cross and Yateley gravel pits 636, Eccup Reservoir 622, Ellesmere gravel pits 608 and Kirby Bellars gravel pit 602. Most birds are found in south-east and central England, the year-round distribution largely following the preferred habitat of open, standing water in lowlands, although the goose is now colonising upland areas of northern England and central Scotland. Numbers are ▶

nests are exceptionally several kilometres (miles) from water they are almost always well hidden by bracken or heather. The female does most of the nest-building, using nearby material to form a low mound of reeds, grass and leaves on a base of twigs and branches. Down lining is added both during and after laying.

The female's solo 28/30-day incubation commences on completion of the clutch and hatching is synchronous. The young feed themselves, are well cared for by both parents (which are often aggressive towards human intruders), fledge at 40–48 days and achieve independence at the start of the next breeding season. Age of first breeding is mostly three years but sometimes two or four. Several families occasionally form a loose flock.

Diet and Feeding Behaviour

The diet is primarily vegetable, including leaves, stems, tubers, rhizomes, roots, fruits and seeds taken mostly by grazing, but sometimes through up-ending or dipping the head under water. Aquatic, marsh and cultivated plants are eaten, especially grass, but also including clover, sprouting winter and spring cereals, sedges, pondweeds, bulrush, stubble grain, kale and some root crops such as mangolds and sugar-beet. Insects and other invertebrates are more important to the goslings. Except where greatly disturbed, most feeding is by day. The Canada goose usually flights to the feeding grounds after sunrise and returns to roost soon after sunset, but where distances are short — as is often the case in Britain — it walks. In urban and park environments it readily takes food handouts.

Movements

Although most populations are highly migratory in their native North America, where they move north to moult and south to overwinter, British Canada geese are still mostly sedentary for much of the year. However, a substantial moult migration to Scotland started in Yorkshire in the 1950s and the habit has been gradually extending to birds breeding further south, especially in the West Midlands but exceptionally from as far afield as Sussex. These non-breeders (about 50 per cent 1/2-year-olds), which would otherwise compete for food, generally arrive at the Beauly Firth in Aberdeenshire from the end of May, peak in July and return from mid-August to mid-September. Smaller moulting flocks in Scotland, as far afield as Caithness and the Northern Isles, are thought to be partly the result of English birds overshooting their intended Beauly destination after following a coastal path.

In autumn and winter some other British Canadas become more mobile and may flight for at least several kilometres (or miles) between roosts and feeding grounds. Then they are more inclined to visit estuaries and saltmarshes, especially in severe weather, when (exceptionally) they may travel very long distances, a few ringed birds having been recovered in north France. Swedish breeders regularly migrate south in late October and November, some wintering in southern Sweden while others move on to Denmark, Germany and the Netherlands (exceptionally to Spain). In mild years they start to return in February, but most go back in March and early April. Sweden is presumed to be the home of July moulting flocks on Hiddensee Island, eastern Germany. Finnish and Norwegian birds are forced to winter south, too, but little is known about their cold-weather quarters.

Individuals of the small eastern races *hutchinsii* and *parvipes* regularly occur in autumn in west Greenland, where *hutchinsii* has bred. These, and possibly the races *minima* and *interior*, are thought to feature along with the positively identified nominate *canadensis* among the small numbers of transatlantic vagrants which turn up in small numbers each year in Ireland and western Scotland, chiefly among Greenland white-fronted and barnacle geese. Indeed, in Ireland most of the noticeably smaller individuals occur on the Wexford Slobs at the same time as large numbers of wintering Greenland white-fronted geese. Furthermore, the Wexford flocks regularly include believed hybrids of Canada × barnacle geese, Canada × white-fronted geese and Canada × snow geese, indicating origin mainly, if not wholly in arctic Canada or Greenland.

CANADA GOOSE

▶ relatively low in much of south-west England and Wales, but increasing there too. Ireland has strong populations (also based on waterfowl collections) at Strangford Lough (truly feral birds) and The Lough, Cork, plus over 400 at Lough Erne and at least 300 elsewhere.

BRENT GOOSE
(Branta bernicla)

TWO races winter in Europe in internationally important numbers. The dark-bellied brent goose (*B. b. bernicla*) winters exclusively in north-west Europe (about half in Britain) and, following dramatic recovery of its population, many British shooters are keen to have it restored to the quarry list. Numbers of pale-bellied brent geese (*B. b. hrota*) visiting Ireland appear to be on the increase too, but the discreet breeding population of Svalbard and Franz Josef Land, which sometimes winters almost entirely at Lindisfarne (Northumberland), remains precariously low.

History and Conservation

Earliest records of the brent in Britain are from the cooler phases of the last glaciation and into the early Holocene, when it might have bred here. Later records are confused because many early ornithologists regarded the brent and barnacle as the same species. Also, although the pale-bellied race was first described in 1776, it is rarely referred to in British literature before the 1950s. However, there is no

BRENT GOOSE
Once known as brant goose (still standard in North America), brand goose, the black goose, ware goose, horie goose, horra goose, rott goose, rat goose, rood goose, road goose, quink goose, clatter goose, crocker, barnacle and brabt

Pennant adopted the name 'brent goose' in 1768, following Ray's use of 'brant goose' in 1678. Branta goes back to Turner in 1544, deriving from the Anglo Saxon *brennan*, meaning to burn, and the Old Norse *brandgas*, for black or burnt goose. The Latin specific *bernicla* (from the French *bernicle*) and many of the old common names also refer to the barnacle goose, with which the brent was often confused.

With a long history of domestication, geese often figured in early literature.
Photo: B. Martin

51

BRENT GOOSE

The brent's breeding habitat is restricted chiefly to low tundra with many pools in the high arctic, where nesting must start before the thaw and the young must leave with their parents within about three months. Away from the breeding grounds and migration routes, it rarely visits fresh water.

doubt that the brent was a common winter visitor to north-west Europe in the eighteenth century. Indeed, in some years it occurred in numbers sufficient to cause serious agricultural damage. For example, in the hard winters of 1740 and 1765, the people of coastal Picardy, in France, were raised to drive the 'immense swarms' from the cornfields, but they failed and the birds only left when the weather changed. In the nineteenth century Morris was but one author who wrote of 'vast multitudes which blackened the ground' in Britain. Not surprisingly, the great flocks became a favourite target for the punt-gunner, apparently up to 300 brent being killed by one double-discharge. Large numbers were taken to market and the brent became a popular table bird.

Despite the huge cull, the species was still widespread and numerous during the early twentieth century. It was largely a natural phenomenon which precipitated sharp decline. In the 1930s probably at least 75 per cent of the big flocks of brent, as well as innumerable wigeon, disappeared from many north-west European coasts when disease of the marine grass *Zostera* removed their main food supply. Numbers remained depressed until the introduction of protective legislation in 1954, by which time the world population of the dark-bellied race had shrunk alarmingly to some 16,500.

Recovery was very slow at first and hampered by the fact that the species is an exceptionally erratic breeder, failing on average to raise any young every other year. But as numbers increased in the 1970s the birds started to feed more on coastal arable land and pasture when their food supplies below the sea-wall were depleted. Now farmland feeding is firmly established, but as the brent population has soared it has been necessary to issue licences to shoot them as scaring devices have become largely ineffective in protecting crops. However, scarers such as gas guns would probably regain their initial effect if used in conjunction with shooting. Unfortunately for farmers, the geese have come to prefer the more reliable and easily accessible cultivated foods. Indeed, the current high population probably depends on them. Furthermore, farm fields are especially attractive to geese in providing relatively level and sheltered feeding sites where large numbers may disperse easily and are not disturbed by buffeting coastal winds. Playing fields, too, are prime targets for their grass and roosting sites, much to the annoyance of sportsmen who find their prized turf fouled by droppings.

Many wildfowlers would like to see the species returned to the general quarry list, pointing out that controlling numbers would alleviate the farmers' problem. However, other sportsmen are against this because they fear that the species' new tameness would result in mass slaughter. To compromise, Sir Peter Scott suggested that shooting should be allowed only inland of the sea-wall, the limited sport helping to drive birds back to their natural habitat. However, the British Association for Shooting and Conservation pointed out that 69 per cent of 47 wildfowling clubs consulted wanted the bird back as a *sporting* quarry species, not simply as a pest to be controlled. In fact, fears of an excessive cull are ill-founded because as long ago as the early nineteenth century it was noted that the apparently tame flocks soon became very wary once a few shots were fired. Also, within the sport the tide has clearly turned against the taking of large bags. None the less, much of the shooting would take place in very public places and some shooters believe that this would jeopardise the future of the whole sport.

As numbers wintering in Britain have increased roughly in proportion to the world population, there appears to be no conservation reason for not restoring the brent to the quarry list. However, as the subspecies are not easy to separate in the field there would clearly have to be regional restrictions to continue close protection of the far less numerous pale-bellied race, whose feeding grounds around Lindisfarne must be carefully conserved. Even if the BASC is successful in winning Government support they point out that it could be at least several years before the brent is in the gamebag again because European Community approval requires unanimous support of member states. Furthermore, European interest is likely to be slight because the only legal bag currently taken is a small one in Germany for crop-protection. However, it is estimated that some 2,000 are shot illegally in France each winter despite protection there since 1966.

Some conservationists fear rapid reversal of factors which have brought brent recovery. Although protection throughout most of the wintering grounds has been significant, they say that the ascendancy is mainly due to a long series of very successful nesting seasons made possible by favourable weather. Not only could this suddenly change but also farm practices might swing against the goose. There is also increasing disturbance and threat of development on coasts and estuaries used by the geese. But then, the same arguments apply to wildfowl which are still shot. Clearly the brent goose is providing a test case which will largely determine the future of wildfowl shooting. If a compromise is reached and wildfowlers regain the right to cull this bird then we will need close monitoring and perhaps more flexible legislation than we have been used to. In the meantime, securing further strategically-sited roosts and alternative feeding grounds will alleviate but not eradicate agricultural pressure. In the Netherlands the brent has become known as 'the goose with the golden feet' because farmers are paid large sums to compensate for crop damage, but throughout Europe there is increasing antagonism to financial solution of conservation problems. Such funds would be better spent on speeding recovery of the *Zostera* beds or sanctuary purchase.

Concern has been expressed that the wigeon has suffered through competition with the brent, but the duck is thriving despite this, having followed the goose in developing the inland feeding habit. None the less, although wigeon numbers are greatly up overall, there has been significant redistribution and some of this is due to brent pressure, causing mixed feelings among wildfowlers. More serious is competition between the pale-bellied brent and the increasing barnacle goose population, which now nests on many of the brent's former breeding islands.

Distribution, Habitat and Population

The three races differ little in morphological characters, but have a wide range of intermediates. The dark-bellied brent is restricted to the Palearctic and prefers grassy tundra near coasts or in river valleys whereas the pale-bellied also favours coastal islands. The nominate dark-bellied race (*B. b. bernicla*) breeds on the arctic coasts of Siberia, from Kolguev Island east to the Taimyr Peninsula and the islands of Severnaya Zemlya. It winters in Denmark, Germany, the Netherlands, Belgium, Britain and France. Black brant (*B. b. nigricans*) breeding in north-east Siberia winter on the coasts of the Yellow Sea in Korea and China, and in Japan. *Nigricans* breeding on Wrangel Island and the Chukotski Peninsula winter on the Pacific coast of the USA and Mexico, where they are joined by breeders from Alaska and western arctic Canada. To the end of 1990 there were 52 accepted records of the *nigricans* race in the British Isles. The pale-bellied brent (*B. b. hrota*) breeds on both sides of the Atlantic in three separate ranges. One breeds in Svalbard and Franz Josef Land and winters chiefly in Denmark, with variable

BRENT GOOSE

In 1990–91 Britain's peak count of 124,067 (February) was a new record. Resorts of international importance (holding 1,700 birds) and their average maxima 1986–91 were: the Wash 21,808, Thames Estuary 20,265, (but with a staggering 33,109 in October 1990), North Norfolk Marshes 10,112, Chichester Harbour 9,816, Blackwater Estuary 8,949, Langstone Harbour 7,474, Hamford Water 5,645, Colne Estuary 5,524, Crouch Estuary 5,057, Medway Estuary 4,135, Swale Estuary 2,876, Portsmouth Harbour 2,885, Pagham Harbour 2,741, Exe Estuary 2,439, north-west Solent 2,251, Dengie 1,975 and Humber Estuary 1,971. Other important sites and maxima 1990–91 were The Fleet/Medway with 2,800 in December and Deben with 2,051 in January.

The entire Svalbard/Franz Josef Land population of pale-bellied brent, which has apparently declined from some 4,000–5,000 in the 1950s to about 3,500, starts the winter in Denmark. Later, numbers varying from about 300 to the whole population (according to the severity of the weather) move on to Lindisfarne, north-east England. Smaller groups sometimes occur in other places, chiefly in south-east England. Recent Lindisfarne counts (December) have been relatively stable: 3,000 in 1986–87, 2,000 1987–88, 3,000 1988–89, 3,000 1989–90 and 2,700 1990–91.

53

numbers in north-east England (mostly Lindisfarne). Another breeds in north and east Greenland and on northern Canadian islands and winters mostly in Ireland.

The world population of the dark-bellied brent appears to have increased substantially since the 1988–89 estimate of 235,000. About half of these winter in south-east England, chiefly on estuaries from the Wash to the Solent. Smaller numbers visit the coasts of Wales, south-west England and northern England. At Lindisfarne they overlap with the pale-bellied brent. Few occur inland. In Scotland it is a passage and irregular winter visitor, in variable but usually small numbers averaging 30–300. In most years about half are subspecifically identified, revealing that between 1968 and 1980 83 per cent of 728 birds were pale-bellied. Probably most of these come from Ireland but some are from Svalbard. Most Scottish dark-bellied brent records are from the eastern half of the country.

Field Characters

The average length is 56–61cm (22–24in), wing-span 110–120cm (43.3–47.2in), and weight 1,270–1,575g (2.8–3.5lb) for the male, 1,090–1,395g (2.4–3.1lb) the female.

Brent geese landing in winter wheat. Growing flocks have caused considerable agricultural damage. Photo: R. Glover

This stocky, duck-sized goose is unlikely to be confused with any other bird except perhaps the barnacle goose, from which it is separated by its all-black head and darker body contrasting with a more prominent white stern. The sexes are similar and there is no seasonal plumage variation. The races are distinguishable in the field. As its name implies, the pale-bellied race *hrota* is much paler than the dark-bellied brent on the lower breast, belly and flanks. The *nigricans* race differs from the dark-bellied in having a much deeper and more prominent white collar, an overall browner tinge, and broader pale bars on the flanks. However, there are many intermediates so stragglers can be hard to distinguish. In all races the juvenile resembles the adult, but lacks the white neck-patch and has bolder barring on the lower mantle, scapulars and wings. The white neck-patch starts to show in the first winter, when the pale wing-bars are still prominent.

The brent goose is highly gregarious, especially in autumn and winter when flocks, often in hundreds, constantly wheel rapidly back and forth between foreshore and inland feeding grounds and roosts. On mudflats they tend to spread out more than when feeding on fields, where they tend to move in tight bunches, almost as one. They seldom fly in V-formation, instead wavering and undulating gracefully in mostly low lines or irregular masses, with quicker wing-beats than larger geese. The brent walks well, with quick, precise movements, and swims readily with its stern high to display the white undertail. During the flightless moulting period it dives readily. In many areas it has become very tolerant of man, often flying back and forth across busy main roads and moving no further than necessary on close approach.

Flocks are often very noisy in flight and on water, but their constant, guttural, rolling *rot* or *rronk* is pleasing and much softer than other goose calls.

Breeding

A monogamous, lifelong pair-bond is believed to be usual. Display has been little observed but includes flashing of the white undertail, considerable head-dipping neck posturing and neck-shaking (in which the white neck-patch appears to be important).

In some parts of the range nests are dispersed, usually within a few hundred metres (yards) of the sea but up to some 10km (6 miles) inland. More commonly they are very close to water and colonial, especially in small, relatively secure groups on coastal islets or islands on lakes. The gander is very territorial and strongly defends a small area around the nest, which is always in the open and no more than a shallow depression on a dry hummock or prominence clear of melt-water. Both sexes line it with grasses and mosses within easy reach, the female adding much down both during and after laying. Old nests are often re-used, but given a new lining.

Because the brent has the longest migration of all geese, the breeding season is short and it is unlikely that the single clutch is replaced on loss, even when the eggs are laid within a week of arrival on the breeding grounds.

The female's solo 24/26-day incubation starts with the last egg and hatching is synchronous. The young leave the nest within two days, feed themselves, are cared for by both parents and probably fledge at about 40 days. They remain with their parents through the first autumn and winter and start the spring migration with them, but disperse before reaching the breeding grounds. Age of first breeding is two or three years.

The breeding success of Siberian *bernicla* is the most variable of all Palearctic geese, the proportion of young in British winter flocks ranging from less than 1 per cent to over 45 per cent. Production is also very erratic among pale-bellied brent, which is why some conservationists still resist restoring the species to the shooting list even though the overall population has made such a strong recovery.

Diet and Feeding Behaviour

The brent's diet consists almost entirely of vegetation. Animal foods such as molluscs, crustaceans and lugworms are occasionally taken, but probably mostly accidentally. A fairly wide variety of plants is mostly grazed or torn and pulled up underwater, but also while drifting. Feeding is chiefly diurnal but related to tides

Clutches of 3–5 (1–8) oval, creamy-white or yellow-white (*hrota*) or green-white or pale-olive (*bernicla*) eggs, averaging 71 × 47mm (2.8 × 1.85in), are laid from the third week in May to the first week in July, but mostly over the last three weeks of June.

A Norfolk study (Summers and Critchley 1990) found that dark-bellied brent spent 74 per cent of the day on grass or arable fields during midwinter, with 44–66 per cent of the observations on grass fields. The geese selected fields with a high percentage of 'live' grass, perhaps through colour, and of these fields those with the shortest grass and the fewest thistles were favoured. Grazing on winter cereals resulted in the loss of about 75 per cent of the biomass of leaves and shoots. Grazed wheat ripened late and average grain-yield losses were 6–10 per cent. In many areas grass is also taken from playing fields and even golf courses as well as valuable pastures.

BRENT GOOSE

and the bird will feed by moonlight. Plants covered by the tide are taken through up-ending or swimming with the head and neck below the surface. At low tide rhizomes are exposed or loosened from mud by grubbing and trampling.

Breeding-ground food includes algae, mosses, lichens and the stalks and leaves of grasses and herbs. In the winter quarters the species has a long history of taking cultivated crops when mudflat foods are exhausted, but this has been of increasing interest as brent population recovery has resulted in serious economic loss. Major change appears to have been stimulated by population decrease related to a dramatic decline of the main food *Zostera marina* in the North Atlantic from the 1930s. Since then *Zostera noltii* appears to have become more important, along with green seaweeds — especially *Enteromorpha* and *Ulva*, which are taken in addition to a variety of saltmarsh plants and grasses, but the choice depends on availability.

Unfortunately, these natural foods have been widely depleted by disease, pollution, development and disturbance, so the greatly increased brent flocks have been forced to feed on coastal farmland. When the favoured eel-grass is largely exhausted at main centres such as Foulness in Essex and Strangford Lough, Northern Ireland, the big brent concentrations disperse to other estuaries, chiefly from early December. In most areas grass and cereals have long been mainstays, but the recent trend towards winter cereals and oil-seed rape has been of special benefit, the young shoots providing both high nutrient levels and more reliable food supplies.

Movements

Dark-bellied brent leave north-east Siberia from mid-August to early September and mostly head west along the coasts of the former USSR to the White Sea, then overland to the gulfs of Finland and Bothnia. They pass through the Baltic from mid-September to early October. Some arrive in Denmark in late September, but most in October. Relatively small numbers remain in Denmark and Germany in November, but move on in colder weather. Others fly direct to their winter quarters in the Netherlands, France and south-east England, where they start to arrive towards the end of September, with the main arrival in November and peak numbers usually during December-February. Early concentration is on estuaries with major natural food sources, but after dispersion in November there is little overall change in distribution unless severe weather ensues, when there may be considerable movement across the Channel. Most leave England and France between early March and mid-April, but stragglers are often seen into early May. They regroup in the Netherlands, Germany and Denmark before the main departures in mid-May, arriving back on the breeding grounds during the first half of June.

Pale-bellied brent from Svalbard and Franz Josef Land flock in late August and start to head south in early September, travelling down the west coast of Norway, to arrive in Denmark in late September and early October. They move on in variable numbers to north-east England (mostly Lindisfarne), usually arriving from mid-October to mid-November, but severe weather may drive more (if not all) over, peaking as late as February. In March and early April they return to Denmark, from where most head north in the second half of May, to arrive in Svalbard in late May and early June.

The pale-bellied brent of north-east and north Greenland and many Canadian

Pale-bellied brent from arctic Canada and Greenland winter around most of the Irish coast, again concentrating on large estuaries and intertidal mudflats with fine sediments but avoiding rocky shores such as those in the south-west and north-east. Inland records are extremely rare. Censuses have produced widely varying figures for Ireland but there appears to be overall increase from some 12,000 in 1960, when shooting was prohibited, to about 20,000 in 1986. The main autumn arrivals are at the west Kerry bays and Strangford Lough, where numbers appear to be relatively stable. Strangford's peak count in 1990–91 (September) was 13,237, with a five-year average 1986–1991 of 12,737. However, numbers at Lough Foyle in October have risen sharply from 1,693 in 1986 to 6,007 in 1990, indicating further population ▶

birds have two main migration routes to the British Isles, chiefly Ireland. One is down the east coast of Greenland, continuing via Iceland; the other down the west coast of Greenland, some birds crossing the inland ice-cap near the Arctic Circle, others continuing down around Cape Farewell and probably bypassing Iceland. Irish arrivals are as early as late August, but the main influx is usually in the second half of October. Once the big flocks have dispersed there is little interchange between resorts, though some move as late as January to western Scotland, where the bulk of records are from September to November. Small numbers of *hrota* also winter in north-west France. The return north starts in early April and many birds stop on the west coast of Iceland from late April to mid-May before continuing north to reach their breeding grounds by early June.

▶ increase rather than mere redistribution. Among other important Irish sites are the Dublin and Wexford estuaries, following a midwinter shift in the centre of distribution since the 1970s, with fewer birds in Kerry and more on the east coast. The dark-bellied brent and black brant are rare vagrants to Ireland.

BARNACLE GOOSE
(*Branta leucopsis*)

IN the absence of knowledge about migration, up to the seventeenth century it was widely believed that barnacle geese miraculously hatched from sea-shells suspended from rotting wood or the legendary 'barnacle tree'. Today we know where they really come from — very restricted arctic breeding grounds, and that the entire population winters in western Europe. The species' dramatic recovery from a world population of some 30,000 in the 1950s to over 120,000 today is one of the great successes of modern conservation.

BARNACLE GOOSE
Once known as bernicle goose, common bernicle goose, bernacle, white-faced barnacle, Norway barnacle, bar goose, rood goose, tree goose, clakis, claik and routhecock

History and Conservation

There is evidence that the species once bred much further south, in parts of South Wales, England and Jersey during the colder phase of the final, Devensian, glaciation, in areas with steep rock outcrops near tundra surface-water. Furthermore, early Holocene and Iron Age records suggest that in postglacial times the wintering area extended much further south-west. During later warm periods, when forests dominated lowland Europe, there were very few areas of open ground where geese could feed. Although there were also much greater estuarine areas before man proliferated, there was already stiff competition with species such as the brent goose. Furthermore, the short-billed, fast-pecking barnacle goose is adapted to grazing on very short swards so the amount of prime habitat, such as that on exposed islands off Ireland and Scotland, has probably always been relatively small.

Because the species has continued to concentrate on a small number of winter haunts and has not yet adapted to new food sources so well as other geese have, it has been particularly vulnerable to persecution. There was substantial decline through market gunning and sport shooting in the late nineteenth and early twentieth centuries, but with improved statutory protection in recent decades there has been steady overall population increase. The Netherlands protected it from 1946 and Svalbard from 1955, when a December–January open season continued in Scotland outside the Solway. The Svalbard stock gained complete protection in Britain in 1954, but the shooting season on Islay did not end until 1981. However, there have been setbacks as the species has been accused of significant local crop

The Latin specific *leucopsis* derives from the Greek *leukos* for white and *opsis* for aspect or appearance, referring to the bird's white forehead and face. Pennant introduced the common name 'bernacle goose' in 1768. In the 19th century 'barnacle goose' became standard, the name 'barnacle' going back to the thirteenth-century *bernekke* and the Latin *bernaca* of Giraldus, circa 1185. In view of the species' early association with Ireland, the name could have derived from the Gaelic *bairneach* for limpet or shellfish. Indeed, when a barnacle is broken open its shape resembles a goose, which is why we have the term 'goose barnacle' (*Lepas anatifera*). Interestingly, ▶

57

▶ Giraldus noted that even 'Bishops and religious men in some parts of Ireland do not scruple to dine off these birds at the time of fasting, because they are not born of flesh'. Apparently, the practice continued into the twentieth century, the 'fish-bird' being considered acceptable fare for Catholics on Fridays.

Irish wintering birds are longer-lived than those on Islay, but only half as productive and include only half as many successfully breeding adults. Some 2,500 barnacles winter elsewhere in Ireland, mostly in Donegal and Sligo. On the east coast, both the Wexford Slobs, where 500 were counted in the 1950s, and Lurgangreen (Louth), where about 100 wintered up to about 1945, were deserted in the 1960s. However, about 50 now visit both Lambay and the Skerries Islands off Dublin.

The peak 1990–91 count of the Svalbard population wintering on the Solway (Caerlavercock) was 12,100 in October, indicating stabilisation with a five-year average of 11,560 1986–91. Smaller flocks counted in October 1990 and likely to have been from Svalbard were 356 at the Loch of Strathbeg, 275 at Gladhouse Reservoir and 115 at Portmore Loch. ▶

damage, especially on Islay, off west Scotland. Numbers there increased from 3,000 to 24,000 between the 1950s and mid-1970s, but by 1983 had fallen back to only 14,000 because so many had been shot. Although numbers have since recovered, conflict remains with unlimited numbers of birds (1,300 in 1990–91) still shot under Scottish Office licence. Furthermore, many of these birds have been killed by paying Guns, which is to be deplored as contrary to the spirit of the law and as an inducement for landowners to continue the cull rather than seek less drastic solutions.

Scaring schemes have attempted to move birds around the island and concentrate them on the SSSIs created on two of the main areas, but the effort has not been co-ordinated so the birds have remained very loyal to their wintering areas. At the moment the only solution, apart from the creation of further refuges, appears to be financial compensation for the farmers. There is no doubt that the geese must be vigorously defended as the Islay flock of Greenland breeders contains such a high proportion of the world population. The designation of Special Protection Areas, the creation of an RSPB reserve in 1983 and management agreements on the SSSIs have given a good start in helping to hold most of the geese away from areas of cattle grazing, but there is a long way to go.

There has also been a steep increase in the Russian population wintering in the Netherlands and Germany, from about 19,700 birds in 1959 to over 45,000 by the mid-1970s, due largely to better protection and additional feeding on recently reclaimed polders. The Spitsbergen population, too, has recently soared, from about 400 in the late 1940s to some 11,000 in the 1980s. This has been made possible by the introduction of statutory protection and the creation of refuges (notably the Caerlaverock NNR in 1957) on the Solway wintering grounds, speeding recovery from severe wartime disturbance and heavy shooting pressure.

Breeding was first discovered off southern Sweden in 1980, on the island of Laus Holmar. Since then there has been steady increase and spread to Gotland and other neighbouring islands. The origin of the birds is unknown but the islands are on the migration route of the Siberian population. It is likely that the geese could not have become established there before farming modified the vegetation.

Distribution, Habitat and Population

The breeding population is confined to four areas: southern Novaya Zemlya/Vaigach Island off northern Siberia, Svalbard (Spitsbergen), southern Sweden (Gotland and neighbouring islands) and coastal north-east Greenland. The Greenland population winters in western Scotland and Ireland, Svalbard birds winter on the inner Solway Firth on the England/Scotland border, and the Siberian and Swedish populations go to the Netherlands and Germany — a few reaching England. Clearly Britain has a great international responsibility for this species.

Small numbers of barnacle geese occur throughout much of England and parts of Wales. Some of those in south-east England are genuine wild birds from the Siberian population, but many have escaped from numerous wildfowl collections. Full-winged flocks breed at some centres, including that of over 200 birds at the Wildfowl and Wetland Trust's Slimbridge headquarters, but they have not yet bred outside the protected areas. Records from north-east England and central and east Scotland mostly involve wanderers from the Svalbard population. Pairs breeding in Iceland are thought to have been escapes.

For breeding, the barnacle goose prefers small islands or skerries and precipices overlooking fjords or slopes rather than low tundra. Such sites must be within commuting distance of suitable feeding grounds — coastal fringes, valleys, rivers and lakes with abundant vegetation. In winter little use is made of intertidal feeding grounds, concentration being on terrestrial grazing. Use of managed habitat varies considerably within the discrete populations.

Field Characters

This goose is readily distinguished from other European 'black geese' — the much larger Canada and the smaller brent — by its creamy-white face contrasting boldly with the black hind-crown, neck and breast. The sexes are similar and there is no seasonal plumage variation. The juvenile has black spots on the forehead, black mottling on the face, a wider black streak between the bill and the eye and upperparts tinged red-brown.

The barnacle goose is highly gregarious throughout the year, winter flocks sometimes numbering thousands. It does not mix much with other geese and is noisy and quarrelsome among its own kind. Like other *Branta* species, it is less wary of man than the grey geese. Although it is more terrestrial than the brent goose, it usually stays close to the sea. It swims well and its flight is as strong as that of other geese, but its wings look more pointed.

Flocks are noisy, with shrill barking — *gnuk* — like the yapping of small dogs, both in flight and at rest. There are also low-pitched conversational feeding calls, given as *hoog, hogoog* and *wrack*. The wings generate a distinctive creaking sound.

▶ The Siberian population, which now winters chiefly in Friesland and islands off the north coast of the Netherlands, and in the Rhine/Maas delta near the Belgian border after drainage of former haunts in western Germany, passed 60,000 in the mid-1980s and has continued to increase. The Swedish population now numbers some 5,000 birds. England's expanding feral population of barnacle geese now numbers over 700.

Breeding

The monogamous pair-bond is mostly lifelong and new mates are replaced. Study of the Solway population found that some 2 per cent of pairs became separated each year, but mostly accidentally through migration. Remarkably, 'divorced' pairs have been know to 'remarry' on relocating each other even if one bird has found a new mate in the meantime. The reason for such a strong bond in all geese is that long-established pairs are three times more likely to breed successfully. Another surprising finding of Myrfyn Owen's Solway study was that young geese preferred to mate with those reared in the same area, even though pairing took place two or three years later. Thorough mixing of the flocks on the wintering grounds shows that this is not merely because birds from the same area are more likely to encounter each other, but perhaps because common environmental 'training' is advantageous in successful breeding. While most obvious in the spring, pair-formation can occur at any time of year.

In an activity known as 'herding', a male singles out a female and continually tries to separate her from the rest of the flock. If there is competition, noisy chases can ensue, sometimes in the air. Display is dominated by the triumph ceremony, which is similar to that of the Canada goose, but with alternate wing-flicking. In this two birds stand alongside each other, facing in opposite directions and 'barking' loudly while pumping their heads up and down. This also helps to maintain the bond between established pairs.

Nesting is mostly loosely colonial (exceptionally as close as 2m (6ft)), but because secure sites are so valued they are probably used in successive years by the same females, each male jealously guarding his mate and nest. Because the

The average length is 58–70cm (22.8–27.6in), wing-span 132–145cm (52–57.1in), and weight 1,370–2,400g (3–5.3lb) for the male, 1,290–2,230g (2.8–4.9lb) the female.

The single clutch of 4–5 (2–9) oval, creamy-white eggs, average size 77 × 50mm (3.03 × 1.97in), is mostly laid from mid-May to mid-June.

Barnacle geese with young. In some areas farmers regard the species as a pest. Photo: B. Martin

barnacle is too small to defend itself against larger predators such as the arctic fox it must choose an inaccessible nest-site, often on a cliff ledge or a rocky island shared with other seabirds. Shelter to minimise heat loss is important too. Tundra ground nests, on snow-free hummocks which avoid meltwater, are more likely on islands where there are no large ground predators. Usually there is very little material available for nest-building, so the female adds droppings to create a low mound around the scrape she has excavated with her claws.

The male stands during the female's solo 24/25-day incubation, which starts on the day before the last egg is laid. When the clutch is complete the female plucks down from her breast to expose her special brood patch and help insulate the eggs, especially when she leaves the nest to drink, bathe and preen.

Hatching is synchronous and soon after the last gosling is dry the whole family sets off for the rearing area. The young may face a drop of up to 60m (200ft) from their cliff nest, but they are so light they do not damage themselves. The only real threat comes from the gulls and foxes which wait below to snap them up before they are reunited with their parents. Predation by gulls is a special threat for island nesters which may have to swim some 2km (just over a mile) to the mainland. Families gradually group together in roving flocks which have a number of feeding areas, rotational grazing ensuring a succession of young, nutritious shoots. The young are cared for by both parents and fledge at 40–45 days. They do not usually leave the family before reaching the breeding grounds in their first spring. Age of first breeding is usually three years, sometimes two.

Diet and Feeding Behaviour

The vegetable diet consists chiefly of the leaves and stems of grasses and other herbs, stolons and seeds of both saltmarsh and cultivated plants. The short bill is specially suited to the grazing of short vegetation, but is also used for probing and pulling up vegetation and stripping seeds from stalks. There is wide seasonal and local variation, with increasing tendency to use pastures sown for cattle in most main autumn and winter haunts. Molluscs and crustaceans recorded in the diet have probably been taken accidentally. Summer diet includes the buds of purple saxifrage and willow, horsetail, sedges, mosses and liverworts, early nesting being essential so that the goslings can grow quickly on the first, highly nutritious flush of vegetation. Feeding is chiefly by day, but in the continuous daylight of the arctic summer birds can forage for 20 hours out of 24.

After the autumn migration, natural seeds and stubble grain provide a rich source of energy to restore condition before winter sets in. When these are exhausted or in short supply the geese often switch to the stems of white clover, which are widely available and especially nutritious before the plant becomes dormant for the winter. During midwinter and early spring grazing is most important and the birds are surprisingly adept at selecting the most nutritious grasses, having discovered the heavily fertilised and improved swards which now abound in their traditional haunts. As feeding flocks tend to be more concentrated than those of any other goose, they can cause serious economic loss at major resorts. Winter feeding sites are rarely more than 5km (3 miles) from the roost.

Movements

All populations are entirely migratory and each has a well-defined staging area. Although Svalbard and Greenland breeders winter within 150km (93 miles) of each other, the two populations very rarely intermix.

Greenland breeders leave from late August to mid-September and migrate via Iceland to arrive in Scotland and Ireland mainly in the second half of October, sometimes early November. There is little interchange between the winter haunts. Northward movement in the British Isles starts in late March and departures begin mid-April, tailing off in mid-May. Most birds return to Greenland in May, having again stopped off in Iceland.

The Svalbard population starts to head south in September, using Bear Island, the southernmost island of the archipelago, as a staging post before travelling down the west coast of Norway and across the North Sea, northern England and southern Scotland to arrive on the Solway in late September or early October, usually peaking within three weeks. During the winter they move only locally, using the area around Caerlaverock, south of Dumfries, from Rockcliffe Marsh 20km (12.5 miles) to the east to the coastal flatlands 20km (12.5 miles) to the west. Most head north in the second half of April, some staying on into early May. They stop at Helgeland on the coast of Norway just south of the Arctic Circle, where they spend two or three weeks before travelling a further 1,600km (994 miles) to arrive back in Svalbard in late May.

In late August and early September the Novaya Zemlya/Vaigach Island population migrates south-west across the White Sea, the Gulf of Finland, Baltic, north Estonia, Gotland and south Sweden, north Germany and south Denmark, to arrive in the Netherlands from October, mixing with the Gotland breeders which are already there. In most years peak numbers are reached in January. A few move on to south-east England, Belgium and north-west France, especially in severe weather. They start to return north in late March, many halting at the North Friesian Islands, where they may stay until late April. In early May about half the population may be found on Gotland, where nesting is already underway. The remainder stop in Estonia. They return to their breeding grounds in late May.

BARNACLE GOOSE

By far the most important site for the Greenland population is the island of Islay, where some two-thirds have wintered in recent decades. A record 30,208 were counted there in early December 1990 and 22,172 in March 1991. It is not known how many birds winter throughout the rest of Scotland, but an international census taking place in 1993 is likely to show substantial increase in overall numbers and the relative importance of Islay. Away from Islay, Greenland barnacles winter in Scotland at a large number of mostly small and uninhabited western islands, from the Sound of Jura to the Pentland Firth, a few sometimes visiting mainland headlands, such as Kintyre and Durness. In March 1991 the only sizeable flock of likely Greenland birds counted outside Islay was that of 375 at Craiglin Lochan. In Ireland Greenland barnacles winter almost exclusively on the west coast. The principal resort is the Inishkea Islands, Mayo, where numbers increased after the human population was evacuated in 1932, but have since stabilised at around 2,000, probably because the maximum carrying capacity has been reached.

EGYPTIAN GOOSE
(Alopochen aegyptiacus)

Once known as Spanish goose, ganser and gambo goose

As its name implies, this is an African species, whose range once extended into the Middle East and south-eastern Europe. It was the main domestic bird in the Egyptian Old Kingdom, which ended around 2300BC.

The current British population is just over 900, centred on Norfolk (notably Holkham Park). Most others are scattered about southern and central England. There are no records for Ireland. The Netherlands has a naturalised flock of some 200–250.

THIS 'sheldgoose' is classified in the tribe *Tadornini*, along with the shelducks, and in many characters is intermediate between the true geese and ducks. England and the Netherlands now have thriving feral populations based on escapes from wildfowl collections.

History and Conservation

First introductions to north-west Europe were probably in the seventeenth century, the earliest record of it in captivity in Britain being from 1678, in King Charles II's menagerie at St James's Park. A century later it was breeding on the waters of several large parks and estates. During the nineteenth century it was well established on lakes in Norfolk — notably on the large Holkham estate, Woburn in Bedfordshire, Bicton and Crediton in Devon, and Gosford in East Lothian. From these centres the bird spread widely, early reports including five on the Farne Islands in 1830, three shot near Glasgow in 1832, nine on the Isle of Man in 1838, a flock on the River Tweed in 1839, four shot on the Severn in 1840, five in Kent in 1846 and two shot in Sussex in 1848. Colonel Peter Hawker bagged three at Longparish in Hampshire in 1823 and two more in the following year, when a flock of 80 appeared at the same place after a great westerly gale.

Although the species rapidly established itself in Britain (officially admitted to the national list in 1971), and later in the Netherlands, its numbers have remained small. Although the adults survive the winter well enough, the main limiting factor appears to be the climate. Modest increase generally follows mild winters and springs, but the bird lays early, as befits its African origin, so a return to cold weather greatly reduces its hatching success. Replaced clutches often fail through competition with another introduced species, the larger and more numerous Canada goose, and feral greylag geese. Poor productivity in Britain is also the result of heavy predation by crows and, more recently, feral mink. Furthermore, feral populations have yet to adopt such a great diversity of habitats as used in their native range. None the less, during the 1980s there was a distinct spread from the Norfolk stronghold into northern Suffolk, along the coastal fringe as well as in the Brecks.

Distribution, Habitat and Population

The main native breeding range is in Africa south of 20°N, extending northwards into Egypt, where it was formerly very abundant in the Nile Valley. Now it is scarce in lower Egypt but recovering north of Aswan following improved but not total protection. Most of these are resident, as is the British population, estimated at 300–400 birds in the 1960s and 1970s. No major change has been apparent since then, but neither has there been a full survey.

The natural habitat is mainly sub-tropical, chiefly on inland fresh water, along rivers as well as around lakes and pools, at widely varying altitudes. In England the concentration is on lowland ornamental lakes and rivers, and in managed aquatic habitats such as the pastures and alder-willow swamps of the Norfolk Broads.

An Egyptian goose characteristically perching on a branch. Photo: E. Janes

EGYPTIAN GOOSE

The average length is 63–73cm (24.8–28.7in), wing-span 134–154cm (52.7–60.6in), and weight 1,900–2,500g (4.2–5.5lb) for the male, 1,500–2,040g (3.3–4.5lb) the female.

The single clutch (replaced after early loss) of 8–9 (6–12) creamy-white eggs, average size 69 × 50mm (2.71 × 1.97in) and rounded at both ends, is mostly laid in late March and April in Britain.

Unlike the true geese, it is thoroughly at home in fairly open woodland, where it nests and flies freely.

Field Characters

Larger than the related shelducks, the Egyptian goose has a heavier bill and longer legs. Among its most striking features are the brown 'spectacles' and white forewing contrasting with black flight feathers. The sexes are similar and there is no seasonal variation other than a swelling at the base of the bill. Juvenile and first-winter birds lack the eye and breast patches, have a yellow-grey rather than pink bill and are generally paler and duller, but with a darker head and hindneck. The only other species with which it might be confused is the ruddy shelduck, which has a similar wing-pattern but is slightly smaller and shorter-legged, with a much more orange-chestnut body and no eye patches.

This duck often perches and roosts on trees, among which it manoeuvres easily in strong, fast flight, but with fairly slow, goose-like wing-beats. It swims well and dives readily, but spends most of its time on land, walking rather sedately. It is gregarious outside the breeding season, occurring in flocks of hundreds or even thousands in Africa, especially during the flightless post-breeding period.

Both sexes hiss but the male's husky calls, likened to a steam-engine, are nothing like the female's often loud trumpeting or harsh quacking.

Breeding

The monogamous pair-bond is sustained from year to year. Pairs usually form in a flock. Courtship has not been well studied and contains many aggressive elements which are not easy to separate from antagonistic behaviour. The male's main displays include ceremonial drinking and lateral swimming to show the yellow under-tail coverts. Both sexes sky-call and engage in the triumph ceremony, usually ending with the wing-spread display.

Most pairs are strong in defence of fairly large territories — about 1 hectare (2.5 acres) at open-water areas. On larger, shared waters each family tends to stay within its own territory, the adults mostly feeding there. There is a wide variety of ground nest-sites, many in thick vegetation and under bushes. Others are in bank holes, among rocks, on buildings and cliff ledges, in old tree nests of other species or in the crown or hollow of a tree, especially a pollarded willow. The female alone builds — a mound of reeds or grass on the ground, a simple depression without material on cliffs and in holes. She adds a lining of leaves or twigs to tree nests and all nests are lined with down.

The female's solo 28/30-day incubation starts with the last egg. Hatching is synchronous. The young feed themselves, are cared for by both parents and fledge at 70–75 days. The exact age of independence is not known, but the young stay with the parents for at least six weeks and sometimes several months after fledging. Age of first breeding is probably one year. In England breeding success is poor, averaging only two fledged birds per pair.

Diet and Feeding Behaviour

The diet consists chiefly of land plants — cultivated as well as wild grass, leaves and seeds. With maize stubble, growing wheat, ground nuts and sweet potatoes on the menu, significant agricultural loss has been reported in South Africa. Stubble grain is seasonally important in Britain, where some insects and snails are also taken. Like geese they often feed in pairs or family groups within larger flocks. In Africa feeding is chiefly nocturnal, mostly over a few hours from sunset, but in cooler Britain it is chiefly by day. Grit is taken to aid digestion.

Movements

Most African birds move only locally, but some make regular, long-distance wet-season movements. In drier parts families often have to move when their water dries up. During the nineteenth century small wintering parties were often reported from the east coast of England, where they were regarded as genuine wild birds, but they could have originated from the feral population in the Netherlands, driven west by greater cold. Today there is no evidence of long-distance movement in Britain. There are occasional records from other parts of western Europe, including France, Sweden and Spain, but it is likely that these are mostly (if not entirely) escapes.

SHELDUCK
(*Tadorna tadorna*)

THE shelduck differs from other British breeding ducks in that the great majority nest very close to tidal water. Among the most conspicuous wildfowl, it has increased substantially this century with the aid of protective legislation.

History and Conservation

The species' early distribution in Britain is unusual in that it occurs around the Torbay area in Devon from the Wolstonian, the second to last glaciation, to the present, in both warmer and cooler phases, But then, during the coldest stages the Channel would have been mostly dry land. Equally surprising for such a maritime species, it also occurs in the last glaciation in the Midlands as well as south-east England. Both its narrow habitat requirements and current discontinuous range suggest relict status, but with considerable ability to adapt and survive. For example, in nesting it has made great use of the burrows provided by rabbits since the mammal's introduction to Britain. Fortuitously, the greatest concentrations of rabbit burrows occur in the duck's favoured sandy soils, especially in eastern England.

The species was described as quite common in eighteenth-century Britain, when its bold colours and readiness to accept domestication made it a favourite with gentlemen forming wildfowl collections. Unfortunately, this same conspicuousness made it popular as a cased specimen and a relatively easy target for wildfowlers, so large numbers were shot during the nineteenth and early twentieth centuries, before the advent of protective legislation. However, sustained increase this century appears to be more than mere recovery from earlier persecution. With the north-west European population having risen from an estimated 120,000–130,000 in the 1970s to about 250,000 in 1980–81, there

Once known as sheldrake, shelldrake, shieldrake, skeldrake, sheld fowl, shell, shellie, scale duck, skeel duck, skeel goose, skeeling goose, skelgoose, bar duck, bargander, bergander, bar goose, burrow duck, burrough duck, bay duck, St George's duck, sly duck, sly goose, links goose, pirennet (*pied ent* = pied duck) and stock annet

65

has been real range expansion too. With numbers building there has been an increasing tendency to colonise inland sites, such as Wisbech sewage farm, six miles from the mouth of a tidal river, since at least 1923. Nesting was first recorded in Berkshire in 1950, Warwickshire in 1970, Worcestershire in 1978 and Staffordshire in 1979. Numbers are probably still increasing but the coastal sector of the population is likely to remain predominant.

As the shelduck is particularly vulnerable to severe weather it is likely that recent ascendancy is at least partly due to climatic amelioration 1900–1950. There was high mortality during the winters of 1962–63 and 1978–79, when there were exceptionally low temperatures throughout north-west Europe, but the long run of mild winters from 1963–64 to 1980–81 provided a great boost.

Increased statutory protection has been important throughout Europe, especially on the German moulting grounds. However, many important breeding and wintering estuary sites are still threatened by development and expansion of leisure activities. There is urgent need for further designation and better management of marine protection areas. Moulting flocks remain at special risk in the event of oil spills and breeding birds are likely to suffer increased predation through the recent rapid spread of mink around coasts.

Distribution, Habitat and Population

The shelduck breeds only in Eurasia, in three separate regions. The greatest part of the range is in a broad belt across southern Siberia from the Black Sea to western China. The other two centres are coastal north-western Europe — around the British Isles, southern Scandinavia, the Baltic and North Sea, and the western Mediterranean — southern France, Italy, Tunisia, Algeria and Spain. Although it is resident along most European sea-shores, Scandinavian breeders migrate south-west and all Siberian birds winter around the south Caspian Sea and in north-west India, Pakistan, southern China and neighbouring south-east Asia.

Throughout the range it favours a warm, semi-arid, and mild maritime climate, avoiding the boreal and sub-arctic zones and only entering the Mediterranean to a small extent. In north-west Europe it mostly ranges no more than 1–2km (0.5–1 mile) out to sea and little farther inland, with only sporadic use of wholly freshwater sites. However, as numbers build there is increasing tendency to breed inland on lochs (some 40–55 pairs on Loch Leven, 25–35 on Loch Lomond and some 30 on Lough Neagh), reservoirs, sewage-farms, valley farms, downs and commons, though rarely more than 20km (12.5 miles) from tidal water. In contrast, in Central Asia it concentrates around salt lakes and marshes in steppe and semi-desert, mostly far from marine marshes and even large inland seas.

Because the shelduck does not breed before at least its third calendar year, a large part of the population — about half in north-west Europe — consists of non-breeding immatures. Breeding occurs around almost the entire British Isles, where there are some 12,000 pairs plus 26,000 non-breeders, concentrating on estuaries and shallow coasts with suitable low-tide feeding areas near to stabilised sand-dunes or grazing marshes for nesting. Ideal nest-sites are close to feeding areas which are small enough for single pairs to defend as feeding territories, thereby providing an exclusive feeding area for the female from pairing until hatching. But territories are not established until prey supply reaches a critical minimum so that pairs can feed easily and have sufficient time for defence. Densities are lowest around rocky coasts and those with cliffs.

Not unnaturally, it has been commonly suggested that the current name and earlier variants, going back at least to the twelfth century, derive from connection with seashells. However, the true origin seems to be in the Old English *sheld*, a dialect word meaning variegated or parti-coloured, referring to the bird's bold plumage with contrasting colours. Common use of sheldrake persisted through the nineteenth century. Many of the popular names reflect the common view of the species as a link between the ducks and geese. The New Latin *tadorna* derives from the French *tadorne* for sheldrake.

The Egyptian goose (background) is scientifically grouped with the shelduck (male left, female right).

SHELDUCK

During the mid-1980s Britain hosted some 60,000–65,000 and Ireland about 6,500–8,000 shelducks in midwinter, which was itself a great increase on the regular 50,000 level up to the early 1970s, but by 1990–91 the peak count for Britain was up to 79,949 (February), with 3,738 in Northern Ireland. The Wash remained by far the most important UK site with an average peak 1986–91 of 18,287. Other resorts regularly achieving the 2,500 level for international importance, and their average maxima 1986–91, are the Medway Estuary 5,930, Dee Estuary 4,740, Humber Estuary 4,630, Morecambe Bay 4,603, Ribble Estuary 4,180, Mersey Estuary 3,396, Severn Estuary 2,983, Forth Estuary 2,794, Chichester Harbour 2,755, Thames Estuary 2,692, and Poole Harbour 2,577. Blackwater Estuary averaged 2,286 and Strangford Lough 2,213. The Swale Estuary held 2,545 birds in January 1991. For details of moult gatherings see *Movements* section.

The average length is 58–67cm (22.8–26.4in — male slightly larger), wing-span 110–133cm (43.3–52.4in), and weight 830–1,500g (1.8–3.3lb) for the male, 562–1,250g (1.2–2.8lb) the female.

In Norway, where it breeds to about 63°N, there has been marked recovery since wartime persecution, and in southern Sweden, where it breeds around large lakes as well as coasts, there has been pronounced recent increase. Scattered breeding resumed in Finland, around the Baltic coast, in 1962, after probable absence since 1888. The small populations in France, Belgium and Germany have increased with the aid of protection, and numbers have risen significantly in the Netherlands (over 3,000 pairs) and Denmark, with recent breeding at many new inland sites in both countries. Breeding is rare and sporadic in Italy and Poland.

The total flyway population in north-west Europe has been increasing too, being some 250,000 birds in the 1980s. The British wintering population varies greatly with the weather, most birds occurring on the muddier estuaries of eastern and southern England, southern Ireland, around the coasts of the Irish Sea and south-west Scotland. Much of northern and western Scotland is vacated in winter. In England there is a scattering of winter records from reservoirs and gravel pits.

Field Characters

No one should have any difficulty in identifying the large, somewhat goose-like shelduck, with similar, bold-patterned plumage in both sexes and only slight seasonal differences. The handsome male's bottle-green head and upper neck contrast strongly with his large, red bill (with swan-like, fleshy basal knob in early spring), predominantly white body banded with chestnut around the breast and upper back, black 'braces', black belly-stripe and black flight feathers. The female differs only slightly in having a paler, black-tipped bill, usually duller head and neck, generally narrower and paler chest-band (with some black markings), weaker and narrower black belly-stripe, and a paler undertail. In eclipse the male loses the bill knob and is duller and less clearly marked, with a brown-black head and white about the face and throat. Then he resembles the non-breeding female. The juvenile is unlike all adult phases, though it occasionally resembles the non-breeding female. It has little trace of any breast-band, more white on the face and its upperparts are mottled dark grey-brown. The only other bird which it resembles is the immature Egyptian goose, which is more brown and buff and has a more pronounced eye-patch.

The shelduck is gregarious except in spring and early summer, often congregating in large numbers during the flightless, post-breeding moult and sometimes in thousands during winter. Although it is less aquatic than other ducks and built more like a goose, it is none the less buoyant. It swims more in channels and creeks than the open sea and dives only when wounded or frightened, but the young submerge readily. On land it is exceptionally agile, walking and running easily about the breeding area, even perching on haystacks, cliff-ledges and buildings. Although it sometimes takes a run, it rises easily from both land and water. In flight, too, it is goose-like, with slow, powerful wing-beats, frequently flighting to feed in V-formation or diagonal lines. On migration, however, it usually flies in straight lines at some height.

It is mostly quiet outside the breeding season, but in the summer it calls frequently from land, water and air, its voice often carrying long distances. The male has a pleasing variety of melodic whistles, which have been likened to the calls of songbirds and the wigeon. In contrast, the female has a low, deep voice, her main repertoire including a harsh, chattering or growling quack, sometimes given as *ak-ak-ak-ak* or *gagagaga*.

Breeding

The pair-bond is monogamous and the strongest among British ducks, pairs mostly persisting from year to year, although some separate on moult migration. The male stays with the female throughout incubation and sometimes helps to tend the young until they are fledged. In courtship pursuit-flights are common. Main displays include the male's upward-shake while throwing the head up, and flicking the head upwards so that the bill aligns with the erect neck (sometimes by female too), both moves accompanied by whistling. Both sexes also bill-dip and have an exaggerated preen-behind-wing display.

In late March pairs start to leave the winter flocks and disperse to their territories, which are usually in about the same place on muddy shores and used only for feeding. A female with a new mate tends to return to her last territory but a male goes to that of his new partner. Recent research has shown that dominant pairs occupy larger exclusive areas (non-overlapping zones) than neighbouring subordinate pairs at high density, regardless of their order of arrival on the mud-flats. The behaviour of dominant pairs may limit the number of broods and breeding success. While maintaining these territories, pairs search for nest-sites, which may be several kilometres (miles) away. Although the species is vigorous in defence of its feeding area, there are no clear territories around the nests, which are often close together, sometimes with several in the same burrow.

Nests are mostly near water, though sometimes up to several kilometres (miles) away, so there is frequent commuting to feeding grounds. Sites are chiefly in holes but occasionally in thick vegetation. Selection depends on local availability. For example, of 100 in Kent 29 were in hollow trees (14 in the base, 15 up to 5m (16.4ft) above ground), 28 in straw or hay stacks (to 8m (26ft) above ground), 27 in rabbit burrows, 23 under buildings and other objects and three in the open. In some areas, especially eastern Britain where soils are sandy, they are entirely in rabbit burrows. In holes the female uses little or no material, but at open sites she gathers vegetation to form a shallow depression, which is always lined with large amounts of down.

The female's 29/31-day incubation starts with the last egg and hatching is synchronous. The young feed themselves and are soon led by both parents to the main rearing area, which may be several kilometres (miles) away. Some broods remain with their parents until fledging at 45–50 days, but most join crèches of up to 100 after just 15–20 days because their parents must undertake moult migrations. Adults left in charge of the crèches, which often contain young of widely varying ages, may be birds with their own broods present, or failed or non-breeders. Some ducklings are more or less independent and in unsupervised groups, but full independence usually comes at or soon after fledging. Although most females first breed on achieving maturity at two years, some males do not breed until four or five.

Diet and Feeding Behaviour

Not surprisingly for a bird with such a discontinuous range, there is considerable variation in the predominantly invertebrate diet, requiring a variety of feeding methods. In north and west Europe small molluscs are most important, but in southern Europe and southern and central areas of the former USSR small crustaceans and insect larvae predominate. In English waters the small snail *Hydrobia*

The single clutch (replaced after early loss) of 8–10 (3–12) rounded-oval, creamy-white eggs, average size 66 × 47mm (2.6 × 1.85in), is mostly laid from mid-April to mid-June in North Sea countries, but from early May in southern areas of the former USSR and more northerly parts of Scandinavia.

During the late 1950s and early 1960s a moulting ground in Bridgwater Bay, Somerset, was used by some 3,000–4,000 birds, possibly Irish breeders, but by 1990 numbers had declined to some 2,000. There were up to 200 on the Humber in the late 1970s and the gathering on the Firth of Forth increased from 300–800 in 1977 to 2,500–3,000 in 1979–80. Numbers on the Norfolk side of the Wash were consistently well ove 1,000 in the 1980s and in July 1991 there were 3,35/ on the Solway.

69

Female shelduck at her nest in a barn. Photo: Dennis Green

ulvae is by far the most important single item throughout the year, one bird from Kent containing over 3,000. However, *Hydrobia* is not widely available at some estuaries and then other foods such as marine worms become dominant. Lesser coastal foods include amphipods, algae, green seaweeds and the leaves and seeds of plants such as sea club-rush, enteromorpha and herbaceous sea-blite. Inland, freshwater snails and earthworms may be significant.

In north-west Europe the shelduck's life is chiefly governed by tides, which regulate the behaviour of the main prey. Thus the duck feeds by day and night, mainly by wading in shallow water or on freshly exposed, wet mud, where the prey is easily accessible, but it also forages on drier, inland areas. Groups of shelducks follow the receding tide, dabbling or swinging their extended necks and heads from side to side with a smooth, scything action as they sift the soft ooze in very shallow water or sieve the wet mud with their lamellated bills. They also dig in mud which has been exposed for longer periods, head-dip in water some 10–25cm (4–10in) deep and up-end in water about 25–40cm (10–16in) deep. The young dive freely but adults only rarely. Foot-trampling helps to bring prey to the surface.

Movements

Shelducks also undertake extensive cold-weather movements, sometimes resulting in large influxes during severe spells. For example, when north-west Europe was in the grip of deep frost during 1978–79 the population wintering in Britain rose from 38,000 in December to 68,000 in January.

The species is migratory, partially migratory and dispersive. In north-west Europe the pattern of migration is affected by major moult movements. In mid-July most adults and non-breeding immatures leave Britain and other north-west European breeding areas to form huge gatherings at traditional sites on the vast mudflats of the German Waddensee — chiefly on the Grosser Knechtsand between the Elbe

70

and Weser estuaries. There they become flightless during their complete autumn moult. Other sites are more transient but some which have rich feeding grounds and are relatively safe from disturbance have acquired regular importance as the overall population has increased.

In September, moulted birds start to return to south-east England and other sites, but some delay until November or early December. By midwinter they have spread north and west from East Anglia, but are replaced by many others which include Continental immigrants as well as British and Irish breeders. Individuals tend to remain faithful to particular routes and often spend several months returning to their breeding grounds.

Juvenile shelducks (which do not moult flight feathers in their first autumn) do not follow their parents to the moulting grounds, but later disperse widely, some even reaching as far as southern France. Adults which have stayed with the young also remain in Britain.

MALLARD
(Anas platyrhynchos)

BY far the most familiar European duck, the mallard has learnt to exploit almost every habitat, both natural and artificial. It is the ancestor of most domestic duck breeds and crossbreeds throughout western Europe and, despite the heavy toll of this most palatable species taken by man and a wide range of predators, it remains numerous.

Once known as wild duck, common duck, stock duck, muir duck, mire duck, moss duck, grey duck and flapper (young)

History and Conservation

This is the most frequently occurring duck in the fossil record of the British Ice Ages, the earliest being from Norfolk, in the Pastonian Glaciation. Subsequently, the climate does not appear to have been a major limiting factor in much of north-west Europe and the species has remained common through both warmer and cooler periods. More significant has been extensive drainage of wetlands since the seventeenth century, which has removed huge acreages of habitat. On the other hand, the species gained somewhat through early agriculture, with field enclosure, wider availability of grain and other food, and widespread creation of cattle-ponds.

It appears to have been domesticated as early as the Iron Age, independently in many parts of its range, resulting in centuries of crossbreeding between tame and wild birds. Furthermore, during the second half of the twentieth century, large numbers have been reared and released for shooting, so estimation of the wild population has never been easy. Of course, many of the introduced birds have survived, thereby facilitating further expansion of an already wide range. More recently, wildfowling clubs have concentrated on habitat improvement rather than rearing and release, but substantial numbers of mallard are now put down by game-shooters to augment inland sport. Such birds are often very inferior quarry because they have lost most of their wildness, so their popularity is likely to wane.

For centuries, when wild meat was more highly valued, vast numbers of mallard were taken for the market. Some were shot and trapped, but by far the most were

During the nineteenth and early twentieth centuries the species was mostly referred to as the wild duck, only the male being called 'mallard'. But following Hartert's example (1912), 'mallard' has again become the standard, returning to medieval tradition. The term mallard is known from 1314, *maulard* too being used in the 14th century, deriving from the Normans and the French *malard* for the drake. Mallard comes from the Latin *masculus* for male and *ard* from the Old High German *hart* for hardy or bold. The current Latin specific *platyrhynchos* refers to the bill, coming from the Greek *platus* for wide or flat, and *rhunkhos* for beak.

71

MALLARD

Ducks (this is probably a mallard) were common quarry when falconry was widely practised. Photo: B. Martin

In 1976 Atkinson-Wiles estimated the population of the western Palearctic at 4–5 million, with 1.5 million in north-west Europe. In 1976 Sharrock estimated the British Isles breeding population at 70,000–150,000 pairs. France's population has dropped significantly to 20,000–40,000 pairs. Other recent estimates include: Iceland – at least 5,000 pairs, Belgium – 10,000 pairs, Netherlands – 150,000 pairs, Finland – 160,000 pairs, and Poland – 100,000 pairs. Up to 1970 there was a slight decrease in Sweden, and more recently there has been substantial decline in Ireland through land drainage, with a recent estimate of 20,000 pairs.

In winter few birds move out of Britain and there is a substantial influx, bringing the total to an estimated January peak of some 500,000 (Lack, 1986). While the 1990–91 National Waterfowl Counts gave peaks of only 214,458 (January) for Great Britain and 10,864 (September) for Northern Ireland, there are thought to be substantial numbers unrecorded on numerous small waters.

The most important resorts and average maxima 1986–91 were Humber Estuary ▶

taken in decoys, which is now illegal. Earlier still, the mallard was a common quarry of the medieval falconer. Yet all this hunting and the continuance of sport today has done little to stop this bird thriving within the British Isles. Other countries have shown increase too, but many have been less willing or unable to control their culling so well and are witnessing substantial decline through hunting pressure.

Even the severe winter of 1962–63 did not appear to have any significant effect on the breeding population, though it did cause regional redistribution at the time. Common Birds Census monitoring has been interesting, but it takes place only on farmland, which is not a key habitat for this species. None the less, this revealed almost doubling of the British population between 1967 and 1976, followed by stability around the new, higher level, with little disruption following the cold winters of 1978–79 and 1981–82, suggesting attainment of maximum carrying capacity for that habitat. Reasons for the increase from the mid-1960s are uncertain. The number surviving from release schemes is thought to have been so small as to have contributed little to the breeding population, but there may be disproportionate benefit through reduction in shooting and predation of wild stock.

Distribution, Habitat and Population

The mallard breeds right across the northern hemisphere, in both northern and temperate zones. In North America it is absent only from the northernmost Canadian tundra, south to Maine and Nova Scotia, though it breeds much further north, in Iceland and along the west coast of Greenland. Although resident in southern California, it does not breed in many southern States. In Eurasia it is absent only from the highest mountains, notably in northern Scandinavia, Sicily, and central Iceland, ranging from Britain and Spain through Russia and Siberia to northern Japan, but avoiding the coldest tundra. In Norway there has been marked expansion northwards since the 1870s, as well as post-1945 increase in

Finland. Britain lies within the substantial area where the species is resident, but many populations in colder areas are forced to migrate long distances to overwinter, including almost all birds in Canada and the former USSR, which mostly move into the southern USA and Europe. Many more easterly birds overwinter from northern India to southern China and Korea. Small numbers breed in North Africa, where there is a slightly larger winter population. There have been many introductions around the world, the most significant being into the eastern USA, Bermuda, Australia and New Zealand.

Throughout the year, this is the most widely distributed species of wildfowl in the British Isles, being absent only from the highest and most barren hills. But densities vary considerably. Almost every type of wetland habitat is used, maritime areas being more important outside the breeding season, but deep water is avoided unless the bird is alarmed. Its adaptability and tolerance of man has enabled it to make extensive use of all types of urban and suburban water, which has been encouraged by free interbreeding with semi-wild stock.

Field Characters

The handsome male is easily identified by his dark, bottle-green head, which is neatly separated from his purple-brown breast by a narrow, white collar, his yellow bill and two curled central tail feathers. The blue/purple wing-bar is edged black and white on both front and rear edges and is the best distinguishing mark of the female, which is mainly brown, spotted and streaked black. In eclipse (mostly July–August) the male resembles the female but has a yellower bill, blacker crown, paler face, neck and upperparts, warmer brown breast and heavier build. The juvenile closely resembles the female, but is duller with more narrowly streaked underparts. If the speculum is not clear the female may be confused with females of other species, but the smaller gadwall may be distinguished by its white belly and white speculum, the pintail by its slender build and pointed tail, the wigeon by its short neck, much shorter bill, whitish belly and obscure green/black speculum, and the shoveler by its much longer bill, shorter neck and wings set far back in flight. Both sexes are easily confused with domesticated and semi-wild individuals, which are mostly larger with excess black or white markings.

Like other dabbling ducks, the mallard swims well and lightly, with the tail cocked. The young dive freely, but the adult only occasionally. It rises easily and almost vertically from the water. Flight is fast, though the wing-beats are shallow and less rapid than those of many other ducks, producing a distinctive whistle. Thoroughly at home on land, it walks and runs easily with almost horizontal carriage. A very gregarious species, but often secretive while breeding.

Only the female makes the familiar, deep quacking like a farmyard duck, but the male has a softer, nasal, single or double *raehb*, a high-pitched whistle and a deep courtship grunt.

Breeding

The monogamous pair-bond is of only seasonal duration, occasional successive pairing among resident birds being fortuitous. Pairing is rare before the end of August, but may be delayed till spring, especially among migratory birds. Although some populations are balanced, there is a general excess of males, which is apparent at hatching and increased by the greater mortality of breeding females.

MALLARD

▶(February) 5,992, Lough Neagh/Beg 5,330 (September), the Wash 4,733 (January), Ouse Washes 4,612 (January), Morecambe Bay 4,144 (October), Swale Estuary 3,844 (January), Dee Estuary 3,752 (December), Martin Mere 3,694 (December), Severn Estuary 3,670 (November). Ireland's winter peak is probably well over 50,000, mostly thinly distributed, but over 2,000 have been counted on the Wexford Slobs. In north-west Europe, only the south-east corner of the IJsselmeer of the Netherlands exceeds the qualifying level of 10,000 for international importance.

The length averages 50–65cm (19.7–25.6in – female averaging larger), wing-span 81–98cm (31.9–38.6in), and weight ranges widely from 850–1,570g (1.9–3.5lb) for the male and 750–1,100g (1.7–2.4lb) for the female.

The single clutch of grey-green or buff, occasionally bluish eggs, average size 57 × 41mm (2.25 × 1.61in), averages 9–13 within a range of 4–18,▶

73

The mallard (male top, female below) is among the ducks which frequently up-end to feed. Photo: B. Martin

▶ those containing over 18 usually being the product of more than one female. Larger clutch size in England may be due to interbreeding with domestic stock. Replacement clutches are common after loss of eggs or young ducklings. The laying interval between eggs is usually 1 day but sometimes 2–3.

The mallard (female upper, male lower) is the ancestor of most domestic duck breeds.

Furthermore, there is a tendency for females to migrate further south. Therefore there are many unmated males in some areas. Coupled with natural promiscuity, this often results in the liaison of two males with one female, frequent desertion and 'adultery', and the pursuit and 'rape' of a female by a dozen or more males. In such situations the females are treated brutally in a mating frenzy and many have been drowned by over-anxious suitors. Yet the pair-bond ends soon after the female starts incubating. Because of the sexual imbalance, the niceties of courtship are often overlooked, but the mallard does have the typically varied display of its family, ranging from bill-dipping and tail-wagging on water to courtship-flights of up to 10 minutes.

The nest is built by the female and is mostly on the ground among thick undergrowth such as brambles, nettles, grass and reeds, and near water, though some may be in dry situations several miles from any stream, pond, marsh, lake, river or reservoir. Sometimes sites are fairly exposed, at the foot of a post or tree, in the crown of a pollarded willow, or in a tree hollow. Others are under boulders or in artificial nestboxes and baskets. Islets are strongly favoured for their greater security from predation. Town sites are often surprising, including building ledges, bridge supports, window-boxes, roof gardens, static water tanks and even moored boats. The shallow nest is made from local vegetation such as leaves and grass, sometimes with small twigs, and lined with down.

A sudden mild spell often induces laying in February in more temperate regions, but early eggs are often lost because lack of cover makes them more liable to predation, even if they survive a return to severe conditions. In Britain most are laid from March to May, occasional autumn eggs mostly being from birds breeding in their year of birth and as young as six months. The season is generally later

and shorter in colder, more northerly areas. Incubation is by the female and averages 27–28 days. The young leave the nest on their first day, feed themselves, and are cared for by the female. They become independent at or just before fledging, at 50–60 days.

Diet and Feeding Behaviour

Much of the mallard's success has been due to its opportunistic feeding, taking a wide variety of both animal and plant foods through varied methods, according to season and local abundance. As a dabbling duck, it thrives in shallows, where it can up-end to take, for example, aquatic vegetation, but it is just as happy seizing floating insects or a passing crust, or taking grain from the stubbles. It can peck potatoes softened by the frost, sieve water for minute animals, graze like geese and even dive for submerged items such as acorns, or strip seeds from plants and shake vegetation to loosen invertebrates. Animal foods include fish such as eels up to 10cm (3.9in) long, innumerable insects, molluscs, crustaceans, amphibians, and sometimes even small birds and mammals. Plant foods include the buds, seeds, leaves, tubers, berries and stems of many aquatic and terrestrial species, though typical saltmarsh vegetation is mostly ignored.

Feeding may be by day or night, according to local availability, tides, weather, disturbance and light level.

Movements

Although most mallard populations are migratory because their summer quarters become frozen in winter, that within the British Isles moves little. Here, most waters remain open and there is adequate winter feed. Mallard are very reluctant to move and generally 'sit out' short freezes. In exceptional conditions there is some movement south and towards the coast, but very little emigration. Furthermore, the clemency of Britain's climate attracts a large winter influx of mallard from colder climes, notably Scandinavia and Iceland. However, some do over-winter in north, east and central Europe where conditions are suitable, such as parts of Iceland where waters are kept open by thermal springs, power stations and sewage effluent near coasts. Where migration is regular there are established flyways. Birds from Denmark, north Germany, north Poland, Baltic states, Fenno-Scandia and north-west Russia winter from Britain and north France to Denmark, a few moving on as far as north Spain. Movements to winter quarters are protracted, starting in August, peaking November–December in west Europe. Winter visitors and passage migrants mostly arrive in Britain from September and October and leave as late as April–May, breeding grounds being reoccupied February–May, according to the thaw in the north and east. Exceptionally, birds visit Britain from 50–60°E. Only a small proportion of the Irish winter population are immigrants.

Moult migrations are fairly common but mostly small-scale and marked among long-distance winter migrants. Among smaller British sites are two in east England used by males from Denmark and the Netherlands. North-west European mallard also frequently take part in abmigration (a spring movement by a bird that had wintered in its natal area and best known among ducks where it is due to early pairing). This is pronounced among artificially reared stock released by sportsmen.

WIGEON
(Anas penelope)

IN contrast to the over-familiar mallard, the handsome wigeon has inspired man for centuries, drawing artists and hunters to our wildest shores, where the bird's great flocks and haunting whistle seem to epitomise wilderness. This has always been *the* wildfowlers's duck, but fortunately the species has prospered, now attracting many bird-watchers as well to the spectacle of the saltmarsh.

History and Conservation

Fossil remains show that the wigeon was present in Britain during the Pleistocene, the earliest record being from the Cromerian Interglacial. How the species fared subsequently we do not know, but it is likely that it was much more numerous before extensive drainage of eastern England got underway in the seventeenth century. Indeed, European literature abounds with references to the vast numbers taken in decoys, trapped and shot for market from the sixteenth century on. Indeed, it was such a familiar and important table bird that there were many special names to distinguish male, female and young, including easterling and lady fowl for the young male and female respectively in the London market.

In view of this abundance, it is most likely that the species did breed in Britain before the first record, of 1834, in Sutherland. The erratic climate of preceding centuries must have suited the subarctic bird at some stage. However, it soon spread south through central Scotland, though lateral expansion was slower, reaching Tweed in the 1890s, Yorkshire in 1897, Cumberland in 1903, Galloway in 1906, Northumberland in 1913, and the Outer Hebrides in the 1920s. This period of rapid expansion seems to have ended by 1950, with subsequent stability and possible recent contraction in Scotland. Breeding records have been few south of the Pennines, some probably involving escapees or birds with slight wounds which could not return to their native haunts. Nesting was reported in Ireland in 1933 and 1953, in only six years this century in the Netherlands, and twice in Germany (first proved 1908).

There has been recent local decline in some countries, but generally this has been due to changing distribution rather than overall reduction in numbers. Indeed, the north-west European population has been increasing steadily since the early 1970s. A run of mild winters may have encouraged this duck, which is particularly vulnerable to severe weather, but much more important in Britain has been increasing use of the rising amount of suitable habitat available, including gravel pits and reservoirs, providing safe roosts near good feeding areas and facilitating exploitation of inland grasses as well as relatively new foods such as sprouting winter wheat as the mainstay marine grass *Zostera* has declined. Equally important has been the creation of sanctuary areas on established sites, all of Britain's top ten now being designated SSSIs. On the Ouse Washes, for example, the winter peak has multiplied by at least four times since 1970, with the creation of refuges and management to provide winter flooding. Wildfowling continues at many wigeon strongholds, but the size of the national cull does not appear to have had a depressive effect on the population. Most important has been increased co-operation between wildfowlers and conservationists to create sanctuaries and

Once known as whew, pandled whew, whistler, grass whew, whewer, whim, bald pate, yellow poll, golden head, black wigeon, lady fowl, lady duck, easterling, half duck, smee duck, winder and cock winder

The name 'wigeon' goes back through various spellings such as 'wigene' to the 'wegyons' of 1513. The most popular alternative has been 'widgeon', even today used by some people, but 'wigeon' became dominant when adopted by Pennant in 1768. It derives from the Old French *vigeon*, traced back through *vibionem* of the Late Latin of Gaul, and has onomatopoeic origin. The Latin specific *penelope* derives from the Greek *penelops* for a kind of duck. There is a Greek legend that Penelope, the wife of Odysseus, was thrown into the sea as a baby and rescued by seabirds.

minimise roost disturbance. Management plans such as that on the Ribble Marshes National Nature Reserve have resulted in both greatly increased wigeon numbers and much better sport.

Distribution, Habitat and Population

One of the world's most successful duck, the European wigeon breeds mainly in subarctic to boreal zones right across northern Eurasia, from Iceland to the Bering Strait, south to England and southern Siberia. To most of this vast range it is only a summer visitor, winter cold driving it south as far as East Africa, central India and Indo-China. Where ice-free shores can be found throughout the year, journeys are much shorter, in hundreds rather than thousands of kilometres (miles). One such haven is the British Isles, which attract about half the north-west European population of 750,000, including almost the entire Icelandic stock (a few are resident). Smaller numbers winter around other North Sea countries, and in France and Iberia.

The British Isles have an abundance of prime winter habitat, especially shallow coastal waters with extensive tracts of tidal mud, sand and saltmarsh, which provide both plenty of food and security for gatherings, with good visibility, as well as general freedom from icing. Flooded grassland and freshwater and brackish lagoons are also attractive. For breeding, fast-flowing streams and rivers are avoided, preference being for shallow waters of medium size and lightly vegetated. Bogs and damp woodland are also used.

Field Characters

The handsome male is easily recognised by his white forewing — the only British duck to have this — his chestnut head and neck, cream-yellow crown and forehead, and grey-pink breast contrasting with white belly and black stern. In silhouette, the short neck, compactness, peaked forehead, pointed tail and narrow wings help to distinguish. In eclipse — mostly late July and August, but also June to November — the male resembles a dark female but retains the white forewing. The female is distinguished from the female mallard by her slimness and small, steel-blue bill as well as the rounded head. She has two colour types — rufous and grey, each plain or barred. The juvenile resembles the female and is not certainly distinguishable in the field. It is much like the adult by its first winter, but the male does not acquire white forewings till its second winter.

The wigeon rises straight from the water almost as well as the teal and keeps tight formation in swift, powerful flight, with rapid beats of the long, narrow wings, which at the downstroke are more depressed than those of the mallard. Though aerobatic, it does not twist and turn as much as the teal. Highly gregarious, approaching flocks are often announced by the distinctive whistling, birds gliding in from considerable height on arched, motionless wings before braking with loud fluttering just prior to alighting. Sometimes they fly in long, straggling lines. Shy and wary, the wigeon swims well, but fairly low in the water, with the neck retracted. It up-ends when necessary, though not often, and when wounded or frightened dives well to avoid capture. It walks and runs easily.

Although renowned for his evocative whistling *whee-OO*, the male has a fairly limited repertoire owing to the similarity of sounds. In contrast, the female's main call is a low, growling purr and she does not quack like most other ducks.

Most British breeding wigeon are found on moorland lochs and pools along the upland spine of the country, from the northern Pennines to northernmost Scotland, with outposts as far afield as the Outer Hebrides and Orkney. But this relatively recently established breeding stock of some 500 pairs, mainly in Scotland, is tiny compared with Britain's winter peak count of 260,000 in 1989–90 plus some 100,000 in Ireland, where there have been only two nesting records. Sites with an average maximum of over 7,500 1986-91, thereby qualifying for international recognition, were: the Ribble Estuary with 40,800 (recent dramatic increase), Ouse Washes 38,029, Lindisfarne 16,908, Lough Foyle 13,920, Dornoch Firth 12,727, Swale Estuary 9,512, and Cromarty Firth 8,324. The 1990–91 peak count was 238,369 (January) for Great Britain and 18,660 (October) for Northern Ireland. During that winter other sites supporting large concentrations but not qualifying for international recognition were: North Norfolk Marshes (12,779, November), Loch Eye (9,815, October) and Loch of Harray (9,200, October).

The length averages 45–51cm (17.7–20.1in) and the wing-span 75–86cm (29.5–33.9in). The average weights are 600–1,090g (1.3–2.4lb) for the male and 530–910g (1.2–2lb) for the female.

The wigeon (male left, female right) is among the most important of quarry species.

79

In Britain the single clutch of 8–9 (6–12) creamy-buff eggs, average size 55 × 39mm (2.17 × 1.53in), is laid from mid-April, at daily intervals, peak laying being in May. Further north laying is later, generally commencing mid-late May in Iceland, for example. Occasional dump nesting occurs and lost clutches are replaced.

Breeding

The monogamous pair-bond is prolonged, though probably seasonal, commencing late autumn, continuing through winter and not usually ending before late incubation. Promiscuity is rare and the age of first breeding one year, sometimes two. The communal courtship, which is less highly ritualised than that of the mallard, often starts in the wintering area, when several males may crowd one female. The male usually starts with a 'burp-display', in which the head is raised, with crest and nape feathers erect, and a whistle uttered while aligned sideways with the female. Further courtship includes upward shakes, wing-flapping, head-turning and pursuit flights.

Early pairing enables more northerly birds to make the best of the short breeding season, the start of which is dictated by the thaw. The female alone makes the simple ground nest hollow from nearby leaves, twigs, stems and grass, lined with down and well concealed in thick cover under overhanging vegetation, scrub, a grass tussock, bracken, rushes or long heather. The species is not colonial but nests may be within a few metres (yards) on favoured sites, such as St Serf's Island, Loch Leven. Irregular nesting in southern England is mostly on brackish or coastal marsh or inland pools near rough ground, but sometimes a few hundred metres (yards) from water.

The 22/25-day incubation is by the female only. The ducklings leave the nest soon after their synchronous hatching, feed themselves, are cared for by the female, and become independent just before or at fledging, at 40–45 days.

Diet and Feeding Behaviour

Wigeon often feed in close association with geese because they are both grazers of saltmarsh plants as well as short, inland grasses on damp fields. In many areas they sleep by day and feed by night, flighting from often huge roosts on the open sea, sandbars, estuaries and lakes, to take advantage of the tides or to avoid disturbance. Unlike other duck, they take little insect food in summer. When its favourite marine grass, *Zostera* (also called eel-grass or wigeon grass), started to decline from the 1930s, as various species of land grass invaded the coastal marshes, the wigeon increasingly turned to inland grazing. Saltmarsh vegetation is taken when exposed at low tide, or by pulling it up by the roots while paddling in the shallows or by up-ending, which it is not too good at. Some observers say that the wigeon has lost a great deal of *Zostera* in competition with the brent goose, whose population has expanded enormously since the 1960s, but others point out that wigeon also benefit in feeding on the brent's leavings. Furthermore, the main wigeon concentrations are further north than those of the brent, which concentrate on the coasts of southern and south-eastern England.

As well as the leaves, stems, bulbils, stolons and rhizomes of plants, some seeds are taken, such as those of sedge and plantain. Also, stubble grain and sprouting winter wheat may be locally important. Other plant foods include blackberries, algae, duckweed and watercress. Animal food may be temporarily important, such as spring flies in Iceland and swarming locusts in parts of the former USSR. Some animal items are probably taken accidentally, but some of significant size, such as *Cardium* cockles at Dornoch, Scotland, crustaceans, amphibians and fish spawn, are taken deliberately. In some areas frequent disturbance masks the real food preferences.

Movements

The wigeon is highly migratory, though there are local resident populations in north-west Europe, including that in Britain, which moves to the coast in autumn, with some drifting towards the south-west and Ireland. Over half the total wigeon population of north-west Europe winters within the British Isles, including most of the Icelandic group and birds from Scandinavia, Russia and Siberia. They arrive from late September to the first half of November, the main influx generally being in early November, but the peak in January after midwinter immigration of Continental birds. As the cold intensifies, birds move further south, some beyond Britain to France and Iberia. Some Icelandic birds have been recovered in east Canada, the USA and Greenland, exceptionally in the former USSR and one in the West Indies. Of the few British breeders ringed, a small number have been re-covered as juveniles in the Netherlands and south-west France, and some as abmigrants in Iceland and Russia. Many Fenno-Scandian and Russian birds winter in west and south-west Europe, especially western Germany, the Netherlands and France, as well as the British Isles, and to a lesser extent Iberia.

Most birds wintering in the British Isles return north in March and April but some do not settle on their breeding grounds till May. Soon after breeding, adult males migrate to special moulting grounds, where they join immatures and non-breeders before migrating to winter quarters.

Wigeon movements are dictated by tides as well as weather. Photo: R. Glover

TEAL
(Anas crecca)

THE teal might be small, but among wildfowl its flying skills are second to none. For centuries it has been a great favourite with sportsmen and savoured by gourmets, from medieval times a familiar sight in the market-place as one of the most numerous and widespread duck in the northern hemisphere.

History and Conservation

The teal has great ancestry in Britain, remains having been found in the peat deposits of Neolithic sites and going back to the Cromerian Interglacial of the Middle Pleistocene of Norfolk, as well as north-western and midland caves in the last glaciation. With forest increase in later warm phases the teal probably declined significantly before becoming much more numerous with widespread felling and access to the bogs of acid moorland and peat, on which it thrives. And although still numerous from the sixteenth to the twentieth centuries, its numbers have declined enormously through widespread drainage, especially in Ireland.

That said, there has been significant winter increase throughout north-west Europe since the early 1960s, though it is not known whether this stems from increases in the breeding population in northern Europe. The species had been at a low point following some severe winters, and estimated trebling of the European population 1967–83 may have been largely due to recovery from the cold weather to which it is vulnerable. However, there has long been a pattern of steady increase following decline in severe weather, and there has been no significant improvement in habitat loss to drainage, so other factors must be considered. Among the most important could have been better legislative protection, the creation of more sanctuary areas and enhanced feeding opportunities, especially in Scandinavia. The bird could have been helped by an increased abundance of aquatic insects, which occurs during the early stages of nutrient enrichment and acidification. Yet there are no figures to suggest that British breeders have been more successful where acidification of fresh waters has been marked. Devotion to some British breeding strongholds has declined significantly this century, but this is thought to be due to changing distribution caused by the teal's opportunism in lowland areas rather than overall decline. It always responds quickly to changing environmental circumstances so it is likely that the very recent run of drought years in south-east England will have had a significant effect on distribution.

Distribution, Habitat and Population

The teal has a vast circumpolar range, breeding in subarctic to temperate zones and wintering in warm temperate to subtropical zones and the edges of the boreal zone in western Europe. North America has a distinct subspecies, *Anas crecca carolinensis*, which is a rare straggler to the British Isles (327 accepted records to the end of 1990), and differs from the nominate Eurasian race in having incomplete yellow face-lines, the addition of a vertical white line between flank and breast, and only a black lateral stripe along the wing edge. The females of the two races are impossible to tell apart. Although the American bird is called the green-

Once known as common teal, speckled teal, jay teal, tael teal and throstle teal

Considering that the teal has been common for thousands of years, it is surprising that it has had so few common names. The current spelling is known from Merrett in 1667 and goes back through *teils* (1614), *tele* (1544), *teale* (1538), *teyle* (1532) and *teele* (1530) to the *teles* of 1314. This is the only common British bird not known ever to have been called by another name. There are no Old English sources but the name was present as *tela* (masculine) or *tele* (feminine) and may be traced through the Low German and Dutch *teeling*. The syllable *tel* is said to be imitative of a call.

An estimated 3,500–6,000 pairs (800–1,500 in Ireland) breed in the British Isles, mainly in the north and west, with a thin distribution and very scarce in the south-west. The breeding population of north-west Europe is estimated at 6,370–9,370 pairs, excluding Fenno-Scandia, where about 80,000 pairs breed in Finland. France has some 500–1,000 pairs, Belgium about 400 pairs, the Netherlands about 750 pairs, West Germany 1,000 pairs and Denmark under 200 pairs.

The tiny teal (female left, male right) is one of the most numerous ducks in the northern hemisphere.

The north-west European winter population is estimated at over 400,000, concentrated in the British Isles, the Netherlands and western France. A further 1 million birds winter around the Mediterranean and the Black Sea. Britain's winter population is variously estimated at 100,000–200,000, of which some 85 per cent are immigrants. The 1990–91 peak count of almost 142,000 (January) was almost identical to that of 1989–90, so the population index remained at a high level. The 1990–91 peak count of 11,483 at Abberton Reservoir in September was exceptional, traditional sites in north-west England being the most attractive over a period. Average maxima at main British resorts 1986–91 were: Mersey Estuary 10,685 (December), Ribble Estuary 5,363 (November), Dee Estuary 5,180 (October), Abberton Reservoir 4,266 (September), Ouse Washes 4,064 (January), Woolston Eyes 3,700 (October), Hamford Water 3,629 (December), Martin Mere 3,220 (September), Cleddau Estuary 2,778 (December), Thames Estuary 2,654 (January), Severn Estuary 2,288 (January), North Norfolk Marshes 2,651 (December), Loch Leven 2,245 (October), Lough Neagh/Beg 2,288 (December), Swale Estuary 2,111 (January), Dornoch Firth 2,052 (December), Humber Estuary 1,862 (November). In 1990–91 other sites exceeding the ▶

The teal (this is a male) can spring from danger with great ease. Photo: R. Glover

winged teal, the name is of no use in separating the two races, as both have the green speculum. The teal's breeding range extends through much of Canada, southwards into the north-western USA, throughout Alaska and from Iceland and Britain across Eurasia to northern Japan. The range becomes discontinuous in France and central Europe and it is virtually absent from southern Europe and the Mediterranean. In most of this huge range the teal is only a summer visitor, the entire population moving south to winter, though some stay on in ice-free pockets, such as in south-west Iceland. British breeders are largely sedentary and joined by large numbers of winter visitors.

In winter the teal prefers shallow water on coastal lagoons, coastal and inland marshes, estuaries, flooded pasture and ponds. They mostly breed near water in dense cover, both near coasts and far inland, with a distinct preference for acid environments. It takes to the smallest pond or drainage dykes where sufficient emergent cover suits its secretive behaviour, and is fairly easily encouraged by active habitat management.

Field Characters

Apart from the vagrant bufflehead, this is the smallest west Palearctic duck and its minute size distinguishes it from all other north-west European dabbling ducks except the vagrant blue-winged teal and summer garganey. The male is distinguished at all ranges by his combination of dark head, contrasting grey body, and black-edged, yellow-buff stern. Both sexes may be distinguished in flight by the clearly defined metallic green and black speculum bordered with white, as well as the very short neck and compact shape. (See *Distribution* section for separation of green-winged teal.) Eclipse males and juveniles resemble the female, but with darker, more uniform upperparts.

The teal is renowned for its rapid reaction to danger, its ability to catapult almost vertically into the air with rapid wing-beats rocketing away with twists, dips and swerves, giving rise to the species' collective term 'spring'. It usually flies low and erratically in a tight bunch or pack, but high and in lines or V-formation when

on migration. It swims well and lightly, but usually dives only when wounded or frightened, and walks clumsily. Though highly gregarious, it is often seen in pairs.

The male's short, far-carrying, bell-like whistle — *crrick-crrick* — is not at all duck-like, but the female has a short, high-pitched *queck*, mostly used when alarmed. In flight, flocks call continuously, the *krit-krit* carrying a long way. The wings make a distinctive whistling.

Breeding

The monogamous pair-bond is of seasonal duration and winter flocks are increasingly of paired birds which later migrate together to breeding grounds. The bond ends when the male leaves the female at the start of incubation. Courtship may begin as early as August, but is not regular until October/November. With the frequent local excess of males typical of the family, a female may have 25 suitors in the spring, but usually 5–7. Males swim rapidly round the female, with frequent short jump-flights. Main displays include head-up, tail-up, down-up, water-flick and burp, all accompanied by courtship calls.

The female alone builds the ground nest in thick cover, forming a slight hollow with leaves, bracken, grass and other vegetation lined with down, generally near water but sometimes up to 150m (yards) away. Though not colonial, nests may be as close as 1m (3ft) apart. Nesting is so sporadic in much of England and Wales that in some areas teal may nest in only two years out of ten.

The 21/23-day incubation is by the female only. The chicks hatch synchronously, may return to the nest for the first few nights, feed themselves and are cared for by the female, always preferring to hide among marginal vegetation. Independence is achieved at or just before fledging, at 25–30 days. Age of first breeding is one year.

Diet and Feeding Behaviour

Where it feels safe the teal feeds throughout the day, but nocturnal feeding, involving flighting to and from a secure daytime roost, is common. This dabbler feeds mainly on the surface in shallows, but also up-ends. Its omnivorous diet varies considerably with season and locality, but seeds, mostly filtered from soft mud, predominate in autumn and winter, with relatively more animal food in spring and summer. Plant food, chiefly seeds of mainly aquatic varieties, has the emphasis on commoner freshwater and saltwater species such as sedges, bulrushes, pondweeds, wigeon-grass, buttercup, milfoil, dock, birch, alder, samphire and sea aster, suggesting little selection by the bird. Grasses, algae, eelgrass and stubble grain are also taken. Animal foods include insects, crustaceans, caddis-fly larvae, water-beetles, water-bugs and annelids, with a special emphasis on chironomid midge larvae and small molluscs.

Movements

Teals breeding within the British Isles are thought to be relatively sedentary, few emigrating during average winters. However, many upland areas of Scotland and northern England are vacated in winter in favour of warmer, ice-free lowland marshes. Generally, there is a southerly or south-westerly drift in autumn. Elsewhere, the species is largely migratory. Large numbers of passage migrants

► qualifying level for national importance were: Irvine shore (7,500, February), Blithfield Reservoir (3,410, January), Alaw Reservoir (2,938, December), Pulborough Levels (2,210 January), Rutland Water (2,187, September), and Alde Complex (2,610, January). Yet nearly 40 per cent of the British wintering population consists of flocks of under 200. Ireland's peak population is estimated at 30,000–50,000 in normal years, but sometimes many more, resorts usually holding over 1,000 including the Shannon Estuary, Cork Harbour and the North Bull at Dublin.

The length averages 34–38cm (13.4–15in), wingspan 58–64cm (22.8–25.2in), and weight 200–450g (0.44–1lb) for the male, 185–430g (0.4–0.9lb) the female.

The single clutch (replaced after loss) of 8–11 (7–15) blunt ovate, yellow-white, sometimes greenish eggs, average size 45 × 33mm (1.77 × 1.30in), is laid from late March to mid-May in Britain, sometimes later further north.

and winter visitors arrive in the British Isles as early as August, but chiefly in September and October, with a tailing off in early November. They come from a wide breeding range and include almost all the Icelandic stock (going mostly to Scotland). The majority of birds from north Russia, the Baltic states, Fenno-Scandia, north Poland, north Germany and Denmark overwinter around North Sea grounds, especially Britain and the Netherlands. As the species is very vulnerable to weather fluctuations, there is considerable interchange between Ireland, England, Wales and the Netherlands, the onset of severe cold causing immediate westward movement, exceptionally to France, Iberia and North Africa. Some British and Dutch birds have been recovered in southern Europe. The spring migration starts late February and peaks March–April, the tundras not being reoccupied until late May.

The scale of moult migrations is very variable, large concentrations being reported in the former USSR, but most British birds appear to moult alone or in small groups.

PINTAIL
(Anas acuta)

ALTHOUGH very rare as a breeder within the British Isles, the pintail overwinters here in internationally important numbers and it is possibly the most abundant duck in the world. The frequency with which it is portrayed in ancient and modern art reflects man's great admiration of its beauty and traditional close association with hunting.

History and Conservation

Though rare among early remains, the pintail occurred as a Pleistocene bird, as early as the Cromerian in Norfolk. As a relatively cold-tolerant species, it probably did well during the cool phases of this millennium, but has suffered through extensive land drainage in recent centuries. Although we know that it was sometimes abundant in winter in the eighteenth century and was commonly seen in the market, as a British breeder it appears to have been a nineteenth-century colonist. The first proved breeding was in Inverness-shire, in 1869. England's first was in Kent, in 1869, and Ireland's in 1917, in County Roscommon. It has now nested in at least 28 counties, but usually in no more than 10 in any one year, and there appears to have been recent decrease, with sporadic records from only a handful of areas. This instability is typical of a bird on the edge of its range.

The wintering population, however, has increased steadily in north-west Europe since the early 1970s, by 100 per cent, but the reasons for this are not clear. Good breeding seasons are thought to have been more significant than changes affecting mortality. Today the greatest threat to wintering birds is land-claim on estuaries, especially linked with barrage construction.

Recent establishment of reserves, creation of SSSIs and the development of conservation policies has helped both breeding and overwintering birds. Yet the species remains relatively local throughout the year, so the creation of further inland sanctuaries will do much to lessen its vulnerability. Fortunately, it is quite easy to encourage with new waters near coasts, as some wildfowlers have found to

Once known as common pintail, pintail duck, winter duck, lady bird, cracker, harlan, thin neck, sea pheasant and sprig tail

The name 'pintail' is derived from the bird's long, pointed tail and appears to have been coined by Pennant in 1768, becoming standard in the nineteenth century. The Latin specific *acuta* means sharp and pointed.

Breeding is very patchy within the British Isles. In recent decades there have probably been well under 50 pairs, occurring most frequently in the Highland and Grampian regions of Scotland, Orkney, East Anglia and north Kent. In Ireland there are only a handful of records from just six counties: Armagh, Antrim, Down, Londonderry, Laois and Roscommon.

The male pintail is easily distinguished from the female by his chocolate-brown hood.

their advantage. Numerically, it has become a relatively unimportant quarry for wildfowlers with the ending of market-gunning and the steep decline in punt-gunning, to which it was particularly susceptible, yet it remains highly valued for the sport it provides.

Distribution, Habitat and Population

The pintail has a huge breeding range throughout the northern hemisphere, in the subarctic to cooler temperate zones of North America and Eurasia, though nesting is sporadic over large areas of the western and southern fringes. It is very locally distributed in parts of Europe but much more numerous in Fenno-Scandia and north Russia. A wide variety of habitats is occupied, including ponds, lakes, floods, inland marshes, boreal marshes and marshy tundra. Except for birds in parts of western Europe and the western United States, the whole population migrates long distances to winter quarters, mainly around the coasts of west Europe, the Mediterranean and Black and Caspian Seas, as well as in northern tropical Africa, southern Asia, the USA and Central America.

Iceland has an estimated 500 pairs, Germany 130 pairs, Denmark 200 pairs, Finland 20,000 pairs, Austria 10–15 pairs, and the western part of the former USSR some 316,000 pairs after a great decline. Norwegian figures fluctuate widely.

There is a clear preference for shallow, open, aquatic habitats which are at least moderately productive biologically. This very mobile species makes great use of temporary floods but generally avoids reservoirs and other artefacts. In winter the emphasis is on sheltered coastal habitats, but nearby inland waters and floods are also used extensively. In some areas there has been increasing use of farmland for feeding.

Field Characters

In silhouette or at long distance the male is unmistakable, with his long, pointed tail, slender body and thin neck. Closer, he is also readily identified by his chocolate hood contrasting with a white neck-stripe and underparts. The female's tail is shorter yet remains a good field mark, and she is distinguished from other ducks by her slender, elegant shape, generally paler and greyer plumage; bold, crescent-shaped markings on flanks, and conspicuous light border on the rear of the secondaries. She is also separated from the female mallard and gadwall by her blue-grey bill, long, pointed wings and obscure speculum. The female wigeon shows some similarities but has a more uniform appearance on water, more compact shape, rounded head and a short neck. The juvenile resembles the adult female but is darker and more uniform, without the pale feather edgings, but with paler cheeks and neck sides, and a dark-grey bill. In eclipse the male resembles the female but has darker, more uniform upperparts.

This gregarious but very wary duck swims well and in tight formation, but only dives when wounded or surprised, generally flying right away at the slightest sign of danger. It rises easily from the water and its flight is direct and rapid with fast wing-beats and great agility, the wings making a distinctive hissing sound. Flight is often in V-formation or long lines. It walks well and gracefully, usually with the long neck outstretched and the tail raised, and can run well.

Generally a quiet duck with a rather limited repertoire. The male's peculiar, low, mechanical, rattling main call has been likened to the sound of a fishing reel or breaking ice. The female has a subdued, decrescendo double quack, recalling the mallard, but other calls are more teal-like.

Breeding

The monogamous pair-bond is of seasonal duration, and although pairing may start during early winter, relationships developed gradually during spring migration are thought to be more lasting. The bond often ends during early incubation. The male is strongly promiscuous in the breeding area. His main courtship includes chin-lifting, water-flicking, burp, and head-up, tail-up displays, often accompanied by a low double whistle, as well as pursuit-flights.

The species is not colonial but nests are often only a few metres (yards) apart in favoured areas. The female alone builds the often fairly exposed nest on the bare ground or in short cover such as rushes and grass, but sometimes under scrub and up to 2km or so (just over a mile) away from water. The slight hollow is usually, but not always, formed with leaves, grass and other vegetation, and is always lined with down.

The 22/24-day incubation starts on completion of the clutch (eggs laid at daily intervals) and is by the female only. The chicks hatch synchronously, feed themselves, are cared for by the female, frequently with the male in attendance during the early stages, and become independent near fledging time, at 40–45 days. Age of first breeding is mostly one year, sometimes two.

The single clutch (replaced after loss) of 7–9 (6–12) ovate, yellowish–white, sometimes yellow–green or even pale blue eggs, average size 55 × 39mm (2.17 × 1.53in), is mostly laid from mid-April in the south to mid-June in the north, according to the thaw.

Diet and Feeding Behaviour

This dabbler takes a wide variety of plant and animal food, chiefly from mud in shallows by up-ending, for which the long neck is particularly well suited. It also feeds when swimming with the head and neck submerged and sometimes dives. On land it picks up grain and digs up tubers and rhizomes with its beak. It often feeds alongside other species of wildfowl. In winter this relatively shy bird mostly feeds inland, at night where disturbed during daytime.

There is significant local and seasonal variation in the diet. On estuaries, for example, although seeds are also commonly taken, small snails of the genus *Hydrobia* appear to be the most favoured food. Yet on the Ouse Washes seeds, especially of common spike-rush, have accounted for over four-fifths of the diet. In many areas field feeding has become common in recent years, notably on arable land around the Washes, cereal stubbles being the main autumn attraction, frosted and waste potatoes and sugar-beet thereafter. Other plant foods include mainly seeds, tubers and rhizomes of sedges, pondweeds, docks, bistort, grasses (including eel-grass) and algae. Animal food, largely insects, includes waterbeetles, chironomid midges, caddis-fly larvae, dragonfly larvae, grasshoppers, molluscs, leeches, crustaceans and tadpoles, but rarely fish. Overall, the emphasis is on animal food in spring and summer in some areas, but mostly on plant food in autumn and winter.

Movements

Most pintail populations are highly migratory, overwintering far south of their breeding range, though relatively little is known about their precise relocation. Certainly most of the Icelandic stock overwinters in the British Isles, joining many

The pintail (this is a male) is possibly the most abundant duck in the world. Photo: Dennis Green

OPPOSITE:
Gadwall (male left, female right): a shy duck, but now increasing.

others from Fenno-Scandia and western Siberia, but the degree of movement of the small British population is unknown. Northern European birds generally move south-west, many overwintering in the Netherlands as well as the British Isles, some moving from the former to the latter in severe cold. Smaller numbers (including some ringed in Britain autumn/winter) progress further south, around the coasts of France and Iberia. A few Icelandic birds have been recovered further south-east than Britain, and in Greenland and Quebec. There is considerable interchange between main flyways in different years. Southerly movement mostly begins in mid-August and peaks mid-September to November, with further weather movements at any time during the winter. The spring migration from west Europe mostly starts late February and lasts through March, tundra breeding grounds not being reached until late May. Moult migrations are of widely varying size and peak in July, when some of the females are free to join the males.

GADWALL
(Anas strepera)

Once known as gaddel, grey duck, gray, rodge and sand wigeon

Merrett's 1667 use of the name 'gaddel' indicates onomatopoeic origin, the spelling 'gadwall' first being used by Ray in 1674 and taken up by Pennant in 1768. The Latin specific *strepera* derives from *strepo* for 'I make a noise' and no doubt refers to the species' frequent, excited quacking.

THIS quiet and cryptically coloured duck has an oddly discontinuous breeding range, which is probably linked with climatic change, but now it is on the increase through a combination of natural factors and deliberate and accidental introductions.

History and Conservation

The species' patchy worldwide distribution may be the result of unusual sensitivity to cold and wet. Although the Eurasian and North American populations are separated by 1,600km (a thousand miles) or more, they are identical and do not merit subspecific status, indicating former much wider distribution which may have been severely disrupted by the last Ice Age. Although found in the

Gadwalls are migratory in
the northern and eastern
west Palearctic, but mainly
resident elsewhere. The
north-west European
wintering population has
been increasing steadily
along with the breeding
population and is now at
least 12,000. Britain's
share is of major
international importance,
counts having risen
dramatically from under
300 in 1967 to 7,497 in
December 1990, though
very few sites hold large
numbers. During 1986–91
the main sites and average
maxima were: Rutland
Water 1,430, Abberton
Reservoir 466, Gunton
Park (Norfolk) 387,
Severn Estuary 321, Ouse
Washes 319, River Avon
(Blashford) 240, Cheshunt
gravel pits 223, Loch
Leven 193, Chew Valley
Lake 182, Stanford Meres
153 – mainly encompassing
those areas where the
initial introductions were
made. Other sites holding
more than 170 1990–91
were Eversley Cross/
Yateley gravel pits (338,
December), Hickling
Broad (312, October),
Bucken/Stirtloe gravel pits
(232, November), Amwell
gravel pits (209, January),
Burry Inlet (177, October),
the Fleet/Wey (171,
January), Langtoft gravel
pits (168, January) and
Hanningfield Reservoir
(165, September).
Ireland's top spots are
Ballycotton and nearby
lakes, Cork (where over
300 have been counted),
Ballyallia Lake, Clare (up
to 180) and Tacumshin,
Wexford (up to 160).

Ipswichian Interglacial of south-east England and in the Iron Age in Somerset, in historic times it appears to have been absent as a breeder in Britain, perhaps due to the colder conditions of the 'Little Ice Age' 1550–1850.

The gadwall was not known to breed in the British Isles before 1850, when a wing-clipped pair was turned down at Narford in the Brecks and subsequently bred. By 1875 there was a substantial population in Norfolk, and by 1895 they had crossed into the Suffolk side of Breckland. Further spread into eastern Suffolk by the 1930s and the Norfolk Broads in the 1950s was probably aided by steadily increasing numbers of immigrants. Since then, further introductions and escapes have encouraged establishment in other parts of England and Wales. Scotland was colonised (perhaps from Iceland) in 1909 and Ireland's first breeding record is from 1933. The species' British success has been mirrored throughout western Europe, with many local increases in both breeding and winter populations. First recorded breeding in France was in 1920, in Germany 1930, in Switzerland 1959, and in Norway 1965.

It has been suggested that, apart from warmer weather, this century's range expansion in western Europe may have been stimulated by severe droughts in the former USSR, which made breeding strongholds among shallow lakes uninhabitable. Such irruptive behaviour may partly account for patchy distribution. Fortunately, no special conservation measures appear to be needed. Growth in water sports has caused some local disturbance, but this has been more than offset by the establishment and better management of wildfowl refuges, and the exploitation of new gravel-pit waters and reservoirs. Wildfowlers take only small numbers and have contributed significantly to the species' spread through release schemes and intensive winter feeding.

Distribution, Habitat and Population

Although extensive in temperate Eurasia and North America, the gadwall's breeding range is well broken and significantly to the south of those of most European ducks. Whereas in North America it has spread eastwards, in Europe it has mainly moved north and west. It is mostly absent from Scandinavia, Finland and the forested taiga of the former USSR, and west of Russia its breeding distribution is patchy in mainland Europe. With continuing increase in some areas, notably westwards, the British population is now probably over 600 pairs. East Anglia is the main stronghold, with further centres in Essex, Kent, Surrey, Gloucestershire, the Isles of Scilly, Lancashire, the Lake District, Yorkshire, Loch Leven (Tayside), Perth and Fife, and irregular breeding as far afield as the Orkneys and the Western Isles. Numbers are much smaller in Ireland, but there appears to have been recent increase, with 20 pairs at Lough Neagh in 1987, over 10 pairs in most years in Wexford and others in Galway, Cork, Clare and Roscommon. The generally small groups in Iceland, France, Germany, Denmark, Finland, Switzerland, Sweden and the Netherlands are also mostly increasing.

In winter some 80 per cent of gadwalls are recorded inland in the British Isles, primarily on shallow lakes, notably flooded gravel pits and reservoirs, though recent range expansion appears to have encouraged use of coastal habitats. Outside the Ouse Washes, floodlands are used less by gadwalls than by other dabbling ducks. In the breeding season habitat choice is more restricted and there is a strong preference for shallow, eutrophic, standing or slow-moving water with plenty of cover and islands or dry banks.

Field Characters

The white speculum is the best field mark for both sexes as no other British duck has this white wing-patch. The male's head and neck plumage is similar to that of female ducks generally, but his generally white underparts are distinctive against the grey breast and black under-tail coverts. The female is much like the female mallard but slightly smaller and greyer, with a grey-brown instead of whitish tail and orange side-panels on the bill. Her clear-cut, pale lower breast and belly contrast with brown flanks in flight, but she is less white than the male. In eclipse the male resembles the female but retains the chestnut on the wing-coverts and is greyer with darker, more uniform upperparts. The sides of his bill become more orange. The juvenile resembles the adult female, but has darker upperparts and boldly spotted and streaked underparts.

This rather shy duck rarely gathers in large flocks and is often overlooked in close vegetation. It swims quite high in the water and walks easily. Although its wing-beats are more rapid and it appears faster, it is slower than the mallard and the whistling of the wings is lower pitched.

The male has a soft whistle and a short, deep, chuckling croak, both varying considerably. The female's quacking is reminiscent of the mallard but softer, more strongly decrescendo, uttered more frequently and gives the impression of greater excitement.

The gadwall (this is a male) – no other British duck has the white wing-patch. Photo: Dennis Green

The length averages 46–56cm (18.1–22in), wing-span 84–95cm (33.1–37.4in), and weight 605–1,100g (1.3–2.4lb) for the male, 470–1,000g (1–2.2lb) the female.

Breeding

The monogamous pair-bond is of seasonal duration and pairing starts in flocks as early as late July, continuing until May. Pairs usually separate between the end of laying and mid-incubation. Males are sometimes promiscuous. Courtship peaks August-October, major displays including head-up tail-up, water-flick, down-up, burp, head-high and chin-lifting, all accompanied by frequent calls. There is also a considerable amount of mock-preening, and pursuit-flights may last several minutes.

GADWALL

The single clutch (replaced after loss) of 8–12 (6–16) blunt oval, yellow-buff, pinkish or light-green eggs, average size 55 × 39mm (2.17 × 1.53in), is mostly laid from early May to early June.

The ground nest is usually less than 15m (yards) from water in dense vegetation such as rushes, tall grass and bushes, but may be 100m (yards) or more away in drier cover such as heather. Though the species is not colonial, nests are sometimes only a few metres (yards) apart. The female forms a slight hollow lined with leaves, grass and down.

Only the female undertakes the 24/26-day incubation, which commences on completion of the clutch. Hatching is synchronous, the young feed themselves, are cared for by the female, and become independent at or just before fledging, at 45–50 days. Age of first breeding is one year.

Diet and Feeding Behaviour

This dabbling duck takes mainly vegetable matter, chiefly the leaves, buds, roots and seeds of aquatic plants, while swimming with its head under water, and rarely up-ending. Sometimes it grazes and takes grain on stubbles. Animal food, some of which is taken accidentally, includes insects, molluscs, worms, small amphibians and spawn, and small fish. Sometimes it takes advantage of the very disturbed water where the coot dives and may even steal the other bird's weed. It feeds mostly by day where undisturbed, but is a restless bird and spends a considerable amount of time flying between its roost and alternative feeding grounds.

Movements

Winter visitors start to arrive in the British Isles from mid-August, reaching a peak in October and tailing off in November. They include the Icelandic stock and birds from south Sweden, north Germany, Poland and west-central Russia. The majority of English breeders, which are largely descended from introduced stock, appear to be mainly sedentary, only a few having been recovered from the Continent. Scottish breeders winter chiefly in Ireland, but also in England. Breeders in France and the Netherlands are probably resident, the latter being joined by substantial winter visitors from more northerly and easterly populations. The spring migration is mainly in March and April. Little is known about the small number of male moult migrations recorded in north-west Europe.

GARGANEY
Once known as garganey teal, summer teal, cricket teal, crackling teal, pied wigeon, pied wiggon, summer duck and crick

The garganey (male left, female right) is entirely a summer visitor to Europe.

GARGANEY
(Anas querquedula)

MOST species of duck are long-distance migrants, but the garganey is the only one which is entirely a summer visitor to Europe. On the Continent its population is stable, and worldwide it is common, but within the British Isles it remains rare on the edge of its range.

History and Conservation

The earliest British records are from the pre-Hoxnian interglacial on the east coast and the Iron Age in Somerset. Subsequently its numbers would have fluctuated widely within Britain and north-west Europe, reflecting the edge-of-range

GARGANEY

The name 'garganey' was first recorded in 1668 (misspelt 'gargane') and the current spelling became established when used by Ray in 1678. It derives from the Italian name *garganello*, used by Gesner in 1555, being based on the onomatopoeic *garg*, from the bird's raucous call. The Latin *querquedula* means a kind of duck.

Since 1980 the British breeding population has generally been in the range 40–60 pairs, East Anglia and south-east England being the strongholds. However, it has nested in 25 English counties and there are occasional large spring influxes, such as a possible 94 pairs in 1982, when there is temporary colonisation west and north. There are only a handful of records from Scotland, Wales and Ireland and overall throughout the British Isles few sites are used annually, and even at these numbers fluctuate widely.

distribution dependent on slight climatic change and availability of prime habitat. Thus it was probably very scarce during the relatively cold phase (the 'Little Ice Age') 1550–1850 and undoubtedly suffered greatly through extensive land drainage over the same period, and especially in this century. With climatic amelioration 1900–1950 in England it increased from a few pairs to about 100 in 10 counties, with occasional breeding in 13 others. Recently there has been gradual decline, but long-term trends are very hard to determine as numbers of this opportunistic species present in Britain fluctuate considerably with the weather. There have been very few breeding records from Scotland, Wales and Ireland.

Numbers are highest in warm springs following wet winters, when plenty of shallow floods remain, so the very recent run of dry winters and cold springs in Britain and much of Europe will have had a serious adverse effect. Better protection and management of inland shallow wetlands and grazing marshes is essential if the species is to survive as a British breeder. It is protected under Schedule I of the Wildlife and Countryside Act 1981, the EC Birds Directive, and Appendix III of the Berne Convention.

Distribution, Habitat and Population

Confined to the Old World, the species breeds in much of Europe north to the British Isles, southern Fenno-Scandia and northern Russia, but is generally local or scarce in the western third and only very sporadic in most of Italy, Iberia and the southern Balkans.

On the Continent the population is much more stable than in Britain with some 5,000 pairs in the Netherlands, 2,000 pairs in Finland, 1,100 pairs in west Germany and some thousands in Czechoslovakia. Norway's first record is from 1862 and it has bred there in small numbers since the invasion of 1947. Sweden has seen great fluctuation over the last century, Belgium has only about 20 pairs and Denmark some 200, but there are good numbers throughout the former USSR. The species is accidental in Iceland, the Faeroes and the Azores.

Within the Palearctic the garganey winters only in the Persian Gulf and southern China. Most birds winter thousands of miles south of their breeding range, in India, south-east Asia and north tropical Africa. Over 200,000 have been counted on the Senegal Delta in West Africa, and up to 480,000 on the Niger Delta in Mali. Worldwide, the species is clearly not under any significant threat.

The preferred breeding habitat is water meadows, grasslands with intersecting ditches and floods, and other shallow freshwaters with sufficient vegetation, especially around the edges. Uplands and windy, rainy areas are avoided and only brief, localised use made of marine and estuarine habitats. Little use is made of artificial sites, but the species is less fussy outside the breeding season and small numbers occur at poorer and more exposed waters, including gravel pits and reservoirs, mainly in September and March. The species is very alert to changes in site biological productivity, whether through climatic variation or human interference.

Field Characters

This dainty little duck is about the size of a teal, with a flat crown and straight bill. Although relatively inconspicuous and easily overlooked in eclipse plumage, it is none the less beautifully and delicately marked. The male is readily distinguished by the broad, white supercilium across his dark head, pale blue-grey forewing edged white behind, and striped, elongated, drooping scapulars. From below, watch for the sharp demarcation between his brown breast and white belly. The female is much like other female dabbling ducks, but is distinguished from the teal by her more distinct dark eyestripe, light supercilium, whiter throat, pale patch at the base of her longer bill, and generally paler plumage. In both sexes the dark leading edge to the forewing is prominent from below. The eclipse male closely resembles the adult female, but retains the much brighter blue-grey forewing and green speculum, and has a whiter throat and belly. The juvenile is distinguished from the adult female by its mottled and brown-streaked lower breast and belly.

In Britain, the garganey occurs mostly in pairs or very small parties, but on migration congregates in flocks of several hundreds, and in tens of thousands in winter quarters. It swims low on the water, up-ends little and dives only when alarmed or wounded. Although it rises easily from water and flies with rapid wingbeats and considerable agility, it does not twist and dip like the teal. It walks quite well but spends little time on land.

Mostly a quiet species, the male has a distinctive, mechanical-sounding rattle which has been likened to the sound of breaking ice — hence the old name 'crackling teal'. The female's main call is a short, sharp, decrescendo quack. The whistle of the relatively small wings is insignificant.

Breeding

The monogamous pair-bond is probably mostly of seasonal duration and of necessity most pairs are formed in winter quarters before the long journey north, some Siberian breeding grounds not being reached before late April. Not surprisingly, therefore, promiscuity is unrecorded and, unusually, the pair-bond lasts throughout incubation. In courtship, which may continue into April–May in the breeding area, the male has a display which is unique among surface-feeding ducks. In its most elaborate form the head is thrown right back so that the front of the crown touches the lower back and the bill points skywards, which is similar to the head-throw display of diving ducks. Other displays are more typical of the group.

The species is not colonial and nests are rarely more than 100m (yards) from water. The female makes a shallow depression on the ground in thick vegetation, using locally gathered leaves, grass and rushes, and lines it with down.

Eggs are laid daily and incubated by the female only for 21–23 days from completion of the clutch, but the male remains nearby throughout and often leads the female off the nest to feed during darkness. Hatching is synchronous, the young feed themselves and become independent at about the time of fledging, at 35–40 days. Age of first breeding is one year. Breeding is difficult to confirm because the birds remain hidden away in thick vegetation for much of the season.

Diet and Feeding Behaviour

The garganey has much in common with the shoveler in that a wide variety of plant and animal foods is taken from rich shallow water mainly through swimming with the head submerged. Hence both species have very restricted habitat requirements. The garganey also up-ends briefly, takes food from the surface and

GARGANEY

The length averages 37–41cm (14.6–16.1in), wingspan 60–63cm (23.6–24.8in), and the average weights are 250–600g (0.5–1.3lb) for the male and 250–550g (0.5–1.2lb) for the female.

The single clutch (replacement probable after early loss) of 8–9 (6–14) ovate, pale-buff eggs, average size 46 × 33mm (1.81 × 1.3in), is mostly laid from mid-April to early May in Britain, but immigration may continue into early June and summer presence is not necessarily indicative of breeding. In Fenno-Scandia and west Russia peak laying is early May.

Male garganey feeding.
Photo: Derek Middleton

snaps at flying insects. Feeding is mostly by day, but sometimes chiefly at night where disturbed.

There is regional variation in the diet, but relatively little seasonal change in proportions of plant/animal foods taken as this strongly migratory species has easy access to both for much of the year. Animal foods include water-bugs, caddis-fly, water-beetles, midges, molluscs, crustaceans, worms, leeches, froglets, spawn and small fish. Plant foods include the leaves, buds, roots, tubers and seeds of aquatic and bankside species, rice and seaweeds, and grasses in floods.

Movements

Only a few stragglers occur from November to February in north and west Europe, where the highly migratory garganey is only a summer visitor. The main northward passage through Europe is in March and April, northernmost breeding grounds being reached about mid-May, but there is significant annual variation according to weather. In an average year birds arrive in Britain from mid-March to early June and most go by late September, only a handful remaining in October. Whether they stay or not depends on the availability of suitable habitat on arrival. Non-breeders may return as early as mid-June. Breeders from Britain, the Netherlands, France and Germany migrate south through France and Iberia, across the Mediterranean to Morocco and Algeria, and then on to their winter grounds, or south-east to Italy and the Balkans before a direct crossing of the Sahara. In parts of the range birds perform a so-called loop migration, taking different routes north and south. Moult gatherings of males are known from late May, notably on the Volga Delta.

98

SHOVELER
(Anas clypeata)

THIS colourful duck is chiefly known for its huge, spoonlike bill, which is superbly adapted for surface feeding. This has enabled it to exploit the world's once-extensive shallow marshes, but sadly such specialisation has made it very vulnerable as so many wetlands have been drained.

History and Conservation

From what we know of its recent history and distribution, the shoveler has probably always fared better during warmer periods, when its preferred shallow-water habitat has been relatively ice-free. Thus its strongholds have concentrated on lowlands and the only early British records are from the south-east, from the Hoxnian interglacial, and from Somerset in the Iron Age. Unfortunately, extensive drainage of the Fens and other swamplands from the sixteenth century on coincided with the 'Little Ice Age' 1550–1850, during which time the species became relatively rare in much of north-west Europe, probably ceasing to breed in many areas, including Britain. In 1801 Bewick noted that it was 'not ascertained' as to whether the shoveler bred in England, 'where indeed it is a scarce bird'. The first British nesting record is from 1840, in Scotland, but it was not until the climatic amelioration of the late nineteenth and early twentieth centuries that there was sustained increase and range expansion. By 1900 it was thought to be breeding in 18 Irish counties, with five further counties added up to 1950, matching the increase throughout western Europe. Iceland's first breeding record is from 1931, and Switzerland's 1917.

The increase is probably still continuing, but, in Britain at least, has slowed since the early 1950s as encouragement through creation of new sanctuary areas has been offset by substantial habitat loss, such as on the North Kent Marshes. Fortunately, the bird's year-round, widespread but localised distribution provides a natural safeguard against single threats to the entire population. Rarely is it numerically significant in the wildfowler's bag.

Distribution, Habitat and Population

The shoveler, or northern shoveler, is the most numerous and widespread of a group of four closely related duck with huge, spatulate bills, the other three being confined to the southern hemisphere but probably sharing the same ancestry. As well as in western North America, the northern shoveler breeds right across Eurasia, but avoids the northernmost tundra zone. In Europe it is sporadic and absent from large areas of the south and west. Except for birds in south-west Europe and the Mediterranean, the entire breeding population is migratory. But in much of Europe, including the British Isles, the population moves out only to be replaced by more northerly and easterly birds.

The north-west European breeding population is estimated at 25,000 pairs, but numbers are subject to frequent change on the edge of the range. General increase this century has been linked to climatic amelioration and, apart from the British Isles, has been most significant in Germany, Sweden, Norway and parts of the

Once known as broad bill, shovel bill, shovelard, spoon bill, spoon beak, beck, scopperbill, whinyard, sheldrake, blue-winged shoveler, blue-winged stint, kertlutock, kirk tullock and maiden duck

The name 'shoveler', also spelt 'shoveller', goes back to the 'shovelere' of 1460, but also originally denoted the spoonbill. Ray used it for *Anas clypeata* in 1678 and it became standard after Pennant in 1768. The Latin specific *clypeata* is derived from *clipeus* for shield and *atus* for provided with, probably being a reference to the white breast which contrasts with the darker body, or to the broad bill.

The British Isles population of 1,000–1,500 pairs is well distributed but very local, being firmly restricted by the specialised habitat requirements — the shallow, muddy waters found only in lowlands. Hence the largest numbers are in the central and eastern countries of England. During 1970–90 the two most important areas were the Nene Washes (Cambridgeshire), with up to 350 pairs, and the Ouse Washes (Cambridgeshire/Norfolk), with 80–300 pairs, though many nesting attempts have been disrupted by spring/summer flooding. In Ireland there are few more than 100 pairs, about 20 of which are at Lough Neagh.

99

SHOVELER

The length averages 44–52cm (17.3–20.5in), wing-span 70–84cm (27.6–33.1in), and weight 475–1000g (1–2.2lb) for the male, 470–800g (1–1.76lb) the female.

The single clutch (replaced after loss) of 9–11 (6–14) buff to pale-green, ovate eggs, average size 52 × 37mm (2.05 × 1.46in), is mostly laid from late April to early May, but throughout May further north.

The shoveler (this is a female) is a highly specialised filter feeder. Photo: R. Glover

former USSR. Recent population estimates include: Iceland — under 100 pairs, France — 600–1,000 pairs, Belgium — 200 pairs, Netherlands — 9,000 pairs, Denmark — 500 pairs, Finland — 4,000 pairs, and Baltic USSR — 3,000 pairs.

Field Characters

The huge, spatulate bill is always the best field mark. The male is also readily distinguished by his contrasting dark-green head; white neck, breast and underwing, chestnut belly and pale-blue forewing. The female's plumage resembles that of other female dabbling ducks, but all the paler areas and feather edges are pink-buff. Her bluish forewing is much duller than that of the male but will still aid separation from the female mallard, as will her green speculum, shorter neck and wings appearing to be set far back, chiefly because of the disproportionate effect of the large bill. The juvenile resembles the adult, non-breeding female, but with underparts more streaked and upperparts more uniform. In eclipse and supplementary plumage the male resembles the non-breeding adult female, but his head and upperparts are darker, more uniform and redder, and in flight his much brighter blue forewing and green speculum distinguish.

The shoveler swims characteristically with its front end low in the water, often with the bill dabbling. It also dabbles while paddling in shallows or mud, and has little need to up-end or dive. On land it is awkward, waddling with the body rather erect, but it rises fairly easily, with a characteristic drumming rattle of wings, and has fast, powerful flight with rapid wing-beats and considerable agility, reminiscent of the wigeon. It is very active on the wing and its pinions make a distinctive whistling.

Mostly quiet outside the breeding season, both sexes have a weak voice. The female has a variety of quacks, sometimes like the mallard's, while the male's main cry is a throaty *took-took*. He also utters a loud, nasal *paay* and wheezy *thic* or *whe*.

Breeding

The monogamous pair-bond is probably mostly of seasonal duration and does not end until near hatching. Pairs form in flocks during the winter, early pairings being less stable. Male promiscuity is weak. Courtship display is much simpler than in most other European ducks and easily overlooked. The male attracts the female's attention with several lateral displays. In three of these, ritualised from feeding movements, the feet paddle rapidly and the back and flank feathers are erect. Display features include fast calls, head-dip, up-end with front of body submerged, head held high, and bathe-and-wingflap. Pursuit flights involve much calling.

The female makes a nest hollow among tall grass, rushes, nettles, heather or scrub, lining it with grass, leaves and down, usually near water and sometimes in exposed situations on grazed moorland or grass banks. Though not colonial, shovelers sometimes nest only a few metres (yards) apart. The 22/24-day incubation is by the female only. Hatching is synchronous, the young feed themselves, are cared for by the female, and become independent at or just before fledging, at 40–45 days. Age of first breeding is one year.

Diet and Feeding Behaviour

The huge bill is extremely specialised for filter feeding with fine, comb-like, intermeshing lamellae along the edges of both mandibles, and great length with wide distal end to increase the amount of water that can be sucked in. This is especially suitable for plankton feeding. Most food is collected from the surface and the duck often paddles quickly through the shallows with the head and neck submerged and thrusting the bill forward and from side to side. It rarely needs to up-end, but dives quite often — certainly more than other surface-feeding ducks. Feeding is often in small groups, birds circling behind each other, presumably taking stirred-up food. Sometimes a single bird will swim in a circle to create a whirlpool which draws up food. Feeding is chiefly by day but also at night where disturbed.

A wide variety of animal and plant food is taken, varying with season and locality. The relative importance of food items is difficult to determine because of widely varying rates of digestion and feeding behaviour. Most important foods overall include small crustaceans, molluscs, insects and their larvae, and seeds of aquatic plants. Lesser items include buds and leaves of water plants, spiders, amphibian spawn and tadpoles, and fish.

Movements

Most shovelers migrate far south to overwinter, western Europe and the Mediterranean being the only parts of the huge breeding range holding birds all year. However, European breeders move out to be replaced by immigrants from the former USSR as far as 60° east. Many winter around the shores of the North Sea. British and Irish breeders overwinter in France, Italy, Spain, Portugal and North Africa, but it is likely that some do not migrate in mild years. Most leave by the end of October, before the main arrivals of birds from Iceland (thought to be the entire stock), Fenno-Scandia, Russia and other parts of northern and eastern Europe. Since the 1960s the migration pattern appears to have shifted to the east, so that most birds now avoid the British Isles. Departure from tropical Africa

It has been estimated that about 100,000 breed, winter or migrate through north-west Europe, and the winter population of the west Palearctic has been put at 1.5 million birds. The British peak count of 8,975 in 1990–91 exceeded the previous season by 10 per cent, whereas the Northern Ireland total was only slightly down at 274. The September maximum fell steadily to 4,482 in March, reflecting the usual pattern. Even though most home breeders overwinter in southern France and Spain, British distribution is much wider in winter. Nevertheless, there is consistent concentration on only a small number of sites. For 1986–91 main-resort average maxima were: Ouse Washes 746, Abberton Resevoir 619, Rutland Water 518, Loch Leven 507, Chew Valley Lake 452, Swale Estuary 342, Woolston Eyes 286. Seven other sites held more than 250 in 1990–91: Severn Estuary (454, August), Queen Mary Reservoir (427, October), King George V Reservoir (360, October), Staines Reservoir (339, October), Stain Hill Reservoir (271, February), Attenborough Gravel Pits (268, October), and Grafham Water (263 February). Ireland's Lough Owel is exceptional, with up to 2,000 of the country's 8,000-plus birds in autumn, though when disturbed they readily move to Lough Iron. Throughout the British Isles there is a clear preference for fresh water, few estuaries holding more than 35.

starts in February and the peak spring movement through Europe is from mid-March to mid-April. British breeders return March-April and virtually all breeders have returned by early May. Males tend to stay late with the females in the nesting season and moult gatherings are less significant than among other surface feeders. None the less, small-scale assemblies are reported from IJsselmeer, Netherlands, and other parts of Europe, with bigger concentrations further east.

MANDARIN
(*Aix galericulata*)

ORIGINALLY introduced to grace waterfowl collections, this beautiful duck is now considered to be more common in England than in its original Far East home, except in Japan. As a tree-hole nester of truly exotic appearance, it provides quite a surprise for the casual observer in its southern counties stronghold.

History and Conservation

Bones found in the Cromerian forest beds of Norfolk have been attributed to this species, indicating its presence in the Middle Pleistocene. The temperate mixed-oak wood of this warmer period would have provided suitable habitat. But then there appears to have been a very long gap before it was introduced just before 1745, though we do know that as early as 200BC Chinese and Japanese Buddhists regarded the duck as a model of fidelity and affection.

First breeding in Britain was in 1834 at London Zoo, from two pairs which the recently formed Zoological Society had purchased for the large sum of £70 in 1830. But it was not until 1866 that the first recorded wild British mandarin was shot near the Thames, at Cookham in Berkshire, and not before the early twentieth century that feral populations became evident. Among these was the Duke of Bedford's at Woburn, Bedfordshire, which numbered 300 by 1914, but shrank by half in each World War due to the difficulties of feeding.

By far the most important of the early collections was Alfred Ezra's at Foxwarren Park, near Cobham in Surrey, which started with four or five pairs in 1928 and soon spread into the very favourable habitat around Virginia Water and Windsor Great Park. By the mid-1970s these had spread further through southwest Surrey to the Sussex border, northwards into Buckinghamshire and Middlesex, eastwards beyond Staines and westwards beyond Reading.

The mandarin's British success is primarily due to its having exploited a vacant ecological niche for a perching duck that eats chiefly nuts in autumn and winter and nests mostly in tree-holes, provision of nestboxes having been very important. However, the abandonment of the instinct to migrate has also been crucial, as it has with the Canada goose. But whatever the reasons, the fact is that Britain now hosts a population of world importance and it may not be too long before British birds are taken to boost the declining native population in China. Yet further licensed releases within Britain must be monitored very closely for any negative impact on the native avifauna. Expansion is unlikely to continue so rapidly as prime habitat is taken up and the exceptional vigour of the initial stock declines.

The species' scientific name *Aix* comes from the Greek for a bird of the goose kind. The Latin *galericulata* means provided with a small cap and alludes to the duck's head colouring and crest. The name mandarin refers to the brilliant and decorative plumage, which has been the main reason for its introduction to many countries.

The shoveler (male left, female right) is easily distinguished by its huge bill.

MANDARIN

The Far East population is estimated at 9,800–10,900 birds, including less than 7,000 in Japan, 500–1,000 pairs in China, 300 individuals in Korea and 750–800 pairs in Siberia. All these birds are migratory, unlike the 7,000-plus individuals now in Britain, where they are probably significantly under-recorded.

The length averages 41–49cm (16.1–19.3in), wingspan 68–74cm (26.8–29.1in), and weight 571–693g (1.3–1.5lb) for the male, 428–608g (0.9–1.3lb) the female.

Distribution, Habitat and Population

The species' natural range in far eastern Siberia, China and Japan has declined greatly this century through destruction of optimum habitat — dense woods containing small lakes. One of the greatest setbacks came with the settlement and clearance of the Tung Ling Forest imperial hunting ground after the Chinese Manchu dynasty ended in 1911. By far the most important British stronghold is that centred on Virginia Water and Windsor Great Park, which holds some 5,000 birds. Current patchy distribution is due to the history of releases and escapes over much of central and southern England. Among isolated populations elsewhere are those in central Wales and Tayside, and there is increasing interest in the wooded river valleys of south-west England. Birds were released under Department of the Environment licence at Somerton, Somerset in 1985–6. There are occasional reports from Ireland. While all types of water surrounded by mature woodland are used, those with thick rhododendron undergrowth are favoured. Winter concentrations form where food is regularly provided for game and wildfowl.

A feral population of some 550 birds has been established in northern California since about 1977, though it is heavily reliant on artificial feeding and nestboxes. The species may also be established in Germany, where 25 pairs were recorded on a west Berlin lake in 1987. Accidentals (probably escapes) have been noted in the Faeroes, Finland, Czechoslovakia, Yugoslavia, Italy and Spain and the Channel Islands.

Field Characters

The handsome male is most distinctive with his red bill, multi-coloured crown and crest, orange 'whiskers', broad white band from bill to nape, maroon breast edged with black-and-white stripes, and orange-chestnut wing 'sails'. The female is far less conspicuous in muted greys, brown and white, yet still distinctive. The juvenile closely resembles the adult female, but is more uniformly coloured, with weaker face-markings. In Europe the only possible confusion is with the female and juvenile feral wood duck, which is usually darker and glossier olive-brown above, has more pronounced white around the eye and is bigger. In eclipse the male mandarin resembles the female but is distinguished by his reddish bill, thicker crest, glossier plumage and yellower legs.

This wary duck is not very gregarious, but is seen in substantial flocks on open water where it is fed regularly. It swims well and buoyantly, often with the tail raised, but seldom up-ends and usually dives only when alarmed or wounded. It perches freely on branches, walks well and takes off easily from land or water, flying fast with rapid wing-beats and agility which, together with the long tail, enables it to manoeuvre among trees.

Noisy only in courtship, the male has a variety of whistles and the female's considerable vocabulary includes gentle rolling and clucking notes and a vibrant *eck* not unlike the call of the coot.

Breeding

The pair-bond is mostly monogamous and may last over several breeding seasons, which is why the species has long been revered as a symbol of fidelity in the Far East. However, males are sometimes promiscuous while the females are incubat-

The exotic-looking mandarin is a surprising sight in quiet backwaters of southern England. Photo: B. Martin

ing, and may form loose attachments with second 'wives'. Pairing mostly takes place from September to February. Pair-bonds are usually temporarily discontinued before hatching and re-established in moulting flocks. The male's communal courtship is elaborate and complex, including bill-flicking threats to each other and 'full-sail' posture with raised crests and upstretched necks while calling. The female plays a leading role in pair formation.

The nest-site, almost invariably a tree-hole but sometimes on the ground in thick vegetation under a fallen branch or bush, is chosen by the female with the male nearby. Grass and leaves may form the base of the shallow depression on open sites, but in holes there is usually little material other than the down lining. Nestboxes are readily accepted.

The female alone undertakes the average 28/30-day incubation, starting with the last egg; hatching is synchronous and the young usually leave the nest within 24 hours. The mother looks up at the nest and calls softly to encourage the well-developed ducklings to parachute down safely, apparently without any fear of heights. Their first feeding area may be over 2km (just over a mile) from the nest, but they are cared for by the female until independence, which they achieve at or just after fledging, at 40–45 days. Age of first breeding is one year.

Diet and Feeding Behaviour

Mostly vegetable food is taken by day and night, on land and from water, by dabbling, up-ending and head-dipping, but rarely through diving. In England the mandarin has particularly exploited autumn and winter beechmast, chestnuts and acorns, found along banks or some way into woodland, and sometimes takes winter grain put out for quarry species. In summer animal food becomes more important, especially insects taken off water and aquatic plants. Other foods include beetles, snails, worms, froglets, small and young fish, and spawn.

In Britain the single clutch of 9–12 (rarely 13–14) oval, pure-white eggs, average size 51 × 37mm (2.01 × 1.46in), may be laid as early as late March, but the main laying period is late April to early May. Two or more females may 'dump' up to 34 eggs in one nest where sites are scarce, in which case only one bird undertakes the incubation. Where there are 30 or more the outer eggs usually get chilled and the nest is abandoned, but a clutch up to 20 often has 100 per cent hatching success. In one exceptional case involving a clutch of 32, 22 ducklings left the nest, and several more eggs hatched but the young subsequently died.

Movements

In Asia the mandarin is migratory and dispersive. Japanese birds are resident, but with some southward shift. The introduced British population is resident, with only local movements, about which little is known. Birds in central Surrey leave their breeding areas from late summer, stay away during the winter and return in spring. Escaped birds appear to be capable of long-distance flight, with one bred in the Channel Islands being recovered in Devon, two from Norway shot in Northumberland in 1962, and one British-ringed bird recovered in Hungary.

RED-CRESTED POCHARD
(Netta rufina)

THIS conspicuous bird breeds only in small numbers in north-west Europe, but its range has increased substantially this century and Britain's small stock may already include truly wild colonists as well as feral birds.

History and Conservation

The species is represented in the British Pleistocene record, indicating early warmer periods with more extensive standing waters, in keeping with the species' current, more southerly main range. Apparent decline in the nineteenth century may have been largely the result of extensive land drainage, but the species would have already been under pressure through the cool phase 1550–1850. Colonisation since then is probably linked with climatic amelioration 1850–1950.

There has been marked spread in France, with the first breeding record in the Camargue in 1894, Forez 1896 and Dombes 1910. Other first breeding records include Belgium 1903, the Netherlands 1942, West Germany 1920, Denmark circa 1940, Italian mainland 1950, Rumania 1958, and Sardinia 1969. In Spain it spread to the marismas of Andalucia 1935–40.

The first recorded occurrence of this species in Britain was at Boston, Lincolnshire, in January 1826, when a male was shot. That winter several others were obtained and some ended up in the London markets. The 1840s brought numerous records, including a flock of 18 at Erith, Kent. Breeding occurred in Lincolnshire in 1937 and Essex in 1958, since when very small numbers have nested, chiefly in southern England. It could be that all British breeding records so far have involved escaped birds as the species' year-round distribution is linked so closely with ornamental wildfowl collections. However, Continental birds visit Britain regularly and colonisation by wild stock seems likely given the species' recent westward European spread.

Distribution, Habitat and Population

The species' stronghold stretches from the northern Black Sea, around the north Caspian and Aral seas, south to Turkmen and east across the West Siberian Plain. Breeding distribution further west, to Spain and England on the fringes, is mostly sparse and patchy. Recently estimated breeding populations are: Britain 5–10

Once known as red-crested whistling duck and red-crested duck

The current name did not become standard until the late nineteenth century, though the species had been widely described in Europe since the eighteenth century. 'Red-headed pochard' would be more accurate. The Latin *Netta* derives from the Greek *nessa* for duck, though *neo* for 'I swim', and *rufina* relates to the red crest.

The introduced mandarin duck (male right) is now more common in England than in much of its native Far East range.

107

The north-west European winter population is estimated at 10,000 birds, with a further 50,000 in the Europe–Black Sea–Mediterranean region. About 50–100 overwinter in the British Isles, mainly within a 150km (93 mile) radius of London, an area containing many waterfowl collections. Recent increase may be due chiefly to more escapes rather than immigration. Much smaller numbers occur in northern England, Scotland (about 20 1953–83), and Ireland (10 prior to 1966 and only 16 1966–86).

The average length is 53–57cm (20.9–22.5in), wing-span 84–88cm (33.1–34.6in), and weight 900–1,420g (1.9–3.1lb) for the male, 830–1,400g (1.8–3.1lb) the female.

pairs (feral), France 500–600 pairs (chiefly Camargue, Dombes and Forez), the Netherlands 25 pairs, Germany over 100 pairs, Denmark 50 pairs (recent decline), Austria 10 pairs, Czechoslovakia 25–45 pairs, and Spain 3,000–6,000 pairs (best area Ciudad Real).

In England, since the mid-1960s breeding has occurred in most years at Frampton-on-Severn and near the Wildfowl Trust at Slimbridge (Gloucestershire), and other pairs have bred at the Cotswold Water Park, suggesting the development of a feral population in the West Country. Breeding has also been reported at Apethorpe (Northamptonshire), Rickmansworth (Hertfordshire) and Kew Gardens (Surrey).

Prime habitat in central Asia consists of substantial, warm, fairly deep, eutrophic lakes fringed with reeds, but with plenty of open water and no surrounding trees. Secondary sites are saline or alkaline pools and lagoons, and the reaches of slow-flowing rivers, all chiefly in lowlands. In western Europe the species has shown greater adaptability in the absence of optimum conditions, taking to smaller, more vegetated waters, even with surrounding trees. However, in Spain habitat is more typical and numbers of birds there reflect this. Overall, little use is made of artificial sites, though there is no special sensitivity to the presence of man. Indeed, in Britain there is strong use of reservoirs (notably Abberton) and gravel pits as well as lakes. Reports from tidal waters are few.

Field Characters

The male is most distinctive with his tapering, bright-red bill and large, rounded, chestnut head (with erectile crest) and upper foreneck contrasting with grey-brown upperparts, jet-black underparts and mainly white flanks. He is easy to identify in flight, too, with contrasting black belly and white, oval flank-patches as well as a pale stripe right across the upper hindwing. Although far more sombre and lacking the all-red bill, the female, too, is relatively easy to identify, with dark-brown cap contrasting with grey-white lower face and foreneck, and a broad, white wing-bar as conspicuous as the male's. The female common scoter has a similar head pattern but lacks the wing-bar, is darker and has a stouter, shorter-looking bill. The female smew shares both contrasting pale cheeks and the white wing-bar, but the latter is confined to the inner wing, and her upperparts and breast are grey. In eclipse, the male red-crested pochard resembles the adult female but retains the all-red bill. His eye is redder and his head appears larger with a more pronounced crest. The juvenile closely resembles the adult female, but is darker and in early autumn has more mottled underparts. Even at this early stage males look bigger-headed through development of the crest.

This duck is gregarious for most of the year, often gathering in large flocks in the main wintering areas. It is more buoyant than other diving ducks but submerges easily. However, it is more inclined simply to submerge the head or up-end like dabbling ducks. As it is adapted to spending more time on land, it walks more easily than other diving ducks, with more horizontal carriage and less rolling. It does share the divers' difficulty in getting airborne, having to patter along the water surface, but once underway it flies strongly with rapid wing-beats.

Generally a rather quiet species, the male's main calls are a harsh, wheezing *bat* uttered throughout the year, and a soft *geng* and a far-carrying *baix* mostly used October–May. The female's hard, grating calls are subject to wide variation, being variously rendered as *gock*, *guk-guk*, and *kurr*.

Breeding

The monogamous pair-bond is of seasonal duration, pairing taking place from autumn to spring. The male is more faithful than other pochards, standing by the female during laying and incubation and accompanying her when she leaves the nest. A few even stay nearby after hatching. Suspected occasional promiscuity probably mostly involves unmated males. The courtship of well-established pairs involves the male feeding the female, sometimes bringing her inedible objects such as twigs. Other pair displays include preening behind the wing, ceremonial drinking and lure-sneezing — uttering the sneeze-call with the head stretched sideways or forwards.

Nests are mostly scattered but have been found only 30m (yards) apart, and the male is strong in protection of his mate. The female uses materials within easy reach to build a ground nest in reeds and other dense vegetation, never far from water and sometimes on matted reeds on water. The simple depression is lined with leaves, grass, rushes and down.

The female's 26/28-day incubation starts with the arrival of the last egg and hatching is synchronous. The young feed themselves, are cared for by the female and become independent at about the time of fledging, around 45–50 days. Age of first breeding is usually two years but sometimes one.

Diet and Feeding Behaviour

This mainly vegetarian duck takes most of its food during the early morning and evening through dabbling and leap-diving in water 2–4m (6–13ft) deep, spending about equal time on each method. It also up-ends and forages with its head submerged.

Items most commonly taken are the leaves, seeds, roots and buds of aquatic plants, and pondweed, algae, hornwort and milfoil. Secondary and more seasonal items are aquatic insects and their larvae, adult frogs, tadpoles and spawn, and small fish. Crustaceans and molluscs are recorded but some may be taken accidentally or even to help grind the plant food.

Movements

Most populations leave their breeding areas in late October and early November (some from late September) to winter well south or west in ice-free areas. Many eastern birds winter in India, Pakistan and Bangladesh, where they may outnumber the quarter to half a million mainly Soviet birds which resort to the Black Sea and Caspian region. Many central and west European birds winter around the Mediterranean, but there are substantial winter concentrations in Spain and southern France, where populations are only partially migratory. The spring return is mostly in late February and March, but the most eastern and northern breeding grounds are not reoccupied before April or early May.

Virtually the entire north-west European range is vacated in winter, though some feral birds remain and wander considerably. The small numbers which regularly turn up in autumn in Britain — chiefly south-east England — are thought to be from the late-summer moult assemblies in the Netherlands, which later move south-west to winter in the north Mediterranean basin. Danish and north-west German birds migrate south and south-west to Mediterranean France

RED-CRESTED POCHARD

The single clutch (replaced after loss) of 8–10 (6–14) broad, rounded, stone-coloured or greenish eggs, average size 58 × 42mm (2.28 × 1.65in), is mostly laid from early May to mid-June. Dump nests containing up to 39 eggs are recorded, and nest parasitism is common. Single eggs to full clutches are laid in the nests of species such as mallard and gadwall even after close sitting has begun.

Group of male red-crested pochards. In Britain distribution is closely linked with wildfowl collections. Photo: Dennis Green

and Spain. Moult migration of immatures and males starts in early June and may lead to substantial gatherings. In Switzerland, for example, some 3,000–4,000 regularly occur around the Bodensee in October and leave in November. This number exceeds the entire north and central European breeding population so must include birds from further east.

POCHARD
(Aythya ferina)

Once known as poker, poker duck, red-eyed poker, red-headed poker, red-headed wigeon, red-headed curre, snuff-headed wigeon, red neck, gold head, blue poker, great-headed wigeon, bull-headed wigeon, dunbird, dun curre, dun air, dun poker, well plum, smee duck, whinyard, wigeon diver, freshwater wigeon, vare-headed wigeon, diver and doucker

In north-west Europe the red-crested pochard (above, male left, female right) breeds only in small numbers, but the common pochard (below, female left, male right) is true to its name.

H AVING colonised much of north-west Europe in the nineteenth and twentieth centuries, the pochard remains a rare breeder in Britain. It does not appear to be under any particular threat, but may be one of the relatively few species of western Palearctic waterfowl currently in slight overall decline. It is often found alongside the tufted duck, but there seems to be no significant competition because the pochard is mainly vegetarian whereas the tufted's food is predominantly animate.

History and Conservation

Earliest British remains are from the Cromerian interglacial and the Iron Age in Somerset. Little is known about the species' more modern history, but there seems little doubt that it did breed in the British Isles before the first record, from Yorkshire in 1844. Tring Reservoirs, Hertfordshire, saw breeding in 1850, and there followed slow expansion, mainly eastwards, at a time of general range extension in western Europe. Scotland was colonised in 1871, with Caithness reached in 1921, and Ireland in 1907. Increase slowed from the 1940s and was patchy in much of England and Wales, with significant decline in Scotland. The introduction of feral birds has speeded colonisation in much of the south-east.

110

POCHARD

While the British breeding population is probably still increasing slightly, there has been recent decline in wintering numbers in some areas. This may be partly due to the clean-up of sewage outfalls. For example, the largest regular flock in Britain — some 7,000 birds — virtually disappeared from Duddingston Loch, near Edinburgh, when the city had new sewage treatment works in 1978. This reduced the pochards' invertebrate food supply and eliminated the waste grain and other food from sewage outfalls which had attracted them to the Firth of Forth. In contrast, continuing water pollution may be a problem in areas such as the Norfolk Broads. The species remains a valuable quarry for wildfowlers, but the national cull appears to have no significant impact on winter numbers. The breeding population, on the other hand, has been held back by its reluctance to use man-made waters, such as reservoirs and gravel pits, to anything like the extent shown by the tufted duck. None the less, increasing numbers have been resorting to artificial wetlands with established biosystems. Sadly, those near towns are subject to considerable disturbance through new water sports.

Distribution, Habitat and Population

The pochard has its main population centres well to the south of those of many other wildfowl species, across the boreal and temperate zones of Eurasia, which may partly account for its spread during the relatively warm period 1850–1950. Drying up of breeding lakes in central Asia may also have acted as a stimulus. Now it breeds from Iceland to eastern Siberia, with isolated populations in southern and Mediterranean Spain, Tunisia and central Anatolia. In the north it reaches the head of the Gulf of Bothnia, but as it is not a tundra species it is absent from northern Siberia. In western Europe breeding remains sporadic in many areas, reflecting sensitivity to climatic fluctuation. Iceland was colonised in 1954, France probably during the early twentieth century, Denmark 1862, Sweden 1849, Finland 1867, Switzerland 1952, Austria 1957, the Netherlands in the early nineteenth century and France probably during the early twentieth century. The main European centres now are the former USSR, Finland, Czechoslovakia, western Germany and France.

Mainly confined to fresh water, the pochard requires thick marginal growth of emergent and waterside vegetation for nesting, preferring large pools, lakes and slow-moving streams, with a strong preference for overgrown islands. In reclaimed coastal marshes fleet type habitat is favoured. In winter some upland areas are vacated. It is not quite so widely distributed as the tufted duck, as it probably prefers larger waters. Furthermore, it generally favours shallower water, yet recent studies have shown that prey-density rather than depth is the key to the choice of feeding site, maximising food intake while minimising energy output.

Field Characters

With his chestnut-red head and neck and very pale grey upperparts and flanks, the male is unmistakable among west European duck, but is similar to the American canvasback and redhead. The female, too, is readily distinguished from other European species by her sloping forehead, hoary face, grey-banded bill, and (when present) line behind the eye. In flight both male and female are separated from the tufted duck by their broad, pale-grey stripe running right across the wing without a white bar. However, there are hybrids of pochard × tufted duck. The juvenile resembles the winter adult female, but has no white streak behind the eye, paler cheeks and neck, and less grey on the upperparts and sides. In eclipse, the male superficially resembles the adult female, but his head and neck are more uniform golden-brown and his back greyer.

This very gregarious duck is often seen in huge flocks, though mostly in small, dense packs. It swims very well but rather low in the water with the tail trailing the surface. Dives are frequent and expert, with a pronounced jump, and uniquely among European duck it sometimes paddles before diving. Up-ending is only occasional. With a heavy body, rather short wings and legs set well back, it has a rather horizontal carriage and walks awkwardly. It prefers to swim rather than fly away from danger and is slow to take off, pattering across the surface for some distance, usually rising into the wind with rapidly beating wings, yet flight is fast and direct, producing a whistling sound. Most flights are in compact groups, but over longer distances they may form long, rather irregular lines or ragged spearheads at greater height.

Mostly a quiet species, the male has a low, soft whistle and the female a harsh growl or croak — *kurr* or *karr*.

Breeding

The monogamous pair-bond is usually of brief, seasonal duration. Most pairs form in the spring and break up during the first two weeks of incubation. Some bigamy is suspected. During courtship the male's head often appears enlarged through raised feathers, and his eyes may blaze red through constriction of the pupil. In preliminary display he sometimes swims with the head only slightly raised, but also shakes and flicks his head and upward-shakes the body. Main displays are head-throw, kinked neck and sneak, accompanied by producing unusually harmonic calls of changing pitch and loudness. Prolonged pursuit-flights may be in a straight line or wide arc.

The ground nest is usually within 10m (yards) of water in thick cover at large, inland stillwaters, but also marshes and slow-moving streams where there is a wide bed of aquatic vegetation. Many are on islets or built up above the water surface among dense reeds or rushes. The pochard has not taken to breeding much on artificial waters, as has the tufted duck. The nest usually has a substantial base, especially over water, the female constructing it from locally available reeds, leaves and other vegetation, and lining it with down.

Eggs are laid one per day, incubated by the female only for 24–28 days from completion of the clutch, and hatching is synchronous. The self-feeding young are cared for by the female and become independent at or just before fledging, at 50–55 days. Age of first breeding is usually one year, sometimes two.

Diet and Feeding Behaviour

The diet varies according to season and locality, but overall the species is mainly vegetarian, taking seeds, leaves, shoots, roots and tubers of aquatic plants in shallow water. A depth of 1–2m (3–6ft) is preferred, but sometimes to about 3.5m (11ft). However, prey-density rather than depth is the key to site selection where animal food is concerned. Most vegetation is taken from submerged plants or from the bottom. Dives are often preceded by a jump, and the deeper the dive the bigger the jump. Most dives average 13–16 seconds, but up to 30 seconds has

POCHARD

The length averages 42–49cm (16.5–19.3in), wing-span 72–82cm (28.3–32.3in), and weight 585–1,300g (1.3–2.9lb) for the male, 467–1,100g (1–2.4lb) the female, with much seasonal variation.

The single clutch (replaced after loss) of 8–10 (4–22, though over 15 probably always two females) broad oval, grey–green eggs, average size 62 × 44mm (2.44 × 1.73in), is mostly laid from mid-April to early May, though right through July in some parts of Europe.

The British wintering population reached about 35,000 (10 per cent of the north-west European wintering population) in the mid-1970s, but may have been as high as 50,000. Some decline followed, but recent counts suggest considerable pick-up. The 1990–91 peak for Great Britain was 37,419 (January), about 4,000 down on 1989–90, but conversely, Northern Ireland had 41,364 (December) 1990–91 and 36,946 1989–90. Among the main UK resorts, Loughs Neagh/Beg are overwhelmingly important, with an average maximum 1986–91 of 31,508. Next most important is Abberton Reservoir, with an average maximum of 2,835 over the same period, followed by the Ouse Washes (2,098), ▶

113

The male pochard's red eye is striking in display. Photo: R. Glover

both approaching the 3,500 level for international importance. Thirteen other sites held over 1,000 during 1990–91. In Ireland, huge flocks dominated by adult males, probably mostly moulting birds, assemble at Lough Corrib and Lough Derravaragh, Westmeath. At Corrib they gather from mid-July and peak counts of up to 22,000 have been recorded in late autumn. Lough Derravaragh peaks a little earlier, sometimes with 5,000–6,000 in September. Dispersal takes place from late October. Apart from Lough Neagh, Ireland's main winter flocks are on the lakes of Clare, Mayo, Galway, Sligo, Donegal, Fermanagh and Westmeath. Flocks over 100 are unusual south-east of a line from Dundalk to Limerick.

been recorded. Also, unlike other *Aythya* species, it sometimes foot-paddles to stir up food before diving. Other feeding methods include up-ending, submerging the head and neck, and surface dabbling in driftlines or shoreline mud. Animal food includes crustaceans, molluscs, annelids, insects and larvae (especially chironomids), amphibians, tadpoles and small fish. Feeding is by day and night. Until recent clean-ups, waste grain and other food from sewage outfalls was locally important.

Movements

Many Russian and Siberian birds winter in western Europe, and around the Mediterranean and Black Sea. Immigrants from northern and central Europe, Siberia and Iceland start to arrive in the British Isles in September, swelling the substantial flocks of moulting birds, mainly males, already assembled. As well as British breeders, these moulting flocks include birds from the Netherlands and Germany and gather in July, 2,000–3,000 regularly occurring at Abberton Reservoir, Essex, up to 1,000 at Rutland Water, Leicestershire, and 4,000 on Lough Cullin, Ireland. Most disperse from October. Many birds are passage migrants and continue into France. Peak numbers are usually present November–January in the British Isles and return migration is mostly from late March to early April, but from February in mild years. It is not known whether British and Irish breeders are migratory, but few are resident on breeding waters and it seems likely that more northerly birds may move some way south. Some British-ringed birds have been recovered in France and Spain. Those breeding in the Netherlands, France and Spain are probably partially migratory, and there is considerable movement of north-west European populations during periods of severe cold as late as February.

TUFTED DUCK
(Aythya fuligula)

A LTHOUGH it is now the country's most numerous diving duck, the tufted was not known to breed in Britain before the mid-nineteenth century. Its recent increase, linked with newly available habitat and foods, has been spectacular and mirrored throughout much of Europe.

History and Conservation

The species was present in Britain during the warmer periods of the Pleistocene, from the Cromerian interglacial onwards. It appears to have been absent as a breeder during the 'Little Ice Age' 1550–1850, its colonisation of north-west Europe coinciding with climatic warming 1850–1950. There is also a suggestion that initial range expansion was linked with increased aridity in south-west Asian lakes.

The first recorded British nest was in Yorkshire in 1849, followed by Notting-hamshire in 1851, Sussex 1853, Perthshire 1872, Kinross 1875 and Ireland 1877. Elsewhere, first records include Iceland 1895, Netherlands 1904 (after a long gap), and Denmark 1904, and in many other parts of Europe breeding is now common where once it was sporadic.

At first, British colonisation was rapid as available waters were taken up, then slowed before further dramatic increase from the 1930s, encouraged by newly created freshwaters, especially reservoirs and gravel pits. But the tufted duck has been fortunate in other ways too. First, it is very tolerant of disturbance and has readily accepted suitable new habitat near man. Second it has thrived on two freshwater shellfish which came to Britain in the nineteenth century and are now common. The zebra-mussel — the only freshwater bivalve with a free-living larval stage, as possessed by marine mussels — was first noticed in the London Docks in 1824 and probably came via timber ships from the River Volga or the Baltic. The

TUFTED DUCK
Once known as black wigeon, curre wigeon, black topping duck, black curre, black poker, magpie diver, white-sided duck, white-sided diver, doucker, dovver, crested diver, gold-eye duck, blue neb and blue-billed curre

The name 'tufted duck' was first used by Ray in 1678, 'tufted' deriving from the Latin *cirratus* found in *Mergus* (diver) *cirratus*, used by Gesner in 1555. Tufted, of course, refers to the long feathers at the back of the head. The name became standard when adopted by Pennant in 1768. The Latin specific *fuligula* refers to the dark plumage, deriving from *fuligo* for soot.

The female tufted duck starts to incubate on completion of the clutch
Photo: Dennis Green

TUFTED DUCK

Britain's breeding population was estimated at over 7,000 pairs in 1986, having quadrupled since 1970. Ireland had an estimated 2,000 pairs in 1972, including 200 on Lower Lough Erne and 800–1000 in the Lough Neagh Basin, where there was a dramatic drop to 300 pairs in 1987. The wintering population has increased dramatically too, trebling between the early 1960s and mid-1980s, when the north-west European wintering population was put at over 500,000. In 1990–91 the peak winter count for Great Britain was 48,425 (January) and 23,138 for Northern Ireland (November), which may be compared with a 1986 estimate of 60,000 for Britain and 25,000 for Ireland excluding Lough Neagh, where there were 30,000 in the mid-1960s, falling to only 8,000 in 1980. Lough Neagh is still by far Britain's most important resort, with a peak count of 22,278 1990–91. With sustained recovery from the 1980s low, this gave Lough Neagh/Beg an average maximum of 19,372 1986–91, which compares with Abberton Reservoir 3,752 (August), Rutland Water 3,585 (September), Loch Leven 2,676 (September) Kingsbury/Cotton Pools 1,641 (November), Loch of Harray 1,537 (October), Severn Estuary 1,079 (February), Walthamstow Reservoir 1,028 ▶

adult is the only freshwater bivalve that can attach itself to the bottom by sticky threads, so it copes well with moving water. The larva, however, would soon be swept away, so the species rapidly took to the increasing number of man-made, static waters, such as docks, canals, reservoirs and gravel-pit floods, where the tufted duck was settling in. Now it is widespread throughout England and southern Scotland and forms an important part of the duck's diet in some areas. The mussel's spread has helped the bird in other countries too, such as in Switzerland, where there was a great increase in the winter population of tufted ducks on Lake Neuchatel following the arrival of zebra-mussels in 1967.

The other invader from the sea to have helped the tufted duck is the Jenkin's spire-shell, naturalised in Britain since being introduced to the Thames Estuary — probably by ship — before 1883. Up to 1900 this little winkle was found only in brackish water, but it soon spread all over the British Isles and has certainly contributed to the tufted duck's colonisation of running-water areas.

However, there has been at least one major blackspot. Sharp decline in the breeding population at Lough Neagh may be due to increased competition for food by roach, which have dramatically increased there.

The general population increase fluctuates but appears to be continuing throughout north-west Europe, where the species remains a popular quarry for wildfowlers. Its prospects seem to be excellent as there is now more pressure on developers to naturalise flooded gravel pits and new expertise in the management of freshwater biosystems.

Distribution, Habitat and Population

The species is widespread and abundant throughout upper-middle latitudes of Eurasia, avoiding climatic extremes, from Iceland, across much of Scandinavia to Siberia and the Bering Strait, but it does not breed in Spain and most of the Mediterranean. In the British Isles it is widespread but mostly absent from areas more than about 120m (400ft) above sea level, or where there are no stillwaters larger than one hectare (2.5 acres). Thus there are few breeders in south-west England, much of Wales, north and west Scotland and much of Ireland, especially the south-east. Preference for waters with low acidity is probably linked to calcium requirements of bivalve prey.

In winter less than 5 per cent are found in brackish and saltwater habitats, and there are few fertile freshwaters in Britain which do not attract them, except those which are acid, and upland lakes and reservoirs. Distribution varies little throughout the years in the British Isles, but most larger waters and those without islands or thick vegetation are not used for breeding. The species' ability to dive to 14m (46ft) or so enables it to use deeper, more open waters than those favoured by many other duck, but deep lakes without any shallow bays are avoided. Although the preferred water size is 0.4–100ha (1–247 acres), the bird is very adaptable and will use anything from a city pond to a quiet river or sheltered coast.

Field Characters

The male is easily recognised by his black-and-white plumage and long, drooping crest at the back of the head. At long distance he may be confused with the male scaup, but at moderate range the latter's grey back and lack of crest should be apparent. Although the female's crest is shorter, it is still long enough to give that distinctive angular look to the head. Her plumage is rather variable, but generally a rich, dark brown to almost black on the upperparts. She may be confused with the female scaup, especially when the white which is often found at the base of the tufted's bill is more pronounced than usual. However, the female scaup's heavier-looking head and lack of crest should help to separate. In flight both male and female tufted are readily identified by the white bar right across the wing. In eclipse the male resembles the female, but is blacker above and whiter below, and never has any white around the bill. The juvenile is duller than the adult female, with less white at the base of the bill and undertail, the male generally acquiring a short crest by December.

This gregarious duck can be surprisingly tame in town parks, but on large waters often very difficult to approach, keeping well out from the shore and sometimes spending hours on the centre of a lake. It swims well, though rather low in the water, and is an excellent diver — usually with a distinct jump, commonly submerging for over a minute. It tends to swim rather than fly away from danger, and has to patter along the surface to take off, though it is better at this than the pochard. When a flock takes off the splashing can be heard a long way off. Flight is straight and rapid, easy and smooth, the wings making a characteristic rustle. The duck walks quite easily, but rather upright.

This is a quiet bird, especially in winter, the most common calls being the male's soft, musical, courtship whistle and the female's harsh, crow-like *karr-karr*, sometimes described as a growl.

Breeding

The monogamous pair-bond is of seasonal duration, sometimes beginning late winter but mostly from spring, and generally lasts until early incubation. The male's main courtship includes throwing the head back while whistling, sometimes with a kinked neck and often preceded by head-shake and head-flick, and followed by a bill-dip and preen behind the wing. Meanwhile the female repeatedly dips her bill into the water while growling.

Although the species is not colonial, there may be nests only a few metres (yards) apart at favoured sites such as on St Serf's Island, Loch Leven. The nest depression, lined with grass, rushes, reeds and down, is usually in thick vegetation within about 20m (yards) of water, but sometimes over it on a reed platform or old coot's nest. On islands, which are strongly favoured for their security, nests may be some 150m (yards) from water. Sometimes they are in the open, usually in gull colonies. As with most ducks, the female builds with materials close to hand and shapes the nest cup with her body.

The 23/28-day incubation is by the female only and begins on completion of the clutch. Hatching is synchronous, the young feed themselves and are cared for by the female, becoming independent at or just before fledging, at 45–50 days.

Diet and Feeding Behaviour

There is considerable variation in this omnivore's diet, according to location and season. Both animal and plant foods, chiefly stationary or slow-moving, are taken mainly from the bottom by diving. Some are taken from emergent plants, from on and over the water surface, and occasionally by up-ending. In coastal areas molluscs often dominate the winter diet, but in spring and summer food is more

TUFTED DUCK

▶ (February), Wraysbury gravel pits 925 (January), Besthorpe/Girton gravel pits 924 (February), Staines Reservoir 919 (November), Kilconquhar Lough 862 (September), Ouse Washes 858 (March), King George V Reservoir 790 (October), Hanningfield Reservoir 676 (January) and Cotswold Water Park West 663 (March). There is significant fluctuation at many main resorts, and other waters which only occasionally hold the qualifying level of 600 for national importance. ▶

The average length is 40–47cm (15.8–18.5in), wingspan 67–73cm (26.4–28.7in), and weight 475–1,028g (1–2.3lb) for the male, 335–995g (0.7–2.2lb) the female.

The single clutch (replaced after loss) of 8–11 (3–22, though over 14 probably means dump-nesting) ovate, pale grey-green eggs, average size 59 × 41mm (2.32 × 1.61in) is generally laid later than that of most wildfowl, beginning in mid-April but mostly from mid-May, and broods are seldom seen before the end of June.

variable. Overall, animal food predominates, main items being crustaceans, molluscs and insects, but also including amphibian spawn, tadpoles, small amphibians and dead or moribund fish. Plant foods include the leaves and seeds of aquatic species, the roots of pondweeds and cereal grain. The zebra-mussel and Jenkin's spire-shell have become particularly important foods since their accidental introduction in the nineteenth century. Bread and other scraps are sometimes taken in town parks. Recent studies have clearly shown that the success of the downy ducklings is closely related to the insect supply. At Loch Leven, for example, most birds hatch when the greatest number of newly emerged chironomids are on the water surface. High densities of coarse fish can deplete the young's food supply, causing significant variation in local population.

Feeding depths generally are considerably deeper than those favoured by the pochard, being mostly 3–14m (10–45ft), but 2.5–5m (8–16ft) is preferred. Although mainly diurnal, feeding may be chiefly nocturnal in relation to local disturbance or weather. Sometimes birds feed and roost at the same site.

Movements

Most birds winter south or west of their breeding range, some reaching well into Africa and India, but a few populations are mainly resident. Although some Icelandic breeders winter on the coast and ice-free inland waters, most move to the British Isles, chiefly Ireland, a few continuing south to France, Iberia and North Africa. Immigrants from Iceland, Scandinavia, Russia and eastern Europe start to appear on Britain's northern and eastern shores from mid-September but do not usually peak till November to February as the most northerly breeders arrive. Many continue into Ireland, and France if the weather is severe. Although breeders of northern Britain mainly move south-west to Ireland, those in southern Britain are probably mostly resident, as are those in France and the Netherlands, though some of the latter will cross to Britain during prolonged frost. Yet the species is relatively cold-tolerant, as in average weather some 70 per cent winter north of a line from the English Channel to the Adriatic, compared with only 10 per cent of pochards. During mild springs the return migration begins in late February and in north-west Europe is mostly over by mid-April, but may carry on until late May in north Russia. Moult gatherings tend to be small and lead to pronounced winter segregation of sexes as the males leave the breeding grounds first.

SCAUP
(*Aythya marila*)

THIS is the most northerly species of the genus *Aythya* and larger than the tufted duck, greater size being advantageous in withstanding a harsh environment. Although a common winter visitor, in the British Isles it nests only rarely, being at the southern limit of its breeding range.

History and Conservation

The earliest record in the British Isles is from County Meath, about AD 800, and

The tufted duck (female upper, male lower) has taken great advantage of the many new, man-made waters.

▶ Within the British Isles only Lough Neagh/Beg achieves the 7,500 international importance level. Elsewhere in Ireland, flocks of over 500 regularly occur at Westmeath Lakes, Lough Ree, the Lough Erne system and in Wexford.

SCAUP
Once known as scaup duck, scaup pochard, silver pochard, mussel duck, black duck, black-headed diver, green-headed diver, golden-eyed diver, blue neb, black headed wigeon, grey-backed curre, spoonbill duck, frosty-back wigeon, dun bird, white-faced duck, bridle duck, covie duck, Norwegian duck, Norway duck, Holland duck and mule

The name 'scaup duck' was first recorded by Ray in 1678 and derives from the northern word 'skalp' for mussel-bed, referring to one of the species' favourite foods. The abridgement 'scaup' first appeared in Latham's work in 1797 but did not become common in writing until the 1920s.

Some 10,000 winter around the British Isles. The 1990–91 peak count for Great Britain was 6,492 in February, when there were a further 1,821 in Northern Ireland. The two sites of international importance are the Solway Estuary with 3,803 in 1990–91 (January) and an average of 2,779 1986–91, and Lough Neagh/Beg with 1,539 (March) and 1,584 respectively. Other sites of national importance and their five-year averages are: Loch Indaal 869, Forth Estuary 619, Lough Ryan 254, Carlingford Lough 251, Dornoch Firth 216, Loch of Harray 196, Cromarty Firth 174, Inner Clyde 173, Belfast Lough 147 and Dee Estuary 147. Further importance counts 1990–91 were Dungeness 245, Hamford Water 219, Loch of Stenness 194, Ribble Estuary 178 and the Towyn-Abergele coast 151. The winter total for all Ireland is about 3,000 birds.

it is likely that the species bred in northern Britain at least during earlier cool phases. Although the first widely accepted British nesting record is from 1897, there is evidence of earlier breeding, such as the female with young observed by Sir William Jardine in Sutherland, in June 1834. Throughout the twentieth century there has been a pattern of sporadic breeding of just 1–3 pairs, chiefly in Scotland and the northern isles.

The Icelandic and Scandinavian populations have fluctuated significantly this century, probably chiefly in response to climatic change, but winter flocks have been increasingly threatened by oil pollution. In Britain and elsewhere, decline has also been linked with the cleaning up of sewage outfalls, which previously boosted the species' food supply. For example, in the 1960s and 1970s the Firth of Forth held 80–90 per cent of the British scaup population, peaking at 30,000 in the late 1960s, but when Edinburgh's sewage treatment works were updated in 1978 scaup numbers dwindled to a mere 50. Recent recovery internationally may be due to better protection and continuing mild weather on the breeding grounds, a trend shared by most arctic and near-arctic nesting wildfowl.

Such rare breeding species are especially vulnerable to disturbance and egg-collecting, so site secrecy is of utmost importance. However, the long-term success of the species appears to be beyond man's control. That said, reduction in oil pollution, safeguarding mussel-beds from exploitation, and designation of new marine protection areas should help. The scaup is now protected in Britain throughout the year but may still be legally shot in Ireland in winter.

Distribution, Habitat and Population

The scaup breeds on the tundra right across the northern hemisphere and winters south along temperate coasts. In North America, where it averages a little larger and was formerly given subspecific status (*A.m. nearctica*), it nests from Alaska across northern Canada to Hudson Bay, with an isolated population at Ungava Bay. In Eurasia it breeds from Iceland through Scandinavia and Russia to Kamchatka on the Pacific coast. To the south, breeding has been sporadic in Britain, Denmark, and central Europe. North American birds winter along the Pacific and Atlantic coasts south to the Gulf Coast, and along the Mississippi and Missouri rivers. In Eurasia it winters along the coasts of western Europe, including south-west Iceland, the Adriatic, Black and Caspian Seas, southern and eastern Asia.

Iceland has some 10,000 pairs, but in the 1950s there were 10,000–15,000 pairs at Lake Mývatn alone. Finland's population has been estimated at 1,000 pairs, the centre shifting from Lapland to the coast, but Sweden's main population remains in the mountains of Lapland, numbers in the south fluctuating greatly this century. In the former USSR the breeding population is relatively stable at 115,000 pairs in the west, of which about 50,000 are in Europe.

The north-west European wintering population is put at some 150,000 birds, with a further 50,000 in the Europe–Black–Sea–Mediterranean region. Among the greatest concentrations are some 50,000 in the Danish Skaggerak, one of the richest wildfowl wintering grounds in the world. Unfortunately, such huge offshore assemblies make the species particularly vulnerable to single oil pollution incidents.

Breeding habitats are mainly low-arctic or subarctic, in tundra and wooded tundra zones, occasionally in open coniferous forest and (Scandinavia only) upland birch country. Waters of every size are used where there is sufficient food and marginal cover, from tiny pools to lochs and rivers, on shores or islets. In winter this is the most exclusively marine of the diving ducks in the British Isles, concentrating around food sources on coasts and estuaries, with smaller numbers on brackish lagoons and inland lakes and reservoirs. Distribution is sparse but widespread, except in south-west England and north-west Scotland.

Field Characters

In Europe the only likely confusion is with the tufted duck, which is similarly patterned, but the male scaup has a grey back whereas the male tufted's is black. However, separating the two females is more difficult. The female scaup has a bold white facial patch, but some female tufteds have a considerable amount of white on the face, so the latter's less steep forehand and suggestion of a crest are better pointers. In summer the female scaup often has a pale cheek-patch. The juvenile closely resembles the winter adult female, but has a narrower band of white around the bill and sometimes none on the forehead. It also has more white speckles on the lower neck and upper mantle, and more uniform upperparts. In eclipse the male changes relatively little and is more readily distinguished from the female than in most other ducks. His head and neck are browner but the upperparts remain grey with black and white vermiculations.

This highly gregarious duck swims well, but quite low in the water with the tail trailing. A compact, broad-bodied bird, it dives easily, even in the rough, deep waters around the coast. However, it struggles to get airborne and a large flock taking off is a spectacular, noisy affair, the wings rustling like those of the goldeneye. Once underway, it flies fast with rapid wing-beats. It shuns land even more than other divers and walks awkwardly.

Outside courtship this species is generally silent and its calls, especially those of the male, are so low as to be audible only over a few metres (yards). The male gives an occasional series of soft whistles and a dove-like *kucku* of varying pitch, while the female scaup has a variety of harsh growls, variously rendered as *kack*, *gock*, *querr* and *karrr*, as well as a soft *chup-chup-cherr-err* and a crooning *tuc-tuc-turra-tuc*.

Breeding

The monogamous pair-bond is of seasonal duration and lasts from as early as late winter until incubation or soon after, when the male deserts. Many pairs are not formed until spring. Promiscuity appears to be insignificant. Major courtship displays by the male includes head-throw and kinked-neck accompanied by crooning and with an enlarged neck. Other displays include hunched-posture swimming, head-flick, head-shake and upward-shake.

The scaup is not colonial, but in very favoured areas nests may be only 1m (3ft) apart. The female alone uses material within reach to form a depression lined with grass or rushes and down, mostly on the ground and always near water, but also over shallow water, and usually well hidden by tussocks, heather, reeds or scrub. Exposed nests are more likely on relatively secure islets. The 26/28-day incubation, by the female only, starts on completion of the clutch and hatching is synchronous. The young feed themselves, are cared for by the female (sometimes with the male in attendance at first), and become independent at or just before fledging, at 40–45 days. Age of first breeding is said to be at one or two years.

The average length is 42–51cm (16.5–20.1in), wingspan 72–84cm (28.4–33.1in), and weight 744–1,372g (1.6–3.0lb) for the male, 690–1,312g (1.5–2.9lb) the female.

The single clutch (replaced after loss) of 8–11 (6–15) blunt ovate, olive-grey eggs, average size 62 × 43mm (2.44 × 1.69in), is laid according to the thaw in the Arctic, but mostly late May to early June in Iceland. In Fenno-Scandia and the north of the former USSR laying is mostly from mid-May to early July.

In Britain some 1–5 pairs have been recorded breeding sporadically, notably in the Western Isles (South and North Uist) and Orkney, but also Sutherland, Caithness, Ross, Angus, Perth, Lincolnshire (1944) and Wales (1988), and an unpaired female laid infertile clutches in Suffolk 1967–71.

Diet and Feeding Behaviour

This omnivorous duck obtains most of its food through diving in water less than 6m (19ft) deep, using only its feet for propulsion. Occasionally it dabbles among shallows and driftlines, and up-ends. Feeding is by day or night, according to tides and local disturbance. In marine areas molluscs, especially mussels, predominate. Secondary animal foods include crustaceans, insects and small fish and their eggs. Aquatic plants, chiefly seeds, can be locally important. Waste grain from breweries and distilleries has been a major attraction at Scottish sewage outfalls, but the abundance of worms feeding on the sewage has also been important.

Movements

Many of the scaups wintering within the British Isles come from Iceland, but substantial numbers of Icelandic birds also visit the Netherlands, far fewer reaching Denmark, north Germany and north France. Small numbers overwinter in southwest Iceland. Birds breeding in southern Sweden and Norway may be resident too, though undoubtedly move to ice-free coasts to winter with migrants from central and northern Norway. Those from Finland, arctic Russia and Siberia migrate west-south-west, many overwintering around the west Baltic, notably north Germany and Denmark. Some continue west to the Netherlands, east Britain and France, especially in cold winters. Birds start arriving around the North Sea in September, but peak movements to the Netherlands and Britain are not before late October as many birds remain as far north and east as the weather permits. Thereafter numbers remain high at most resorts throughout the winter, peak counts generally occurring late in the season with further arrivals. Unless the weather is unusually mild, maximum numbers are present at many British Isles sites throughout February and the main spring return gets underway about mid-March. Mostly only small moult gatherings occur in western Europe, though up to 1,000 have been recorded on the IJsselmeer in late July.

EIDER

Once known as edder, common eider, eider duck, St Cuthbert's duck, great black-and-white duck, dusky duck, dunter duck, dunter, dunter goose, colk, crattick, cudberduce, culverts and coo-doos

The name 'eider' was coined by the Danish naturalist Worm in 1655, being a phonetic representation (in Danish spelling) of the Icelandic *aeour*, derived from the old Norse *aeoarfugl* for down bird. Ray adopted 'eider' in 1678 and in 1768 Pennant introduced 'eider duck', which became standard until the twentieth century, during which there has been steady reversion to plain eider. The Latin *Somateria* derives from the Greek *somatos* for body and *erion* for wool, while the Latin *mollissima* means 'very soft'.

In northern Europe, chiefly Iceland and islands off Norway, stone buildings and other artificial cavities and boxes are provided as nest-sites and the eider colonies are protected from foxes, dogs, mink and gulls which commonly take the eggs and kill or disturb the sitting females. In Iceland some sites are marked by fluttering flags, which are said to resemble the wings of gulls, in whose colonies eiders like to breed because predation is lower among a mass of other birds. Also, in east Greenland some eiders have even taken to ▶

EIDER
(Somateria mollissima)

MAN has harvested down from the eider's nest for many centuries. Indeed, as early as the eighteenth century the term eiderdown was synonymous with quilt. Because of this 'farming' the bird has been widely protected and is now the world's most abundant sea duck, despite significant local persecution by hunters and shellfishermen.

History and Conservation

The only very early British remains are from a Sutherlandshire site early in the last glaciation, but there are records from an early human settlement in Scotland. In early nineteenth-century Britain the eider was generally restricted to Shetland, Orkney, the Scottish islands and parts of the north-east coast, but there is no doubting the bird's long-term success in north-west Europe. The old name St Cuthbert's duck reflects association with the saint on Lindisfarne (Northumberland) in Saxon times and the species has been protected in Iceland at least since the thirteenth century.

Despite the duck's arctic association, there has been sustained increase and range expansion southwards since the mid-nineteenth century, during a period of prolonged climatic amelioration. This appears to be chiefly the result of much wider legal protection. During the late nineteenth century the eider colonised most of the Scottish mainland coast and in 1912 first nested in Northern Ireland (Donegal), where increase has continued. Britain's most southerly breeding colony, Walney Island in Morecambe Bay, was established in 1949 and Europe's most southerly outpost, the Netherlands, was settled in 1906. More recently, expansion appears to be continuing in north-west Europe, but more locally as there appears to be a climatic limit. In the past colonisation of many areas was preceded by the presence of substantial numbers of summering birds (mostly immatures) in inshore waters, but over the last few decades there have been large gatherings off eastern England, from Yorkshire to Sussex, and in the Burry Inlet (Glamorgan) without any signs of nearby settlement.

The harvesting of eider down has not necessitated true domestication of the duck, but the wild bird's breeding sites are managed and predators controlled. Only laying females of wildfowl species pluck down from their breasts for nest lining, to protect the eggs from cold and dehydration and for camouflage while the parent is away. But down is not found in significant quantities in the few species where both sexes incubate and the eggs are very large or never uncovered. All duck down is superior to synthetic materials for insulation properties, lightness and elasticity, but eiderdown is the very best, the edges of its plumules interlocking to create a dense mass capable of repeated compression and release without damage. Whereas 1.5kg (3.3lb) of synthetic fill can provide adequate insulation in a sleeping bag down to $-7°C$, the same weight of eiderdown gives enough warmth down to at least $-35°C$. The down is first collected from the nests soon after incubation has started, but the duck replaces this within a few days. A second collection is made after the ducklings have left the nest, but that batch is generally soiled and mixed with vegetation so it needs careful cleaning before use.

Because of the economic importance of duck down to relatively poor, isolated communities, the Icelandic government has imposed increasingly severe penalties on those who take eiders or their eggs for food, but complete protection was not achieved until about 1900. Thereafter there was a significant increase in both eider population and down production. But from the 1940s the numbers of eiders in Iceland and some other parts of the range, notably Russia, started to fall. The reasons are unclear but are probably ecological, perhaps involving increased pollution and greater predation by gulls, which are encouraged by the new sewage and rubbish dumps, and feral mink which originate from fur farms. Fortunately, this decline is partly offset by southerly expansion.

Although the eider is protected in most of its European range, hunting is still a significant regional problem. The species is shot in Denmark, and numbers are declining in Greenland, where thousands are killed each year. Apparently eider numbers generally can accommodate a limited cull, but not in the spring or alongside significant egg collection.

Eider increase has not been welcomed in parts of western Scotland, where mussel farming is economically important. Both man and birds welcome this 'free' food, but recent complaints have led to the issue of licences to kill the ducks.

Distribution, Habitat and Population

The eider spends most of its life on or near the coast, its range encircling the North Pole in the northernmost latitudes. Because it has adapted successfully to arctic conditions it is largely resident, wintering displacement being mostly within the breeds on the islands of the Canadian archipelago, around the coasts of Green- Those which breed around Scandinavia, the North Sea and the British Isles are of the nominate race *S.m.mollissima*, while further north *S.m.faeroeensis* is confined to the Faeroe Islands, where it is resident. The most northerly race, *S.m.borealis*, breeds on the islands of the Canadian archepelago, around the coasts of Green- land and Iceland and east to Spitsbergen and Franz Joseph Land, but must vacate parts of this hostile environment to winter south to eastern Canada and north- eastern USA. There it overlaps with the more resident race *S.m.dresseri*, which breeds along the east coast of North America north to Labrador's Hamilton Inlet. *S.m.sedentaria* occurs further west, around Hudson Bay, while *S.m.v-nigrum* frequents both the Alaskan and Siberian coasts of the Bering Sea.

Iceland's breeding population is put at 200,000–300,000 pairs and some 300,000 pairs are estimated to breed in the Baltic areas of Sweden, Finland and Estonia. Other recent estimates include Norway's 100,000 pairs, Sweden's 60,000 pairs (increasing through cessation of spring hunting), Finland's 90,000 pairs, France's 1–10 pairs and west Germany's 700 pairs. Denmark's stock had in- creased rapidly from about 1,500 pairs in 1925 to some 7,500 pairs in 1970, but there was a major setback with about 28,000 birds killed by oil pollution in the Kattegat 1969–71. The Netherlands, too, has been troubled by oil pollution: ascendancy from some 10 pairs in 1925 to 5,756 nests in 1960 was followed by sharp decline to 1,329 in 1968, which was linked with chlorinated hydrocarbons from the Rhine. Control measures brought increase to 1,919 nests by 1970.

Some 200,000 winter around the Waddensee (Netherlands and west Germany), probably well over 250,000 around Norway, about 50,000 in Iceland and about 750,000 in the Baltic–Kattegat–west Jutland region.

In the west Palearctic the eider is entirely coastal and marine. Viable breeding

EIDER

▶ breeding near tethered husky dogs which keep predators away, resulting in an increase from two nests in 1955 to 1,292 in 1975.

The European breeding population, on coasts from Iceland to the White Sea and south to Britain, is estimated at 650,000, while the British population was estimated at 15,000–25,000 pairs in 1976, making it the country's second most abundant breeding duck. Since then there has been overall increase but some local decrease through abnormal mortality, such as a 25–30 per cent decline in Shetland's moulting flock 1977–84. The entire stock is confined to northern Britain. The species is common around many parts of western Scotland's islands and mainland coast, Orkney and Shetland, but most of the really big breeding groups are in east Scotland, including some 2,000 pairs at the Sands of Forvie (Aberdeenshire) and about 3,000 pairs between Fife Ness (Fifeshire) and Goudon (Kincardineshire). There are over 1,000 pairs on the Farne Islands as well as small numbers on the Northumberland mainland and Walney Island (Lancashire). In Ireland the eider breeds around the northern coast from ▶

125

▶ the Copeland Islands, Down, to Inishmurray, Sligo. Numbers there are still relatively small, but there has been sustained increase and expansion. There have been about 100 pairs on the north-east coast since 1977. In 1981 126 birds, including 90 juveniles, were recorded at Inishmurray. In the same year two females and two ducklings were seen off Kerry in the south-west.

The length averages 50–71cm (19.7–28in), wing-span 80–108cm (31.5–42.5in), and the average weights are 1,384–2,875g (3.1–6.3lb) for the male, 1,192–2,895g (2.6–6.4lb) the female.

Eider ducks: common (foreground, male left, female right), king (centre, male left, female right), Steller's (background, male).

colonies can only exist where there are sufficient concentrations of shellfish in accessible waters, which leads to somewhat patchy distribution. Preferred coasts are sheltered from strong winds and waves and have easy landing, steep rocky and spray-swept areas being avoided. Islands, skerries and reefs with sheltered approaches are favoured where there is adequate protection by rocks, stones, herbage or trees. However, such sites are not always available in the high Arctic and then nests are often close together, the eiderdown's great insulation assisting hatching even on frozen ground. Fresh water is hardly ever visited and land is used only for nesting and resting as close to the sea as possible.

Field Characters

Even the brown female is readily identified by the species' bulk, roundness, short neck and large, triangular bill, with the eye set far back. Her warm-brown plumage has straight bars and is darker on the back than on the head and body. The only difficulty is in separating her from other eider species. The male is easily recognisable, being basically white above and black below, with a black panel through the eye and a pale-green patch on the nape. In eclipse he is uniformly sooty-brown, but his wing-coverts remain white and his pale supercilium and chest base are usually clear. The juvenile is like a dull adult female and lacks speculum markings.

This highly gregarious duck spends much of the year in flocks on the sea, sometimes many thousands together from October to March. It swims well but leisurely, often with its head retracted, and it spends quite a lot of time preening and loafing on reefs, sandbanks and shores, where it walks with a slow, rolling gait. Take-off is laboured but flight is powerful, with regular wing-beats as flocks depart low over the water, mostly in single file.

The eider is an exceptionally noisy duck, flocks being most vocal during courtship in autumn and spring. The male's low cooing calls have great carrying capacity so that they may be heard above the sounds of wind and waves. A large flock in full cry is most impressive and at times mystical. The female's variety of loud, grating growls are also far-carrying, being variously rendered as *gog*, *kok* and *qua-qua-qua*.

The single clutch (replaced after loss) of 4–6 (1–8, but more than 8 usually two females) blunt ovate, grey-green (sometimes green, buff or, rarely, blue) eggs, average size 77 ×52mm (3.03 × 2.05in), is laid from early April in England and the Netherlands, but usually late April and early May in Scotland, late May in Iceland and late May/early June in the west of the former USSR.

Europe's winter population is estimated at 2 million, about 4 per cent (80,000) of which occur in the British Isles, chiefly near the breeding areas in northern Britain, but also all around the English and Welsh coasts, especially eastern. Only a few birds occur inland, where they are blown by rough weather. The 1990–91 national counts recorded a peak of 44,232 (February) for Great Britain and 1,382 for Northern Ireland (December), the former being 7 per cent down on the previous year. The only site in British waters holding around the 20,000 level for international importance is the Tay Estuary, with a five-year average peak of 19,075 to 1991, though it has varied considerably from 6,000 in 1987 to 30,000 in 1989. In 1991 there were 20,300 in the Outer Firth of Tay. ▶

Breeding

The monogamous pair-bond is of seasonal duration and a few males are promiscuous. Pairing begins in autumn and continues right through to spring — as late as May on the Farne Islands. The male usually deserts at the onset of incubation but in some colonies, such as in Iceland and Spitsbergen, he may remain faithful until hatching. In courtship the male coos a lot while contorting his head, and has a bill-toss display in which the head is thrown back and the bill briefly held vertically. In neck-jerk display the head is thrust up and forward while the bill is depressed.

Isolated nests are not rare, but the eider is generally colonial, nest density sometimes being very high — as many as 250 per hectare (2.5 acres) in ideal habitat. Pairs remain in flocks on the sea until the time comes for nest-site selection, in which the male accompanies the female. There is no true territory, the male merely defending a small area around the nest, which is usually near the seashore but may be up to about 3km (2 miles) inland. The site is always on the ground and frequently sheltered by vegetation or rocks, but sometimes they are completely exposed, especially on islands where they are relatively safe. Some colonies contain over 3,000 nests, which are often mixed with those of arctic terns and gulls. The female uses material within easy reach, including grass and droppings, to make a slight hollow which is lined with the famous down. Where an old nest is re-used a permanent cup and rim may be formed.

Colonial laying is highly synchronised — for example all within three weeks in Scotland, where the onset is apparently independent of spring temperatures. However, in arctic areas such as Spitsbergen, where all laying occurs within 1–2 weeks, commencement is governed by the appearance of snow-free ground. Clutch size increases with nest-density and where isolated nests are in tern colonies. The male is often in attendance during the female's 25/28-day incubation, which starts in earnest with the last egg. When the female is off the nest the eggs are covered with down, but she is away less often than other wildfowl. Hatching is sychronous, the young feed themselves and are cared for by the female. Where breeding is dense the broods often gather into crèches of over 100, which are accompanied by females, and in these the parent-young bond becomes tenuous or non-existent. Most young become independent at 55–60 days, sometimes earlier, and fledge at 65–75 days. The age of first breeding is mostly three years.

Diet and Feeding Behaviour

The eider's strong bill is well adapted to a diet consisting mostly of shellfish and crabs taken chiefly through surface-diving but sometimes through head-dipping and up-ending in shallows. In diving this duck does not leap forward but simply submerges its head and half opens its wings before slipping below, using its feet for propulsion. Most dives are in water less than 3m (10ft) deep and take less than 40 seconds, but sometimes last well over a minute down to 20m (66ft). Most prey is immobile or slow-moving and sometimes the eider uses its feet to excavate a small crater in the sea-bed before probing with its beak. This powerful tool can easily tear prey from rocks or dig it out of the sand or mud. Some items are swallowed underwater, but others, such as mussel clusters or crabs, are brought to the surface and violently shaken apart. Some feeding takes place at night as the cycle is governed by tides as well as day-length. There is also seasonal and local variation in the diet.

In marine areas, molluscs — especially the blue mussel and other bivalves — and gastropods (especially periwinkles) dominate. Also crustaceans (mainly crabs) and echinoderms (mainly sea-urchins and common starfish). Other foods of occasional importance are cuttlefish, sea-anemones, actinarians, alcyonarians, polychaetes, insects and fish eggs. Small quantities of fish recorded are probably taken when main foods are not available, or opportunistically, where dead or caught in nets. Plants are important to the incubating female, which takes berries, leaves, seeds and green algae. At first, ducklings frequently concentrate on small crustaceans and insects, but blue mussels become increasingly important. Of 50 stomachs from the Firth of Forth, Scotland, November–March, 94 per cent contained blue mussels, 24 per cent shorecrab and 10 per cent periwinkle.

Movements

The eider is only partially migratory and dispersive. Only the most northerly populations make substantial winter movements, which are not generally necessary in north-west Europe. British and Irish breeders rarely move over 200km (124 miles). There is no regular emigration of British-bred birds, with only a few recoveries from Denmark, Sweden and Finland, the Baltic probably being the main source of birds wintering in eastern England. However, Britain's winter visitors also include some from the partially migratory Dutch population.

The Icelandic and Faeroese populations are almost entirely resident, though some Icelandic birds move south to winter within the island. Many Norwegian birds, too, move very little, staying close to their coastal breeding grounds, but in the Baltic there is substantial movement related to moult migration. Very large flocks gather off south-west Jutland, in the German Waddensee and on the Danish Kattegat, most apparently coming from Finland and southern Sweden, some from southern Norway. Having moulted some move on to winter in the Waddensee with Dutch birds. Overall, westward movement may be significant as late as January in severe weather. Very few birds — mostly singles — make substantial inland movements, though since the 1950s there have been some regular migrations to inland Germany and Switzerland — notably over 300 birds on the Bodensee — related to an increase in mussels. Spring movements may start in late February in mild years, the most northerly birds reaching their breeding grounds in late April or early May, depending on the ice.

KING EIDER
(Somateria spectabilis)

THIS bird of the northernmost tundra has only rarely bred in north-west Europe, but it is a regular winter visitor to Scandinavia and Iceland and an accidental to other parts of north-west Europe.

History and Conservation

Traditionally, the species has been subject to small-scale hunting by isolated peoples in its breeding range, the low-flying bird being relatively easy to bring

The name 'king duck' was used by Pennant in 1785 and remained in common use throughout much of the nineteenth century even though Fleming introduced 'king eider' as early as 1828. The BOU adopted the current name in 1883. It derives from the bird's occasional association with a flock of common eiders, among which this striking bird appears as 'king'. This is reflected in the native Faeroese name *aeoukongur* and the Icelandic *aeoarkongur*. The Latin *Somateria* derives from the Greek *Somatos* for body and *erion* for wool, and *spectabilis* means visible or remarkable, reflecting the bird's colourful appearance.

down with primitive missiles. As with most rarities, it tended to be shot for collections when it turned up near habitation in Victorian times. More recently it has been shot on a large scale in a few parts of its range, such as 12,000–14,000 annually in Ostrov Kolguyev in the 1950s.

Despite living in such a harsh environment, its population is remarkably stable and it is likely that its range was more extensive in earlier cold phases. The few records of nesting well south of its normal range include Trondheimsfjord, Norway, in 1957, 1960 and 1961 (perhaps the same pair), and an egg was taken on the Aland Islands, Finland, in May 1883. Early literature also suggests that it could, exceptionally, have bred in Britain. Morris (1850), for example, wrote in his History of British Birds: 'In Orkney it is a rare occasional visitant, and has been known formerly to breed on Papa Westray'. It is interesting to note that in recent decades an increasing number of adults have joined rafts of summering common eiders (mostly immatures) off Scotland, fuelling speculation about possible interbreeding, which already occurs regularly in Iceland. In 1979 and 1980 a male mated with a female common eider on Arran, but the outcome is unknown. A likely hybrid was seen off Loch Fleet in 1981.

The only significant modern threat is from sea oil-pollution, especially to one of the species' spectacular moult gatherings.

Distribution, Habitat and Population

The hardy king eider has a circumpolar distribution north of the Arctic Circle, within a few hundred miles of the North Pole, the only notable gap being around Iceland (excepting occasional interbreeding with common eider) and Norway, where the Gulf Stream makes it too warm. It breeds in Spitsbergen, from Murmansk across the coastal tundra of Siberia to the Bering Straits, among the Canadian archipelago and along the northern coast to Hudson Bay. Surprisingly, Labrador and southern Greenland are too mild, but this remarkable bird does breed on Greenland's east, west and north coasts. The former USSR's population has been estimated at 1–1.5 million adults.

In winter it moves only as far as the nearest open water, at the edge of the pack ice. This means it must leave the frozen Canadian archipelago and the Siberian coast, to gather off the coasts of eastern America, sometimes south to New England, along the shores of the Bering Sea, and off the coasts of south-west Greenland, west Iceland, Norway south to about Kristiansund, and Kolskiy Poluostrov in the north-west of the former USSR.

The duck is also an accidental in Finland, Sweden, the Faeroes, Jan Meyen, Bear Island, the Netherlands, France, Denmark, Germany, Poland, Hungary and Italy.

The king eider clearly avoids the milder influences of the North Atlantic Current and even wintering birds are mostly content to find open water in the Arctic Ocean, staying farther offshore than the common eider. But whereas the latter is overwhelmingly a coastal breeder, the king eider ventures far inland across the tundra. This very adaptable bird commonly faces abrupt seasonal changes of diet and habitat and is often attracted to less rocky shores — even muddy estuaries and bays. During the summer it commonly resorts to freshwater pools, lagoons, and even rivers. In the northern tundra some of these are ice-free for as few as 60 days a year, compared with a minimum of 80 days needed for the breeding cycle, necessitating early evacuation of the young to the coast. Nevertheless, the species apparently maintains a stable, high population. The variety of tundra used is very

varied, ranging from patches of grass, moss, lichens, peat-hummocks and herbage to swampy hollows and sand or shingle spits, but dry situations are favoured and shrubby or tree-grown areas avoided.

The male king eider – a rare breeder in north-west Europe. Photo: E. A. Janes/ZAP

Field Characters

This large duck is slightly smaller, shorter-billed, more compact and less ungainly than the common eider. The bulbous-headed male is unmistakable with his contrasting body plumage — pinkish white in front and black behind, red-orange bill and multi-coloured head, chiefly blue-grey, orange and pale-green. In flight his white wing-coverts on black wings are noticeable and his black back will distinguish from the white of the common eider. Female adults and juveniles are difficult to separate from common eiders, but may be distiguished by warmer plumage with crescentic markings. The females also have different limits to the feathering on the edge of the bill and the female king eider has a pale eye-ring. The juvenile is separated from the adult female by its duller and more uniform upperparts. Males have variable plumage over the three years to maturity, but display an obvious frontal shield from their second summer. In eclipse the male's head shield shrinks and is insignificant, and his plumage is uniformly sooty, usually with pale lower cheeks, throat and chest, but his wing-coverts remain white.

Outside the breeding season the king eider is highly gregarious and winters in large flocks, often with other eider species. The flight silhouette is slightly more compact than the common eider's, the male's head and neck being less noticeably extended. Flight action is similar but a little quicker and lighter. It swims and dives well, often far offshore in deep water.

The female's slurred, grunting croak is more like the calls of other ducks than that of the common eider, and the male's cooing is more tremulous, but the species is rather quieter.

The average length is 47–63cm (18.5–24.8in), wing-span 86–102cm (33.9–40.2in), and the average weights are 1,367–2,013g (3.1–4.4lb) for the male and 1,213–1,923g (2.7–4.2lb) the female

The single clutch (replacement probable after early loss) of 4–5 (3–7) (larger numbers by two females) elongate oval, pale-olive eggs, average size 67 × 45mm (2.64 × 1.77in), is mostly laid in late June in Spitsbergen and the arctic regions of the former USSR, according to the thaw.

Breeding

The pair-bond is of seasonal duration, generally being formed late — at the end of April or early May. The male deserts during early incubation. In Iceland the

KING EIDER

species forms mixed pairs with the common eider, whose courtship is similar. The male's main displays include cooing, neck stretching, thrusting the head forward and upstretching.

This is a solitary nester, the site usually being near water, which is often a freshwater lake or pool and up to 50km (31 miles) (exceptionally to 100km — 62 miles) inland. Small islands are favoured for the generally exposed ground nest, which is sometimes sheltered by a rock or other prominence. The female lines a slight hollow with scraps of vegetation and down.

The male is often in attendance during the start of the female's 22/24-day incubation and the eggs are covered with down when the nest is vacated. Hatching is synchronous, the young feed themselves and broods gather in crèches in areas of high density. The ages of fledging and independence are not known, but are almost certainly relatively early as the whole breeding cycle must be a race against time despite continuous summer daylight. Age of first breeding is three years.

Diet and Feeding Behaviour

There is seasonal and local variation in the diet, but it is almost entirely animal. Some plant food is probably ingested accidentally, though eel-grass *Zostera marina* is taken deliberately, as are the leaves and stalks of grasses and other tundra plants on the breeding grounds. Chief items are molluscs, crustaceans and echinoderms, ranging from relatively large mussels, crabs and sea-urchins to planktonic species, but also fish spawn, insects and their larvae. The latter are especially important to the young, which first feed only in fresh water, where they also take crustaceans, and probably plant food.

This duck feeds gregariously by day, chiefly through surface- diving with partly opened wings, and reputedly in depths to some 55m (180ft). In shallows, up-ending and head-dipping are likely.

Movements

Most populations migrate long distances to escape unbroken winter ice, but some move surprisingly little. Breeders of east Siberia, Alaska and arctic Canada west of Victoria Island overwinter around the Bering Sea, whereas those from the rest of arctic Canada and north-west Greenland winter from south-west Greenland to Labrador and Newfoundland, a few reaching as far as the Great Lakes and New England. North Russian and (presumably) some from Novaya Zemlya and Spitsbergen, winter from the White Sea to arctic Norway. Some of these move down the Norwegian coast and occur sporadically in all months around North Sea countries, including the British Isles. One bird from east Greenland has been recovered in Iceland.

Spectacular moult migrations include some 100,000 males and immatures from Canada and Greenland which gather in the Davis Strait between the Atlantic and Baffin Bay, involving journeys of up to 2,500km (1,553 miles). Males reach even the most distant moulting grounds by early July, peak movement being in the second half of the month. Autumn migration proper lasts from late August to October and the spring return depends on the thaw, ranging from late March to the end of June.

The British Isles receive a small number of vagrants in all months, mostly around Scotland, but also in Ireland and along the east coast of England. Since 1950, Shetland has been the most popular resort, up to eight birds being seen there in 1973 and 1974. The largest group recorded was of three males off Loch Fleet, where they were often seen 1975–78. Other records have been widely scattered. Since 1965 Scotland's maximum for one year has been 13. Great Britain had a total of 215 records to the end of 1990. Ireland had only five records prior to 1966. Most accidental records are of the very obvious adult or near-adult males, the females and juveniles both being remarkably similar to the female and young common eider and easily overlooked. Therefore it is likely that the species is considerably under-recorded in the British Isles and around the North Sea, especially as the males comprise a minority of the total population and are much less likely to venture far from their breeding grounds.

STELLER'S EIDER
(Polysticta stelleri)

PHYSICALLY, this duck is very different from the other eider species, so it has been placed in a separate genus. Breeding is very rare in the west Palearctic, but this great wanderer is a regular winter visitor to northern Russia and Norway, from where birds occasionally straggle south to temperate latitudes.

Once known as Steller's western duck, western duck and western pochard

This is one of several birds and mammals named after the German zoologist and traveller George W. Steller (1709–1769), who was the first to describe it. The Latin Polysticta *comes from the Greek* polus *for many or much and* stiktos *for dotted or dappled, which is appropriate for the female but misleading for the very different male.*

History and Conservation

Little is known about its early history but, as with all rarities, small numbers were shot as curiosities when they wandered to north-west Europe after the introduction of reliable guns. Morris, for example, records (1850) the shooting of a male at Caisted, near Yarmouth, Norfolk, on 10 February 1830, and another at Filey, Yorkshire, on 15 August 1845. He also noted the killing of a few others in Sweden, Denmark and Germany.

Females with young were seen at Varangerfjord in 1924 and breeding has been intermittent in Norway since then. Adults in breeding plumage and young have also been recorded on Novaya Zemlya.

There are no breeding records from the British Isles. The first vagrant was reported in Scotland on 5 January 1947, when two males were seen off Gairsay, Orkney. Between 1947 and 1986 there were 16 recorded in Scotland, including a male on Vorran Island, South Uist, which was accompanied by two females, on 13 April 1974. The number of North Sea and Baltic records appears to have declined since the nineteenth century.

The species does not appear to be under any significant human threat but substantial decline in parts of the range since the nineteenth century may be linked to warming of the arctic seas.

Distribution, Habitat and Population

This duck's main breeding range is restricted to the coastal tundra zone of north-east Siberia and northern and south-eastern Alaska. Breeding is sporadic in west and central Siberia and northern Europe. The east Siberian population is estimated at over 100,000 adults.

The entire population is migratory, but even in winter it is rarely found south of the Arctic Circle. All Alaskan breeders and most from Siberia winter around the southern Bering Sea, from the Alaskan Peninsula, through the Aleutian Islands to coastal Kamchatka, and south to northern Japan, where it is rare. Much smaller numbers winter regularly on the coasts of Murmansk and Finnmark, with up to 2,000 on the Varangerfjord. Westerly movement is governed by yearly variations in the pack-ice, but birds are found in northern Europe in all seasons and it has been suggested that colonisation may be taking place in Finnmark and northern Russia.

During the breeding season, Steller's is the least maritime of the eiders and favours moving several kilometres (miles) inland to nest, usually among pools of varying size and shape along the coastal belt of the tundra zone. Otherwise it requires clear water off clean, rocky shores, bays fed by fresh water or areas near sea-ice.

The length averages 43–47cm (16.9–18.5in), wingspan 70–76cm (27.6–30in), and the average weights are 500–1,000g (1.1–2.2lb) for the male, 750–1,000g (1.7–2.2lb) the female.

Field Characters

This compact sea-duck lacks the sloping forehead and triangular bill of the other eiders and is considerably smaller, its general shape being more indicative of a dabbling duck. The male is readily identified by his unique combination of white head with black eye-patch and buff underparts neatly divided by a black collar. In flight at long range he may be distinguished from the male long-tailed duck by his white inner forewing. The uniformly dark-brown female is more mottled than other female eiders, from whom she is also distinguished by her head and bill shape and strikingly white underwing. Like the male, she has a mallard-like blue-and-white speculum. At long range, her pointed tail held clear of the water will separate from the female goldeneye and scoter. In eclipse the male resembles the female but his upper wing-coverts remain white and he has a paler head and barred chest. The juvenile resembles the adult female but has paler, warmer plumage, especially the heavily barred underparts, and the back feathers are paler tipped.

Steller's eider is highly gregarious outside the breeding season, winter flocks sometimes numbering thousands. It is much more mobile and restless than the common eider, from which it is also distinguished by its narrower wings. The species takes wing easily and readily, especially at the sight of predators. Its flight action is light and fast, often at considerable height and with frequent changes of direction carried out in unison. The roar of a large flock taking off can be heard over a kilometre (or half a mile) away and once under way the wings produce a characteristic singing. Steller's swims and dives well and walks much more easily than other eiders.

The few observations suggest that the species is relatively quiet and it lacks the gentle cooing of other eiders. The male growls softly, and in winter flocks the apparently noisier female utters rapid, rippling, throaty calls variously rendered as *qua-haaa*, *cooay* and *aaaaaaar*.

Breeding

The single clutch (replacement unknown) of 6–8 (5–10) blunt ovate, pale-olive or olive-buff eggs, average size 61 × 45mm (2.40 × 1.59in), is usually laid in late June or early July in Siberia.

The monogamous pair-bond appears to be usually of seasonal duration and, although courting may continue into April, most pairs form in winter flocks and leave for the breeding grounds together when the thaw permits. Unlike other eiders in winter, pairs of Steller's rarely leave flocks for long, except for copulation. The male deserts during early incubation. He does not call in display. His main courtship on water features rearing-up, the head and body swinging back until the body is almost vertical; an exaggerated upward-shake starting with the head held forward rather than in line with the body, like the common and king eiders, and ending with a fast backward jerk; rapid sideways swinging of the bill, and neck-stretching. Courtship-flights are common during communal courtship and may last several minutes.

Apparently colonies are less frequent than in common eider and most nests are well scattered, exposed on low hillocks or peat ridges surrounded by swampy vegetation such as sedges and mosses, or well hidden among grasses, sedges or birch/willow scrub near standing water. The female lines the hollow with grass, lichens, moss and down.

The incubation period is not known, but the female alone sits from the laying of the last egg, the clutch is covered with down when she leaves the nest, and hatch-

ing is synchronous. The young feed themselves and are cared for by the female, though broods sometimes gather in crèches. The fledging period and age of independence are not known, but the age of first breeding is thought to be three years.

Steller's eider – an occasional straggler to temperate latitudes. Photo: Eric and David Hosking

Diet and Feeding Behaviour

The diet is predominantly animal with some plant food taken accidentally, though vegetation, including crowberries, can be important for juveniles. Most food consists of aquatic, saltwater invertebrates, especially small molluscs and crustaceans, but also including echinoderms, worms, brachiopods and small fish. At freshwater sites insects, particularly midge and caddis-fly larvae, may be important.

Most food is taken by day through expert diving from the surface with the wings open and birds often submerging simultaneously. Unlike the common eider, it rarely brings prey to the surface. Shallows are visited more frequently in spring and summer, where this adaptable bird wades and swims, up-ending, dabbling and feeding with its head submerged.

Movements

This bird's movements are characterised by their unpredictability, being largely determined by yearly variations in the ice cover. Significant changes in migration routes this century may be linked with climatic amelioration. Breeding grounds are mostly vacated from mid-July to mid-October and the spring return takes place from April to mid-June according to the thaw. But the overall picture is rarely clear with summering non-breeders common in some areas.

Moult gatherings can be spectacular, such as the estimated 200,000 which assembled in Izembek Bay, Alaska, 1957–62, when those from the Lena Delta moved about 3,200km (1,990 miles) to moult within their winter range. Rafts of up to 100 moulting birds have been seen at Varangerfjord during early July, but most Alaskan moulting grounds fill up in August. Varangerfjord regularly hosts wintering, summering and moulting birds, the erratic numbers apparently being determined by weather further east.

Most accidentals occur in the Baltic and adjacent North Sea countries. Records include Sweden, Finland, Poland, Germany, Denmark, France and Spitsbergen. Within the British Isles most occur in Scotland, notably Orkney and South Uist, but also including Fair Isle, Sutherland and Aberdeen. There were just 13 accepted records for the British Isles to the end of 1990.

135

HARLEQUIN
(Histrionicus histrionicus)

THIS colourful diving duck depends on the roughest, cold waters, whether river torrents or the sea. Within Europe, it breeds only in Iceland but is a vagrant to other parts.

History and Conservation

Because the harlequin has two isolated populations it was once thought that there were two subspecies, but this has now been discredited. The current range is probably a relict of much wider distribution in earlier, colder phases, when the bird probably bred across much of northern Europe. In recent times it has not suffered unduly through loss or alteration of its largely inaccessible, rugged habitat. However, it became necessary to introduce full protection in Iceland following excessive export of eggs for aviculture after 1945.

The number of vagrants to European countries appears to have declined since the nineteenth century. The British Isles has a relatively high number of accepted records — presumably through proximity to Iceland, but even here you can almost count them on two hands. Morris (1850) mentioned a number shot in Norfolk, Devon, Cheshire and Banffshire as well as two sold in the London market and one seen in Orkney.

Currently, the species does not appear to be under any particular human threat, apart from the world-wide problem of oil pollution jeopardising all seafowl. This is a very hardy bird which commonly recovers from the broken bones that are a natural hazard in its active lifestyle.

Distribution, Habitat and Population

The only European breeding area is in Iceland, where some 3,000 pairs use most of the country, avoiding one narrow, central strip. The world's two main populations are in north-east North America, from Alaska to the Mackenzie and south through the Rockies to Idaho; and through much of eastern Siberia, from Kamchatka south to Japan and west to Lake Baikal. There is also a strong population in north-west North America, in east Baffin Island, and across Labrador to Maine, and another around the coast of south-west Greenland. In winter they mostly move to the nearest ice-free coast, often involving only short trips.

In the west Palearctic very small numbers of accidentals have occurred in Spitsbergen, Norway, Sweden, the former USSR, Germany, Poland, Czechoslovakia, Austria, Switzerland and Italy as well as the British Isles (11 accepted to the end of 1990).

This hardy duck thrives in cold, continuously turbulent waters, including rapids and waterfalls, but usually avoids ice and glacier-fed rivers. In Iceland, just south of the Arctic Circle, it ascends even the highest streams, but reaches far greater altitudes in America's Rocky Mountains. Direct run-off waters support only small numbers as they provide little food, but the harlequin can be abundant along rich, spring-fed rivers and lake outlets, such as the Laxa River, which originates in Iceland's Lake Mývatn. In winter it is confined to the coast and almost always within a few hundred metres (yards) of lava shores and largely inaccessible headlands beneath steep cliffs, where it can rest on rocks. Sandbars, shingle, sheltered bays and man-made habitats are shunned.

Field Characters

This small, compact duck has a distinctive high forehead, small bill, short neck and pointed tail. The male is especially easy to recognise with his bold harlequin pattern of white marks on head, neck, breast and scapulars, which contrast strongly with his mainly dark grey-blue plumage and chestnut flanks and head-stripes. The sombre female is less distinctive, being blackish-brown except for a pale lower breast and belly, but she does usually have two clear light patches in front of the eye and a round white patch on the ear-coverts. At long distance she may appear all-black, when she is distinguished from the common scoter by her much smaller size, tiny bill and rounded body. The female velvet scoter also has pale face patches but is separated by a white inner hindwing as well as larger size and longer shape. In eclipse the male superficially resembles the female but is much blacker, tinged on the back, and retains his white wing and face feathers. The juvenile closely resembles the adult female, but its upperparts are paler and more olive.

The length averages 38–45cm (15–17.7in), wing-span 63–69cm (24.8–27.2in), and weights 582–750g (1.3–1.7lb) for the male, 520–562g (1.1–1.2lb) the female.

Outside the breeding season, this gregarious duck occurs in mostly small, compact parties on the sea or flying about the coast, and is relatively easy to approach. It is very buoyant and swims high in the water, habitually jerking its head at each leg stroke and raising and lowering its pointed tail. It is a most accomplished and fearless diver, sometimes plunging into rough waters from rocks or flight. It can even walk along the bottoms of rivers, holding steady against strong currents with its head lowered and wings closed. This agile bird springs easily into the air, even from rough water, and its flight is fast with rapid wing-beats.

The voice is necessarily varied and strong against the constant rush and roar of wind, waves and torrents, many calls having little in common with most other ducks. The male easily increases the pitch and volume of his squealing and whistling to suit conditions or state of excitement. But he does have quieter notes, including a low, piping recalling the common sandpiper. The female's voice can be particularly harsh and includes a persistent *ek-ek-ek-ek*, a high-pitched tern-like call, and *giak* in response to the male.

Breeding

The monogamous pair-bond is generally of seasonal duration and most pairs are formed in winter flocks before leaving the sea. However, some pairing takes place upriver from April to mid-June. Promiscuity appears to be rare and the male usually deserts at or soon after the start of incubation. Despite the male's bold plumage pattern, visual display appears to be unimportant, the emphasis being on calls, in contrast to most sea-ducks. In display, both sexes nod and contort the head. Secondary male courtship includes mock-preening, head-throwing, wing-flapping and peering under the water with the head submerged.

The single clutch (probably replaced after loss) of 5–7 (3–10, but 11–12 probably two females) blunt ovate, yellowish eggs, average size 58 × 41mm (2.28 × 1.61in), is mostly laid in late May or early June in Iceland, where late eggs are present mid-July.

Most nests are well scattered in clear territories, but may be concentrated around rich food sources, such as some 50 pairs along just 5km (3.1 miles) of the Laxa River, in which case substantial defended areas are much less distinct or even absent. The ground nest is usually in a well-concealed hollow among low,

Harlequin and young in the rough waters of Iceland. Photo: Eric and David Hosking

dense vegetation, but sometimes among scrub and rocks or in a rock cavity — even behind a waterfall. Few are more than 5m (16ft) from water. Using materials within easy reach, the female makes a simple depression with grass and twigs, lined with down.

The female's 27/29-day incubation starts with the last egg and hatching is synchronous, from mid-June onwards. The young feed themselves, are cared for by the female and fledge at 60–70 days. After fledging, most broods accompany their mothers downriver to the sea, where they soon achieve independence but do not usually return inland before first breeding at two years old.

Diet and Feeding Behaviour

Almost entirely animal food is taken chiefly in coastal shallows and rivers through short surface-dives with half-open wings. The harlequin also head-dips and takes food from the surface, but rarely up-ends. Even the ducklings show no reluctance in plunging into rough river water.

Chief winter foods are molluscs (mainly periwinkles, blue mussels and nerite) and crustaceans, with smaller numbers of annelids, fish and spawn. In spring and summer, insect larvae (mainly caddis-fly and mayfly) and small crustaceans are most important. Insects and their larvae are vital for the young, which also take some plant food.

Movements

The origins of the vagrants to western Europe have been the subject of considerable debate because there is no clear evidence that birds emigrate from the nearest breeding population, in Iceland. As a high proportion of European accidentals occur in the Baltic and as far north as Spitsbergen and the White Sea, there may be westerly drift from east Siberia. It is also suggested that European vagrants may come from North America, where Canadian harlequins often wander extensively, sometimes as far south as Florida.

In Iceland (where birds tend to move from the north and north-east to the west and south-west) and elsewhere all harlequins leave inland waters to winter on the nearest ice-free coast. Siberian birds which migrate to the coasts of the Bering, Okhotsk and Japan seas include breeders from the entire Siberian range, many of which must travel hundreds of kilometres (miles). Greenland breeders move small distances south. Northernmost breeding grounds are vacated from early September to early October and reoccupied during the second half of May. Where only short distances are involved the spring return is leisurely and often follows the courses of rivers in stages rather than direct overland routes. In Iceland, before such movement gets underway birds drift from exposed coasts to bays and fjords and may gather in substantial numbers at river-mouths.

HARLEQUIN

LONG-TAILED DUCK
(*Clangula hyemalis*)

As this hardy and handsome bird lives farther offshore than the other sea-ducks it is hard to monitor, yet it is probably the most numerous of the arctic breeding ducks. Sadly, its ability to dive deeply for food often leads to its getting caught in fishing nets.

History and Conservation

This is the earliest recent species identified in the British Pleistocene, from the Lower Pleistocene Norwich Crag Formation. It also occurs in the last glaciation in Derbyshire and the early Holocene on the South Wales coast. Over the last two or three centuries the species appears to have bred only very rarely in northern Britain. There were claims for Shetland in 1848 and 1887 and Orkney in 1911 and 1926. However, since then individuals and pairs have continued to summer around Scotland and breeding has been suspected on a number of occasions, notably in the Outer Hebrides in 1969.

There seems little doubt that this species bred more extensively in north-west Europe, including Britain, during earlier cool phases. Steep decline this century in Iceland and much of Sweden and Norway has coincided with climatic amelioration, but there have been other important factors. The wintering population in particular is constantly threatened by oil spillage, especially in the Baltic, where long-tailed ducks formed the bulk of 30,000 seabirds killed in just one incident off Gotland. Orkney, too, is a potential disaster area, with large roosting flocks near fixed oil-terminals in Scapa Flow. Marine pollution also depletes food stocks, as does increasing exploitation of shellfish. Proposals to dredge the Moray Firth for mussels are a particular worry. Long-tailed ducks still often feature among the many diving birds which regularly get trapped and die in fishing-nets. If anything, the problem is getting worse as trawlers increasingly venture farther afield. Water sports, too, are an increasing problem as ever-growing numbers of yachtsmen and power-boats take disturbance farther out to sea, to areas where this species once found peace. As with other sea-ducks, there is urgent need for designated marine conservation areas. World-wide, the species has been hunted extensively, but it has not been on Britain's quarry list since implementation of the Wildlife and

LONG-TAILED DUCK
Once known as long-tailed hareld, northern hareld, sea pheasant, ice duck, sharp-tailed duck, swallow-tailed shieldrake, mealy bird, calloo, calaw, coldie, coal-and-candle-light, col-candle, and darcall

The current name was coined by Edwards in 1750 and has been dominant in Britain ever since. The Latin *Clangula* alludes to the species' frequent and often sonorous calling, which is also reflected in the main American name 'old squaw'. *Hyemalis*, too, refers to the species' garrulousness, a characteristic shared with the hyena. In 1801 Bewick remarked that the 'vast companies' which roosted off the Orkneys made 'such a noise, as in frosty weather may be heard some miles'.

The British wintering population is estimated at 20,000–30,000, mainly occurring along the east coast of Scotland and around the northern and western Isles. For many years flocks of a few hundred have been recorded regularly at sites in Orkney, Shetland, Aberdeenshire, St Andrew's Bay and the Firth of Forth, but recently the Moray Firth (notably the Riff Bank and from Nairn to Burghead) has clearly been the most important resort with some 10,000–20,000 birds. Over 15,000 were counted at the Burghead roost in mid-February 1982. Orkney's population peaks at around 6,000, with a further 5,000 or less around the rest of the British Isles. Lindisfarne (Northumberland) had a five-year average peak count of 441 to January 1991. The Eden Estuary held 360 in December 1990. In Ireland only some 18 sites attract more than 10 birds and none have achieved counts above 68. Most types of coast and estuaries have birds from time to time, but there is a clear preference for areas with extensive soft-bedded shallows or shoals offshore. However, even in areas of high abundance they are usually well dispersed in small flocks. Rocky shores, such as those around north-west Scotland, are avoided.

Countryside Act 1981 and only a few were shot here anyway. However, the same legislation failed to plug the undesirable legal loophole which permits the establishment, from captive sources, of feral populations of wildfowl which usually only winter in Britain, so now the long-tailed duck is one of the species which is breeding 'at large'.

Distribution, Habitat and Population

The long-tailed duck has a continuous circumpolar breeding range from Iceland and Norway through Fenno-Scandia and the north of the former USSR to the Bering Sea, Alaska and northern Canada, south to Hudson Bay and Newfoundland, and all around Greenland. The majority of these 15 million or so birds winter well to the south of their breeding range, though some move only short distances to ice-free coasts. Most west Palearctic breeders are within the former USSR, where there may be as many as 5 million birds. In Iceland there are an estimated 100,000–300,000 pairs. Elsewhere in Europe, it breeds from central-southern Norway along the Swedish border, and across Lapland and the Kola Peninsula. Finland has about 500 pairs including the small, isolated populations around the Baltic coast. Breeding is on skerries and islands as well as inland on larger land masses. The habitat ranges from islets in saltwater fjords to inland dry tundra near standing water. Wooded tundra and the fringes of coniferous forest are avoided, but it readily uses uplands, ranging south in Scandinavia among the willows and dwarf birches in the arctic-alpine zone.

This species is notoriously difficult to census because so many birds spend much of their time well offshore. Therefore recent apparent increases are probably largely the result of improved monitoring, which has concentrated on roost counts. The winter population of western Europe is estimated at about half a million, most of which are concentrated around north Norway, the southern Baltic and eastern Denmark. They also occur all around the Icelandic and Norwegian coasts, parts of the Dutch coast and the British Isles.

Field Characters

This rather small and well-proportioned bird does not usually mix with other ducks and is unlikely to be confused with other species in its predominantly marine habitat. Most unusually, it has distinct summer and winter plumages as well as eclipse and first-year plumages. The handsome male is relatively easy to identify at all times with his long tail, but whereas in summer he is mainly dark-brown with whitish face-patch, belly, flanks and undertail, in winter he is predominantly white with a dark-brown cheek-patch, breast-band, back, tail and wings. He also has transitional autumn (about September to November) and early summer (about May to June) plumages, which are linked with the changing habitat. The only other duck with which he might be confused is the pintail, which is larger, has an all-dark head and white breast and haunts mainly fresh water. The female has a pointed tail, too, but lacks the long streamers which give the species its name. During the breeding season the female is distinguished by her clearly defined white neck-band, dark-brown back and predominantly sooty-black head with a short, pale stripe behind the eye. During the winter and two intermediate phases she is much paler generally, especially about the head, but the patchy head pattern characterises all plumages. The juvenile is fairly easily distinguished from the similar adult female, being duller with less clearly defined plumage.

Outside the breeding season, this restless species is gregarious, forming winter sea flocks of all sizes. It swims buoyantly and dives with great agility, even in rough conditions. The male often trails his long tail along the surface, but raises it in alert, and when he is very excited it is almost vertical and partly expanded. This duck is not at all shy yet takes flight frequently for no apparent reason. It rises easily and generally flies low over the water, the wings unusually downcurved and with an odd beat almost entirely below the horizontal. It gives the impression of swinging from side to side so that the contrasting white underparts and dark upperparts flash alternately. Rather than gliding in like most ducks, it often drops suddenly, breast first, which may be an adaptation to rough waters which do not allow a gentle approach. Occasionally it dives from the wing. There is no regular flight formation, but sometimes it forms straggling lines. Apart from when nesting, it rarely visits land, but when it does it walks quite easily in an upright manner.

This is an unusually vocal duck, the male's calls being exceptionally melodious, recalling some swans and geese. They have been likened to many things, from bagpipes and bugles to the baying of hounds, which defy description on paper. The female is equally noisy but her calls lack the penetration and harmony, being mainly low and more typically duck-like, with some quacking.

The length averages 40–47cm (15.7–18.5in) plus up to 13cm (5.1in) elongated tail feathers in male, wing-span 73–79cm (28.7–31.1in) and weight 616–955g (1.4–2.1lb) for the male, 510–879g (1.1–1.9lb) the female.

Breeding

The monogamous pair-bond is of seasonal duration and strong, with the possibility that some pairs re-form in successive years. Pairing starts in November and is mostly completed by February in the winter quarters, but some pairs are not formed until early May. The male is not generally promiscuous and usually deserts his mate during the first half of incubation. Courtship is characterised by great activity and frequent calling as parties of 10–15 males crowd one female on the sea. The lateral head-shake is the male's most common display, the flashing black-and-white plumage being conspicuous for up to 150m (yards) in good light. The next most frequent display is the head-toss over the back while calling. His courtship also includes kicking to raise the rear end with the tail vertical, wing-flapping, upward-shakes and ritualised bathing.

The single clutch (sometimes replaced twice after loss) of 6–9 (5–11, but to 17 by two females) ovate, olive-buff eggs, average size 54 × 38mm (2.13 × 1.50in), is mostly laid in late May in Iceland but from late May to early July in Lapland and arctic regions of the former USSR, depending on the thaw.

Long-tailed duck – male in winter plumage. Photo: R. Glover

Nests are mostly fairly well dispersed, but some large lakes hold several pairs and there may be loose colonies on relatively safe islands, where they often associate with other species, especially terns. Sites and territories are often traditional and the male is strong in defence of his half-hectare or so patch (about one acre). The ground nest is rarely far from water and usually in scrub or thick vegetation, but occasionally in the open or in a rock crevice. The female scantily lines a slight depression with vegetation and down.

The female's solo 24/29-day incubation starts with the last egg. The nest is normally vacated twice a day, sometimes for long periods, but the eggs are always covered with down when the female is away. Hatching is synchronous, the young feed themselves and are cared for by the female, but some broods amalgamate in the charge of one bird. Independence is achieved at or soon after fledging, at 35–40 days. Age of first breeding is two years.

Diet and Feeding Behaviour

In Britain little is known about this bird's predominantly animal diet, mainly because the species' tendency to feed well offshore (chiefly by day) makes observation difficult. But there is no reason to suggest that it differs significantly from elsewhere, concentrating on molluscs, crustaceans and small fish in winter. The long-tailed duck is an expert diver and has been caught in gill-nets down to 55m (180ft), though depths of 3–10m (10–33ft) are most common. It often throws its head back and then forward as it plunges underwater from the surface, its tail fanned and wings slightly open in dives generally lasting 30–60 seconds. In salt and brackish water foods include blue mussels, cockles, clams, periwinkles, dog-whelk, amphipods, isopods, mysids, small crabs, annelids, echinoderms and fish such as cod, flatfish, sticklebacks and gobies. Small amounts of plant material include algae, eel-grass and wigeon-grass, most probably taken accidentally. Some spilt grain is taken from loading ships. Molluscs remain important in freshwater areas in summer but are widely supplemented by insects and their larvae (chief food of young) as well as fish, moss and the tubers, roots, leaves, seeds and berries of plants.

Movements

Most birds which winter around the British Isles are thought to come from Fenno-Scandia and north-west Russia, but a few may come from Iceland. The bulk arrive in the first half of October but numbers build right through to December as more birds are pushed south-west and perhaps west from the Baltic in severe weather. Many Icelandic breeders do not emigrate but move to the nearest coast and may be joined by some of the Greenland population, some of which have been recovered in Denmark while others winter in the Greenland seas. Most Fenno-Scandian birds probably move to the north Norwegian coast in September and October while the majority of north Russian and west Siberian birds migrate to the southern Baltic from October, peaking there in November and December. For both North and Baltic seas the main spring return is from mid-March. Icelandic and west Greenland birds may be back on their breeding grounds as early as late April, but in east Greenland, Spitsbergen and northern Russia reoccupation may not be possible before mid-June. In their pre-spring migration assemblies they are more likely to occur on fresh water in Scotland.

The harlequin duck (above: male right, female left) and long-tailed duck (below: male upper, female lower) are both at home on rough water.

East Siberian birds regularly migrate 1,000km (620 miles) south of their breeding range and gather in large numbers to moult, but most west Palearctic males moult alone or in small flocks near their breeding grounds, movements starting in late June. Flocks build August-September when the females join them.

One of the reasons why long-tailed duck populations have been hard to monitor in British waters is that they tend to feed quite far out and only flight to inshore, but deeper water, roosts at dusk, which is the best time to count them. Even so, the pattern of daily movements is extremely variable.

COMMON SCOTER
(*Melanitta nigra*)

Once known as scoter, black scoter, black diver, black duck, surf duck, scoter duck, sea duck, sea hen, doucker and whilk

The name 'common scoter' was introduced by Yarrell in 1843 and replaced 'black scoter', previously plain 'scoter' since the sixteenth century or earlier. 'Scoter' could have evolved through a written or printed error in reference to 'sooter', deriving from the bird's dark plumage and suggested by the German name *Russente* — soot duck. Another suggestion is that scoter derives from the Old English *sceotan*, meaning to move quickly, referring to the species' habit of flying fast and low — almost scooting — across the waves.

ALTHOUGH it is abundant world-wide and often assembles in huge numbers, the common scoter spends most of its time at sea and some mystery still surrounds its movements. Within the British Isles it remains a rare breeder, having apparently colonised in the nineteenth century.

History and Conservation

This duck is well represented in the Pleistocene of eastern England, from the late Cromerian interglacial onwards. Further remains are from Iron Age Somerset. Although breeding was not confirmed in Britain before the nineteenth century, there seems little doubt that the common scoter previously bred here, as suggested by Derbyshire cave remains dating from the last glaciation. Northern Britain is on the southern limit of this bird's wide breeding range, which is mostly beyond the Arctic Circle, so its fortunes here will almost certainly have fluctuated widely with climatic variation.

Britain's first authenticated breeding record is from Sutherlandshire in 1855, but the species could already have nested there as few people visited this remote region at the time. In any event, others were breeding annually in Caithness in the 1860s. Steady expansion followed, to Inverness-shire and Argyllshire in the 1880s, Shetland 1911, Ross-shire 1913, Perthshire 1921, Dunbarton/Stirlingshire 1971 and Dumfries and Galloway 1986. However, breeding has been sporadic at most Scottish sites and overall numbers have remained small.

Northern Ireland was colonised in 1905, when a pair nested on Lower Lough Erne, County Fermanagh. Thereafter numbers there increased steadily, to 7 pairs in 1917, about 50 by 1950 and 150 in the late 1960s. Then the increase stopped and there was a marked decline in the 1970s and 1980s. This may have been due to a reduction in the food supply through water nutrient enrichment, leading to poor productivity, but increased predation by crows and magpies and especially feral mink is at least a contributing factor. Birds were first seen at Lough Conn, Mayo, in 1938 and the community established there in 1948 has maintained its numbers despite a drop in water levels. Others were first seen at Lough Cullin, Mayo, and Lough Ree on the Shannon in 1971. In both Ireland and Scotland the bird's status has been confused through poor monitoring of relatively remote haunts, which seem to change frequently. There is insufficient information to give a clear picture of population trends.

As recently as the nineteenth century scoters were commonly netted in many countries, including France, where they were sold to Catholics as a substitute for fish. Now those ignorant days are long past, yet many scoters are still accidentally netted by sea-fishermen. Today oil pollution (especially in the Baltic and North Sea) and commercial exploitation of food sources are the main threats to large winter assemblies, and moulting flocks may be disturbed by increased recreational activities. Hopefully, recent moves towards establishment of marine conservation areas will address these problems. In Scotland afforestation is probably the main threat, leading to removal of nesting habitat, increased predation and changes in water quality through acidification and fertiliser run-off, which generally reduce or change food sources.

Distribution, Habitat and Population

The common scoter breeds right across northern Eurasia, from Iceland and northern Britain through Scandinavia and Siberia to Kamchatka. In North America it breeds in western Alaska, but then there is a huge gap across most of Canada before the much smaller populations around the shores of Hudson Bay, Ungava Bay and Newfoundland. The Lena and Yana rivers in northern Siberia divide the two subspecies described — Eurasian birds of the nominate race *M.n.nigra* and east Siberian/American birds *M.n.americana*. Those in eastern North America winter from Newfoundland to South Carolina and around the Great Lakes, while Alaskan breeders spread south from the Aleutians around the coast from southern Alaska through Canada to California. Eurasian birds winter on both Atlantic and Pacific coasts, in two widely separated areas — from northern Norway south around the North Sea, France, Iberia and Morocco, down to the Equator; from Kamchatka south around Japan, Korea and China. To the end of 1990 there were only 6 accepted records of the *americana* race in the British Isles.

Iceland has an estimated 500 pairs in the north. Norway's population appears to have declined recently in some areas, especially the north, whereas Sweden's appears stable. Finland, too, has seen decline, to about 500 pairs.

This species tolerates a wide range of habitats within low-arctic and boreal limits. Breeding areas may be substantial distances inland and well away from fresh water on tundra or heath, from open, upland slopes to wooded, lowland islets and slow-moving rivers. In northern Scotland there is a clear link with peatland lochs of low acidity and high conductivity (an index of dissolved salts), where favoured foods thrive.

Outside the breeding season the duck is predominantly marine, feeding and resting in mostly well dispersed groups, chiefly in waters 500–2,000m (500 yards–1 mile) from land, where the maximum depth is 10–20m (33–66ft) and food both abundant and easily reached. Sandy sea-beds are strongly favoured and it is very tolerant of strong currents and rough water. However, its distribution is subject to dramatic change in exceptional weather. For example, there was a massive decrease off Ireland following the easterly gales and severe cold of January 1963 and winter 1963–64, which depleted marine life. Only small numbers turn up on inland lakes, reservoirs and gravel pits.

Scotland has at least 100–115 pairs, the main strongholds being Caithness and Sutherland with over 50 pairs, Inverness-shire about 30 pairs, Islay some 7 pairs and Loch Lomond 4–6 pairs. In addition there are scattered pairs in north Perthshire, Ross and Cromarty and Shetland. There has been steep decline at Lower Lough Erne, Northern Ireland, from 152 pairs in 1967 to 21 in 1986. However, the Irish population overall appears to be slowly expanding its range. Lough Conn had 28–30 pairs in 1968 and at least 29 in 1983, while Lough Cullin had over 24 pairs in 1983, Lough Ree over 30 1984–85 and Lough Corrib 7 pairs 1983–86. Breeding has also been confirmed or is suspected at a number of other sites.

Field Characters

This compact duck has a deep bill, thick neck and pointed tail. Its plumage is in-

145

COMMON SCOTER

The average length is 44–54cm (17.3–21.3in), wingspan 79–90cm (31.1–35.4in), and weights 642–1,450g (1.4–3.2lb) for the male, 600–1,268g (1.3–2.8lb) the female.

conspicuous and birds easily go unnoticed among the waves, especially as they are reluctant to take flight. Apart from the yellow on his upper bill, the male is entirely glossy black, though his underwings and belly are greyer. The male of the American race has much more yellow on the bill, including the base as well as the smaller knob. Male velvet and surf scoters are distinguished by white patches on wings and head. The dark-brown female is separated from female surf and velvet scoters by her pale cheeks and upper neck, and from the female red-crested pochard (occasionally on sea in some parts of range) by uniform wings and generally darker plumage. The male is mottled black from his first December until adult plumage is acquired in his second autumn. Juveniles and first-winter females resemble the adult female, but have whiter underparts and paler upperparts. Male juveniles have a small patch of orange-yellow around the nostrils.

Outside the breeding season this wary species is highly gregarious, often in large, very mobile flocks on the sea. It swims buoyantly with its tail cocked, but sinks the body when alarmed. It takes off more easily than the other scoters, the wings whirring loudly, and usually flies in long, low, straggling lines with rapid, whistling wing-beats. Sometimes flocks fly at altitudes of several hundred metres (yards) or suddenly plummet from considerable height on closed wings with a rushing sound. Except when nesting, this duck rarely goes ashore and walks with an awkward, upright gait.

Noisier than other scoters, flocking birds often whistle, hoot and pipe simultaneously at varying pitch, which from a distance produces a haunting but pleasant murmur. Generally, the male's calls are more metallic, even bell-like, recalling curlew and plover, whereas the female's are harsher. However, difficulty remains in separating calls of individuals and sexes among distant flocks. The male's main calls have been rendered as *pju, wheeu, cour-loo* and *tu-luk*, and the female's likened to a door with a rusty hinge or even the voice of the coot.

Breeding

The single clutch (sometimes replaced after loss) of 6–8 (5–11) ovate, creamy-buff eggs, average size 66 × 45mm (2.6 × 1.77in), is usually laid from late May to late June in the British Isles but to mid-July in the Arctic, where laying is controlled by timing of the thaw.

The monogamous pair-bond is of seasonal duration. Pairing starts in winter flocks but is often delayed until spring. Male promiscuity is common. The male usually deserts soon after the start of incubation. In courtship the male calls frequently, sometimes with his bill held open for at least several seconds. His main displays include short rushes across water with the body flattened and neck held forward, neck-stretching, upward-shakes, wing-flaps, short flights and tail-snap, in which the tail is fanned and suddenly raised vertically or thrust forward over the back.

Nests are usually well dispersed at inland sites near still waters or sluggish rivers, but sometimes well away from fresh water among tundra vegetation, dwarf heath, heather and bramble. There is a preference for areas with a good view of approaching danger but some nests are protected by tall shrubs, trees, or rocks. Sometimes several pairs nest close together on wooded islands on larger lochs, such as at Lomond and other more southerly Scottish sites. The ground nest is generally well concealed in thick vegetation, the female using materials within easy reach, lining the hollow with grass, lichens, moss and down. Little is known about territories (if any), but the male is strong in defence of the female.

Scoters are among the most maritime of ducks. Below: common scoter (male left, female right). Top left: surf scoter (male left, female right). Top right: velvet scoter (female left, male right).

The 30/31-day incubation, by the female alone, starts with the last egg and hatching is synchronous. The young feed themselves, are cared for by the female and become independent at the time of fledging, at 45–50 days. Many broods fledge on the loch to which they were taken soon after hatching, but others spend

146

The winter population of western Europe and North Africa is believed to exceed 1 million, though the whereabouts of some large gatherings remain a mystery. Concentrations vary greatly from year to year and national counts differ widely from authoritative estimates because so many birds go unrecorded well out to sea. The British Isles, for example, probably hosts some 25,000–50,000 (about half around Scotland) whereas the 1990–91 count produced a peak of only 9,072 (February) (including velvet scoter) for Great Britain and 2,480 (November) for Northern Ireland. The bulk tend to gather in a few large flocks off the mouths of major estuaries. The Moray Firth is the only British area currently of international importance, often holding 5,000–10,000 birds, but large flocks are regular at Carmarthen Bay (where there were 25,000 in 1974), St Andrew's Bay, the Firth of Forth and Lindisfarne. Smaller numbers are found off many coasts in most months and this is the most likely sea-duck to be seen. Only the most exposed and rockier coasts are clearly avoided, notably around northern and western Scotland, north Devon and Cornwall and parts of Ireland. In recent years Ireland's largest flocks have occurred on the east, north-west and west coasts, notably at Dundrum Bay, Down (up to 2,570), Donegal Bay (to 1,650), Curracloe, Wexford (to 1,350) and Clogher Head, Louth (to 1,200).

a considerable time at other lochs or in coastal waters before independence. Two or more broods may gather together. Age of first breeding is 2–3 years.

Diet and Feeding Behaviour

Most food is taken by day in dives lasting less than 30 seconds in water 1–4m (3–13ft) deep, but depths to 30m (98ft) have been recorded. There is seasonal and local variation, but overall, in salt and brackish waters the predominantly animal diet consists chiefly of molluscs, especially the blue mussel, but also cockles, clams, other bivalves, gastropods, periwinkles, dogwhelk, laver snails, sand-eels; occasional crustaceans, especially amphipods (shrimps), isopods, small crabs, annelids and echinoderms. Feeding birds drift along with the tide, current or wind and then fly back to their original station.

Molluscs, especially mussels and pond-snails, are also taken in freshwater areas, along with insects and their larvae, annelids, small fish and their eggs, and the seeds, roots and tubers of chiefly aquatic plants. The species is also an opportunistic feeder, for example in taking netted fish and a wrecked cargo of horse-beans off Heligoland. Ducklings eat mainly adult insects, larvae and plant seeds.

Movements

Most populations migrate substantial distances. Some, such as Icelandic breeders, depart from early September to early October, but peak autumn movement (after the moult) is in early November in the Baltic and right through November into early December in the North Sea. At first males dominate western flocks, but the proportions of females and juveniles increase steadily until the passage ends in December. Most birds wintering off the Norwegian coast are probably local breeders.

Once the major assemblies are settled at British sites there seems to be little interchange. The wintering grounds of the small British Isles breeding population are not known, but the nesting areas are deserted. Spring return takes place from late February to April in the Atlantic and North Sea and April–May in the Baltic, but the most northerly breeding grounds are not reoccupied before late May.

Moult movements are extensive, but the destinations of many birds are not known, partly because the species tends to moult further out to sea and in deeper waters than other sea-ducks. The largest known assemblies, totalling several hundred thousand birds, gather in Danish waters but only account for a small proportion of the birds regularly seen on the move. For example, in late summer there is a passage of a million or so along the German North Sea coast, and in early autumn large-scale movements are often seen along the English Channel. Many of the birds in these flocks breed in Fenno-Scandia and Russia and winter off the French and Iberian coasts. They are also the likely source of most birds wintering within the British Isles. Icelandic breeders, too, disperse widely, around France and Iberia as well as Britain and Ireland. Recent late-summer moult gatherings around the British Isles have been largest off east Scotland, especially in the Moray Firth and the Firth of Forth, sometimes exceeding 1,000. But here, too, the picture is confused and certainly subject to frequent change. For example, there were up to 2,000 on the Solway in July during the 1960s, but now the area holds few. Without co-ordinated counts it is likely that many of the birds are recorded at least twice.

VELVET SCOTER
(*Melanitta fusca*)

THIS sea-duck nests widely in Fenno-Scandia but breeding has not been confirmed in the British Isles, where it is a winter visitor in localised concentrations. It often goes unnoticed among flocks of the more abundant common scoter, but the two species differ significantly in both appearance and lifestyle.

Once known as velvet duck and white-winged scoter

History and Conservation

There are no records from Pleistocene Britain, but it did occur in Somerset during the Iron Age and in Scotland during the Dark Ages. Breeding in the British Isles has been suspected on a number of occasions, the last time being in Shetland in 1945. It has also probably bred in the Faeroes and Spitsbergen.

The Baltic breeding population increased during the warm phase 1920–50, but there has been recent decrease through over-shooting and disturbance. Oil spillage (especially near moulting and wintering flocks), human exploitation of the duck's food sources (notably recent proposals to dredge for mussels within the Moray Firth) and increasing coastal recreation are continuing major international threats. Designation of marine conservation areas should address these perils.

Based on the bird's soft plumage, the name 'velvet duck' was coined by Ray in 1678 and remained in use until Fleming introduced 'velvet scoter' in 1828. The Latin specific derives from *fusco* for 'to blacken', being descriptive of the plumage.

Distribution, Habitat and Population

The velvet scoter breeds right across northern Eurasia from Norway to Kamchatka, as far south as 50°N and principally in the east. It is absent from Iceland, Greenland and eastern North America, but breeds widely from Alaska to Husdon Bay, south to the US border. Much of this vast, chiefly inland range is frozen in winter, so most birds migrate substantial distances. Eurasian birds either go west, mostly around the coasts of Norway, the southern Baltic and the North Sea, or east around the Pacific coasts of Japan, Manchuria and southern Kamchatka. North America's breeding population splits widely too, wintering down the Pacific coast from the Aleutians to Baja in California, and the Atlantic coast to South Carolina, with widely varying numbers around the Great Lakes.

The subspecies *M.f.fusca* breeds in Europe and western Asia, *M.f.stejnegeri* in eastern Asia, and *M.f.deglandi* in North America.

In Finland some 5,000–8,000 pairs are mainly in the archipelago, the northern inland population having declined markedly through hunting. Sweden, too, has seen substantial decrease. Norway's population is largely in the centre and north of the country.

The species is an accidental in Iceland, Spitsbergen, Bear Island, the Faeroes, Hungary, Greece, Yugoslavia, Bulgaria, Rumania, Israel, Italy, Portugal, Algeria, Morocco and the Azores.

In winter this is the least numerous of west Palearctic sea-ducks, with an estimated 150,000–200,000 in western Europe, the main known concentrations being in eastern Danish and southern Norwegian waters. As with the common scoter, there is significant yearly variation in numbers visiting individual northwest European countries and main resorts.

VELVET SCOTER

In its breeding habitat the velvet scoter is much more adaptable than the common scoter, using more wooded as well as open country at higher altitudes, especially in higher-middle latitudes. It frequents inland lakes, pools and rivers in the wooded tundra and taiga as well as wooded shores and skerries around the Baltic. Generally, it nests closer to fresh or brackish water than the common scoter.

In winter it is predominantly maritime, though mostly rather closer inshore than the common scoter. It concentrates along exposed coasts where food is easily accessible, especially in sandy shallows such as those off east Scotland. It is more likely than the common scoter to turn up on a small number of inland British sites, but only in very small numbers and usually single birds.

Field Characters

Being predominantly black, the male closely resembles the common scoter, but is distinguished by his wing-patch (especially in flight) and, at close range, his crescent-shaped, white eye-patch and greater amount of yellow on the bill, which has an orange-pink nail. The first-year male is variably mottled black until adult plumage is acquired in the second autumn. The white wing-patch is the best way to distinguish the female, too. At close range she may also be separated from the female common scoter by two variable, small pale patches on the face rather than entirely pale cheeks. The first-year female and juvenile resemble the adult female, but have more mottled white underparts, more distinct white patches on the side of the head, and are generally paler and browner.

The velvet scoter is quite gregarious for much of the year, but mostly occurs in parties of fewer than 20, and even in winter birds of the European race rarely gather in groups of more than 100. It is generally tamer than other scoters and less inclined to avoid rough water between rocks and islands. Although equally expert at diving, it is less buoyant than the common scoter and struggles to become air-borne. In mostly low, noisy flight it appears heavy, but sometimes gets above 20m (66ft) or so. On land it is noticeably clumsy.

This is a much quieter bird than the common scoter and flocks do not generally call in concert. The male's calls include a ringing *skryck-lyck* or *vak-vak* in courtship and a hoarse, growling *koarr* in flight. The female's repertoire includes an excited *braaa-braaa-braaa* and a sharp *kerr-kerr*.

Breeding

The monogamous pair-bond is of seasonal duration, pairs forming in flocks in winter and after spring passage while awaiting the thaw. The male usually deserts during late incubation, some males staying to defend females with broods. As with other scoters, pair-courtship is similar to communal courtship, though the male is quieter. His main displays include low-rush, upward-shake, neck-stretch, head-shake, tail-snap, ceremonial drinking and bowing. Unlike the common scoter, the velvet does not appear to engage in courtship flights, but does pursue underwater for 15–20 seconds.

Nests are mostly well dispersed, but sometimes among colonies of gulls and terns and occasionally only a few metres (yards) apart on relatively safe islets. A small, ill-defined territory is defended. The site is usually well concealed among ground vegetation within 100m (yards) of water but may be as much as 3km

(2 miles) away. Occasionally it is quite exposed at the foot of a woodland tree, but very rarely completely in the open. Nestboxes are sometimes used. The female alone uses materials within easy reach to build a shallow cup with a rim of leaves, twigs and grass lined with down.

The female alone incubates for 26–29 days from the laying of the last egg. Hatching is synchronous, the young feed themselves and are cared for by the female, sometimes with male nearby. However, the parent-young bond is loose and even small ducklings will live alone. Some gather in crèches in the care of one female. Independence is mostly achieved at 30–40 days and the fledging period is thought to be about 50–55 days. Age of first breeding is two to three years. Breeding success is often poor, with high chick mortality due mostly to loose family ties and high vulnerability to bad weather.

Diet and Feeding Behaviour

The diet is a little more varied than that of the common scoter, probably because this species tends to feed more near the coast. Again, the concentration is on molluscs, which may comprise over 80 per cent (by volume) of the winter diet in salt and brackish-water areas. Most important are the blue mussel, dogwhelks and cockles. Among crustaceans taken are small crabs, isopods and amphipods, while echinoderms include starfish and heart-urchin. Other coastal foods include annelids and small fish. At freshwater sites molluscs are supplemented by insects (chief food of small ducklings), small fish and annelids, as well as plant seeds, buds, leaves, roots and tubers. More exceptional foods include fish roe and frogs.

Most food is taken through daytime surface-diving with partly open wings, mostly in water to depths of only a few metres, but occasionally to 30m (98ft) and taking over a minute. Sometimes it dabbles in driftlines and groups often appear to dive synchronously, though this would rarely be to mutual advantage as most food items are static or very slow-moving.

Velvet scoter (above) and common scoter (below) killed by oil. Sea ducks are often victims of pollution incidents. Photo: Dennis Green

The single clutch (replaced after loss) of 7–9 (5–12, but more usually two females) ovate, creamy-buff eggs, average size 72 × 48mm (2.84 × 1.88in), is mostly laid from mid-May to mid-June in Fenno-Scandia and the north-west of the former USSR, but mid-June to early July in the arctic regions of the former USSR.

151

Movements

Although it must travel long distances in colder parts of its range, in north and north-west Europe this migrant tends to stay closer to its breeding haunts, chiefly moving to coastal waters. Unfortunately, its movements are relatively hard to monitor as the species tends to keep offshore and is often overlooked among much larger assemblies of common scoters.

Within the west Palearctic moult gatherings are very variable, but there are usually several significant assemblies, notably some 45,000 in Limfjorden and Kattegat, Denmark, in late July. These are 80 per cent adult males with smaller numbers of immatures, adult females arriving in August and September. Overall, numbers within British waters are small, proabaly with only a few hundred present off east Scotland during late summer and autumn. These increase steadily with the onset of autumn migration proper and the further south-westerly movement of birds which have moulted elsewhere, but in some years do not appear to peak until well into April. As common scoters mostly peak by early February and decline thereafter, velvet scoters may then become the dominant species in mixed flocks. Females and juveniles mostly vacate Fenno-Scandia and north Russia in September and October, pronounced passage through the Baltic occurring in October and November. No significant movement is apparent south of the English Channel. The spring return starts in early March but is generally later than that of the common scoter, peak passage through Sweden and Finland not occurring until mid-May, when there are still big flocks off Denmark. The most northerly breeding grounds may not be reoccupied before mid-June.

GOLDENEYE
(Bucephala clangula)

ORIGINATING in North America, the highly successful goldeneye has extended its range throughout Eurasia, quickly exploiting new suitable habitat. As a recent colonist in Britian it remains a rare breeder, the majority of birds still relying on the provision of nestboxes.

History and Conservation

Mostly a more northerly bird which could have bred during cooler times, there is little very early evidence of the goldeneye in Britain, though it was present in Somerset in the Iron Age and in Norfolk in the Cromerian interglacial. Except in severe winters, it was a scarce winter visitor to England in the nineteenth century, but common around coastal areas of Scotland, where it probably bred during the 'Little Ice Age' 1550–1850.

Throughout the range, destruction of old forests with natural nest-sites has caused some decline, but birds have readily accepted nestboxes in forests near water, such as in Sweden and Finland. Indeed, Laplanders once provided many boxes to procure eggs. Nowadays, site safety is not a great problem with widespread help from landowners, notably the RSPB and Forestry Commission in Britain, where almost half the breeding population nests on nature reserves or SSSIs.

GOLDENEYE
Once known as goldeneyed garrot, buffle-headed garrot, pied wigeon, whiteside, gowdy duck, brown-headed duck, greyheaded duck, mussel cracker, freshwater wigeon, rattlewings, whistler, pied curre, curre, diver, doucker, douker, popping wigeon, diving duck, gingling curre and morillon

Not surprisingly deriving from the bird's brightyellow eye, the name 'golden-eye' appears to have been coined by Ray in 1678 and standardised following adoption by ▶

None the less, there are threats to the goldeneye's survival as a British breeder, quite apart from the lack of natural nest-holes in the absence of large wood-peckers, and competition for holes with the jackdaw and, more rarely but increasingly, the pine marten, which is recolonising lost ground. A small number of eggs have been taken for collections. Also fishermen have been inadvertently spending too much time near some nests, occasionally leading to desertion. Furthermore, heavy stocking of lochs with rainbow trout may deplete invertebrates on which the goldeneye feeds, and some waters have been poisoned to remove coarse fish before restocking with rainbows. Any effects on the goldeneye of acidification of upland waters are not yet apparent. But provided the nestbox supply meets demand while more deciduous trees are planted and retained along rivers and near lochs, and allowed to mature to provide natural hollows, the goldeneye should eventually colonise a large area of northern Britain. It is still legally shot in Britain in winter but the number bagged is very small.

The male goldeneye's courtship is one of the most elaborate among ducks. Photo: Dennis Green

▶ Pennant in 1768. The Latin *Bucephala* derives from the Greek for 'bull-headed', while *clangula* refers to the distinctive sound made by the bird's wings.

Distribution, Habitat and Population

The goldeneye breeds widely across North America, from Alaska to Newfoundland as far south as the US northern border and to the treeline in the north; in Eurasia from Fenno-Scandia and the Baltic states across northern Russia and Siberia, eastwards to Kamchatka and northern Japan. It also breeds locally in Germany, Poland and Czechoslovakia as well as Scotland, but not in Greenland and Iceland, where there are no suitable trees. It winters on ice-free inland waters and coasts south to France, the Balkans, central Asia, China and the southern USA.

For breeding, the goldeneye prefers mature forest with hollow trees near food-rich waters of medium depth, with substantial areas of open water free from vegetation, which means it is restricted to a fairly narrow belt dominated by coniferous forest. A wide range of water is used, from still lakes to fast-flowing and

First recorded nesting in Britain was in Cheshire in 1931–2, in rabbit burrows on the Dee Estuary, but this might have involved injured birds unable to fly back to their usual breeding haunts. True colonisation of Britain started in Inverness-shire in 1970, where nestboxes had been provided as an experiment, and has apparently been encouraged by climatic ▶

The male Barrow's goldeneye (top) is distinguished from the male common goldeneye (below) by his crescent-shaped rather than round cheek patch. The females of the two species (common goldeneye centre) are much harder to separate.

▶ cooling since 1950. With widespread provision of nestboxes in new forests where trees are not allowed to mature and provide natural holes, the population increased to some 50 pairs by the mid-1980s, chiefly in Scotland. Since then rapid increase has continued, some pairs also occurring in Cumbria, and a few natural nest-sites are now used.

The length averages 42–50cm (16.5–19.7in), wing-span 65–80cm (25.6–31.5in), and weight 750–1,245g (1.6–2.7lb) for the male, 500–882g (1.1–1.9lb) the female, the male being significantly larger.

The single clutch of 8–11 (5–13) blunt ovate, blue-green eggs (sometimes replaced after loss), average size 59 × 43mm (2.32 × 1.69in), is generally laid from early April to mid-May in north-west Europe, though as late as mid-June in Fenno-Scandia and Russia.

even turbulent rivers and estuaries. In winter there is some bias towards marine habitat. In Scotland at least, the goldeneye has been strongly attracted to sewers and other waste-discharge sites. During severe weather there is gravitation towards the coast as inland waters freeze.

Field Characters

Unless at close range, the bright-yellow eye is not a prominent field mark, but the high-crowned, 'triangular' head will identify both sexes even at long distance. While the shape is accentuated by elongated crown and nape feathers, it has been suggested that the underlying dome's large air sinuses above the skull carry a reserve supply of air which may enable the bird to prolong its dives. The handsome male has a glossy green-black head, a distinctive circular white patch between the bill and eye, and striking, mainly black-and-white body plumage. The female has a chocolate-brown head, with no white patch, but her white collar often neatly separates the mottled grey upperparts. In flight, both sexes reveal the conspicuous white square on the black wing, though the female's is partly or completely broken by two black lines. In eclipse the male resembles the female but usually retains some green feathers on his darker brown head with blacker lores, and has more white on the wings. The juvenile resembles the non-breeding adult female, with no collar, and is duller. Among young birds the male is often already noticeably larger than the female in the first winter, with little or no white on the scapulars (none on female) and the collar is poorly defined. Adult plumage is not acquired until the second winter.

Although seen in large flocks at some favoured sites, the goldeneye is less gregarious than other ducks, mostly occurring in small parties and not mixing with other species. Among winter flocks males are often in a distinct minority. The goldeneye swims well and lightly, but when alarmed sinks the body, extends the neck and puffs out the head feathers, preferring to swim away or dive, which it does frequently, rather than take flight. This restless bird rises more easily than the other diving ducks, directly into the air rather than pattering across the water, but it may strike the surface several times with its feet when there is little or no wind. Flight is strong, fast and generally rather low, on rapidly beating wings which produce a characteristic whistling rattle, loudest in the male. Even though it walks better than the other divers, with erect carriage, it is still awkward on land, which it rarely visits. During the breeding season the female flies directly in and out of the nest-hole and often perches on nearby branches.

This is a very quiet bird, except when displaying, its calls being supplemented by the rhythmic whistling of its wings, often heard over 1km away. The male has a harsh, wheezing *zeee-ZEEE*, a quieter *rrrt*, and a soft *rrrrrrrt*, while the female's repertoire is said to include a growling *kurr*, a faint *eeuu* or screech, a whistling *peep-peep* and a hoarse *ah-ah-ah*.

Breeding

The monogamous pair-bond is of seasonal duration, pairing starting in winter and continuing into spring. The male deserts during incubation. In wide-ranging elaborate courtship the male swims around or alongside the female while lifting his head straight up or back, sometimes calling and kicking up water, often preceded by jerky neck movements.

The British breeding
population is virtually
confined to Inverness-
shire, where at least 85
occupied nests were
recorded in 1989. Pairs
have also been seen in
north-west England,
where they may have bred.
At least one pair has
recently been seen in
Northern Ireland and up
to 30 birds have summered
on Lough Neagh,
suggesting possible future
colonisation of Ireland. In
Finland this is the
commonest diving duck,
with over 50,000 pairs,
and in Sweden it is the
most abundant freshwater
diving duck.

The winter population
of northern and central
Europe was estimated at
200,000 in 1977. The
largest number occurs in
Denmark, where over
100,000 have been
counted, birds from
Finland and further east
having joined some 12,000
gathered earlier on
moulting grounds. In
Great Britain the
population peaked at
17,102 (February) 1990–
91, with 15,201 in
Northern Ireland in the
same month, both counts
well up on 1989–90.
Loughs Neagh/Beg
represent the only
internationally important
site within the UK, the
1990–91 peak of 13,591
greatly exceeding the
qualifying level of 3,000.
The resort's average
maximum 1986–91 was
11,521, compared with
1,542 for the Forth
Estuary, 685 Inner Moray
Firth, 627 Abberton
Reservoir, 561 Belfast
Lough and 544 Maidens
Harbour/Turnberry. Ten
other sites have average
maxima over 250, and a
further seven passed that
figure 1990–91.

As natural tree-hole nest-sites have become scarce, the species has readily accepted nestboxes throughout much of its range, but sometimes a rabbit burrow or cavity under rocks or logs is used. Holes with open tops, such as in broken tree stumps, are preferred to those with side entrances, but in some countries tree holes excavated by black or pileated woodpeckers are widely adopted, mostly at heights of 10–15m (33–49ft). The site is always within easy access of freshwater feeding grounds, but exceptionally may be several kilometres (miles) away from a lake or stream. The female shapes the nest depression with her body and lines it with wood chips, feathers and down.

The 29/30-day incubation is by the female only, starts on completion of the clutch and hatching is synchronous. Most broods stay in the nest for a day or two before parachuting to the ground and being taken by the female to the rearing area, which may be some 2km (about a mile) away. The young feed themselves and are cared for by the female, becoming independent at about 50 days and fledging at 57–66 days. First breeding is at two years, slowing colonisation.

Because sites are often scarce, two or more females frequently try to use the same nest-hole, with disastrous results. Also, if a goldeneye shares with a red-breasted merganser it is inevitably the goldeneye which gives up. Sometimes mergansers will hatch goldeneye eggs, but resultant ducklings have no parental care.

Diet and Feeding Behaviour

This diver takes predominantly animal food, mostly in depths to 4m (13ft). Dabbling and up-ending are rare. Primarily molluscs, crustaceans and insect larvae are taken from the bottom, the strong bill probing among stones on the beds of rivers and lakes, and in midwater. Dives average 15–20 seconds, but 36 seconds has been recorded, the larger males being more proficient. Most food is swallowed underwater, but some larger items are brought to the surface. The diet varies considerably with locality and season and also includes small fish, frogs, tadpoles, earthworms, water shrews, leeches, shrimps, algae, and the seeds, roots, tubers and leaves of aquatic plants. In winter, it more commonly feeds in brackish and salt water, concentrations occurring at waste outfalls, where grain and other vegetable matter from breweries and food-processing plants appear to be the main attraction. Mostly a day feeder, the goldeneye is also active at night where disturbance or tides dictate, especially in winter when grounds are far from roosts.

Movements

While most goldeneye populations are migratory, many birds move only short distances to winter on the nearest ice-free coasts, including those around southern Sweden and Norway, and a few in south-west Iceland. Most breeders from Fenno-Scandia, Poland, north Germany, the Baltic states and north-west Russia winter around the Baltic, Denmark, the Netherlands and the British Isles, progressively smaller numbers occurring from Belgium to southern France. In severe weather there is increased gravitation towards coasts as inland waters freeze over.

When weather permits, some British birds remain near their nesting areas all year. Recent summer concentrations at Inverness and on the Beauly Firth probably consisted chiefly of non-breeders and moulting drakes from the home breeding population. Large numbers of birds from Scandinavia and western Russia start to arrive in the British Isles from mid-September, initially dispersing

widely, but later tending to concentrate at major sites as the cold weather intensifies, with a south-westerly drift. Adult males tend to migrate shorter distances, perhaps because these larger birds are better able to withstand cold, and juveniles move most of all, thereby partially accounting for winter sexual segregation. The spring return is early, from mid-February on average, most birds having left their winter quarters by late March, and even in Lapland the breeding grounds are reoccupied by mid-May. Little is known about moult migrations, but males arrive at the large assemblies in south Sweden and Denmark from early June and numbers peak in August with the arrival of females.

BARROW'S GOLDENEYE
(Bucephala islandica)

P RIMARILY a Nearctic bird, Barrow's goldeneye does have a breeding outpost in Iceland, but it is only a rare straggler to the rest of Europe. However, it may have been often overlooked as it closely resembles the common goldeneye.

History and Conservation

Little is known about the species' history, apart from the fact that its meat was never popular with hunters, which is just as well as it is a very sedentary bird which could easily be exploited. It has been suggested that the current very restricted and discontinuous range is the relict stage after earlier widespread distribution, perhaps the result of competition with the common goldeneye. Indeed, this is the only *Bucephala* duck present in Iceland, where the commoner bird does not breed, a fact reflected in the Latin specific *islandica*.

The male recorded at Irvine, Ayr, in late 1979 was the first British report accepted by the rarities committee, but with categorised doubt as to whether it was a genuine vagrant. The 1913 Shetland record was not accepted and subsequent occurrences in England have been regarded as escapes.

Distribution, Habitat and Population

The species' main population is restricted to north-western North America, from southern Alaska through the Canadian Rockies to Washington State, with only a few outposts (all at altitude) southwards. There is a huge gap between these birds and those on the Labrador coast near Ungava Bay. Then there is another great gap before the tenuously established population in south-west Greenland, and yet another separating that in Iceland, where some 800 pairs at Lake Mývatn are the only breeders in the west Palearctic.

Unlike the common goldeneye, Barrow's will breed away from trees, using cold, but ice-free inland waters of the subarctic and arctic-alpine zones, yet compared with most wildfowl its habitat requirements appear inflexible. Lakes and pools of all sizes are used when they are of medium depth, with little floating or emergent vegetation and sufficiently productive, strongly alkaline waters supporting a rich supply of prey being preferred. River rapids and torrents are also frequented. Throughout its range, distribution changes little the year round.

The species was named after Sir John Barrow (1764–1848), who was Second Secretary at the Admiralty, a founder of the Royal Geographical Society and promoter of Arctic exploration who selected naturalists for many naval expeditions. The name Barrow's goldeneye was first used in 1831, in a book on North American animals, called Fauna Borealis Americana.

The length averages 42–53cm (16.5–20.9in), wing-span 67–84cm (26.4–33.1in — the male rather larger), and weight 1,191–1,304g (2.6–2.9lb) for the male, 737–907g (1.6–2lb) the female.

The Barrow's goldeneye (female left, males centre and right) starts to pair in winter flocks. Photo: Dennis Green

Field Characters

The male has the same shape and general appearance as the common goldeneye but has a purple rather than green gloss to the head, a crescent-shaped rather than round white patch in front of the eye, and has less white on the upperparts, appearing blacker overall. The females and young are more difficult to separate, but the Barrow's has a shorter, deeper bill, usually with more yellow at the tip, and its forehead is almost vertical, with a distinct mane producing an oval-shaped rather than triangular head. In flight both sexes of Barrow's show less white on the wing. The non-breeding male resembles the female but has an all-black bill and greyer head.

Its general habits are similar to those of the common goldeneye, but it is probably a more proficient diver, making greater use of fast-flowing waters. A quiet species outside courtship, its lack of vocal repertoire being supplemented by the 'singing' of its wings, which may be distinguished from that of the common goldeneye in being quieter, less metallic and slightly higher pitched through having a marginally faster wing-beat. The male's calls are a feeble, grunting *ka-KAA* and a clicking; the female utters a slurred, growling *arrr arrr*.

Breeding

The pair-bond appears to be monogamous and of seasonal duration, pairing starting in winter flocks and continuing into spring on inland breeding waters. The male deserts during incubation. Courtship is similar to that of the common goldeneye, including the head-throw and kick display and rotary pumping. Males are highly aggressive towards each other and threaten with necks lowered along

the water, frequently following up with underwater attacks and beating each other with their wings while rising breast to breast. Females, too, show such behaviour.

Nest-sites are much more varied than those of the common goldeneye, but are mostly in holes and crevices. In North America the majority are in old woodpecker and flicker holes in decaying trees or stumps, but in Iceland lava and rock crevices are necessarily favoured. Some are in thick vegetation overhung by scrub, and others in nestboxes — even on houses in Iceland. Water is rarely far away. Little nest material is used in holes, but in vegetation the down lining may have a substantial base of grass and leaves gathered by the female.

The 28/30-day incubation, by the female only, starts on completion of the clutch, and hatching is more or less synchronous. The ducklings are brooded in the nest for a day or two, but soon learn to feed themselves and are cared for by the female until they fledge at about 56 days. Like the common goldeneye, Barrow's will often lay in the nests of other duck species where sites are scarce. Age of first breeding is two years.

Diet and Feeding Behaviour

Barrow's goldeneye takes mainly animal food through diving in shallow inland and coastal waters, rarely by dabbling and up-ending. In winter molluscs and crustaceans predominate, but in summer insects and plants are more accessible and widely taken. Lesser items include fish eggs and pondweed seeds. Feeding methods are similar to those of the common goldeneye.

Movements

The species is unusual in making only the shortest possible migrations to wintering grounds on the nearest ice-free waters. Some populations are resident. Many Icelandic birds winter in their breeding areas, but some move to relatively warm inland and coastal waters, especially from north to south. As a result vagrants to the Faeroes, Norway, Spitsbergen, Russia, Finland, Britain (only one accepted record), Germany, France and Poland are extremely rare, some possibly of New World rather than Icelandic origin.

SMEW
(*Mergus albellus*)

THIS handsome duck is the smallest of Europe's 'sawbills' and does not breed within the British Isles, though it is a regular winter visitor in small numbers. Indeed, this bird of the far north ventures into temperate zones only as far as the nearest ice-free waters and remains a rare sight for most Europeans.

History and Conservation

The smew is well represented in the British fossil record, occurring from the Cromerian interglacial onwards, and from the Holocene to beyond the Iron Ages.

SMEW
Once known as smee, smee duck, white nun, white wigeon, white merganser, smew merganser, white-headed goosander, lough diver, magpie diver, pied diver, ▶

SMEW

A group of female smews – popularly known as 'redheads'. Photo: R. Glover

▶ red-headed smew, weasel duck, weasel coot, vare wigeon and small herring bar

The name 'smew' is known from the seventeenth century, when it was but one of many in common use for this species. However, it was then secondary to some used for the predominantly white male, especially 'white nun', and did not become standard until Pennant chose it in 1768. This Norfolk word is said to imitate the whistling of the bird's wings, but more probably the name originates through being a variant of 'small', used adjectivally throughout northern Europe — eg *smee* in English and *smiehe* in Old German. The Latin *Mergus* denotes a seabird or diver, from *mergo* 'to dip' or 'to plunge', while *albellus* is the diminutive of *albus* for white, suggesting whitish.

Little is known about its status in recent centuries, but it was almost certainly much commoner in northern Europe during the 'Little Ice Age' 1550–1850. During the early nineteenth century small numbers were regularly shot throughout the British Isles and it was said to have bred on Orkney. There was certainly some range expansion during the last century, when the population in northern Sweden was established. Norway's first breeding record is from 1925, but since then there has been no significant increase in north-west Europe. The main breeding range, in northern Russia, has contracted northwards through loss of habitat.

Since the 1950s the British wintering population has fallen from several hundreds to fewer than a hundred in many years. However, there are occasional invasions when numbers approach former levels, when cold weather pushes birds westwards from their main wintering centre in the Netherlands.

Like the goldeneye, the smew takes readily to nestboxes and this should help to arrest decline in areas where widespread felling has removed many tree-holes. In the British Isles the species is now fully protected.

Distribution, Habitat and Population

The smew breeds only in the boreal zone of the Old World, from northern Scandinavia, where it is rare, through its north Russian stronghold to the Sea of Okhotsk in the north Pacific. Further outposts are the Kamchatka Peninsula, northern Japan, the Asiatic shores of the Bering Sea and, oddly, well to the south along the lower Volga, near the north Caspian Sea. As it requires mature trees with nest-holes, close to cool, fresh water (still or gently flowing), the open tundra is totally avoided. It remains very rare in Sweden and Norway but much more plentiful in northern Finland. No reliable figures are available.

In winter it flies south into temperate zones, but only as far as necessary, to where waters are not continuously covered with ice. In the mid-1970s the total west Palearctic winter population was estimated at 75,000 birds, and that of north-west Europe is probably over 10,000, the bulk of which occur in the Netherlands, in the IJsselmeer and along the Rhine. Much smaller numbers are scattered around the North Sea, central Europe and the eastern Mediterranean. Much larger numbers overwinter further east. French and British winter numbers appear to be dependent on cold weather driving birds west from Holland. In Britain most occur in the south-east on large or fairly large fresh waters, including reservoirs. They are very uncommon in Scotland and extremely rare in Ireland.

Field Characters

Only slightly larger than the teal, the smew has a slight crest and a steep forehead, and its striking plumage makes it easy to identify in both sexes and at all ages. The male is especially beautiful with predominantly white plumage patterned black — hence old names such as 'magpie diver'. In flight the white is less noticeable and he appears more piebald. The female's face mask is less distinct than the male's, but her rufous-brown head-cap contrasts well with her white lower face and throat. The remainder of her upperparts and tail are grey. In eclipse the male resembles the female, but retains a large white patch on the wing-coverts and his back is blacker. The juvenile is like the adult female but its white wing-coverts are tinged grey-brown and it lacks the black lores. Confusion with other ducks is most unlikely, though the male could be overlooked as a small gull and the darker female for a small grebe.

Gregarious for most of the year and generally found in small flocks, the smew takes flight easily and manoeuvres skilfully among trees on its breeding grounds. Its flight is fast, with powerful, even wing-beats generating a humming whistle, groups travelling in oblique lines or Vs, and sometimes in bunches like teal. It swims very buoyantly, dives rapidly, easily and frequently, and walks well with upright carriage.

Little is known about this quiet bird's calls. In courtship the male utters a low, mechanical rattle reminiscent of the sound of fingernails drawn along a comb, while the female incites with a harsh *krrrrr krrrrr*. She also has a low, single or repeated *wok* or *quok*.

Breeding

The monogamous pair-bond is of seasonal duration, some pairs being formed in late winter, but most during the spring migration. The male deserts during incubation. In display he raises his crest, puffs out his breast and pumps his head and neck back over his mantle, frequently following up with a skyward stretch.

The natural nest-site is a tree-hole, often excavated by black woodpeckers, but as forests have been cleared increasing use has been made of nestboxes, usually those put out for goldeneyes. The female's 26/28-day incubation starts on completion of the clutch and hatching is synchronous. The young feed themselves but are cared for by the female. The fledging period is not recorded and the age of first breeding is thought to be two years. The smew's agility on the wing enables it to breed on and around many small waters ignored by other ducks, especially flooded woodlands where prolonged take-off is impossible.

SMEW

During the 1990–91 season there was clearly a substantial cold-weather influx between the January Great Britain count of 67 and the February count of 270. Among the main sites were Rye Harbour with 22, Stain Hill Reservoirs with 21, and Goldhanger and King George VI reservoirs, each with 18. Wraysbury gravel pits had 15 and Dungeness 12 in December, while Marlow gravel pits had 10 in February. However, the smew is always difficult to monitor accurately because, although it is very conspicuous, it is also very mobile so that some individuals are likely to be counted more than once. Allowing for this, the average British Isles winter population is estimated at less than 100 birds.

The length averages 38–44cm (15–17.3in), wing-span 55–69cm (21.7–27.2in), and weight 510–935g (1.1–2lb) for the male, 500–680g (1.1–1.5lb) the female, the male being significantly larger.

The single clutch of 7–9 (5–11) ovate, cream or buff eggs, average size 52 × 38mm (2.05 × 1.50in), is mostly laid from mid-May to mid-June on a scant depression lined with down.

Diet and Feeding Behaviour

The smew takes predominantly animal food chiefly by surface-diving in water less than 4m (13ft) deep. Most dives take less than 30 seconds and prey is brought to the surface. Feeding is diurnal and often synchronous in small groups. In winter and early spring the concentration is on fish, a wide variety of salt- and freshwater species being taken, including salmon, trout, roach, eel, gudgeon, bleak, sticklebacks, minnow, pike, turbot, carp, plaice, sand-eel, sandsmelt, herring, blenny and bream. These are both bottom-feeding and pelagic species, and mostly small, but eel to 29cm (11.4in), trout to 14cm (5.5in), carp to 10cm (3.9in) and perch to 11cm (4.3in) have been recorded.

In late spring, summer and autumn insects form a major part of the diet. These are mainly aquatic, both adults and larvae, and include dragonflies, caddis-flies, chironomids and water-beetles. Other animal foods include molluscs, crustaceans, marine polychaetes and frogs. The leaves, seeds and roots of marine and saltwater plants are sometimes taken, including duckweeds and *Zostera*.

Movements

In winter this northerly breeder must migrate south and west to the nearest open water where there is reasonable access to fish, which means discontinuous ice cover is sometimes acceptable. The total wintering around Germany, the Netherlands, Denmark and Britain is too high to comprise solely Fenno-Scandian birds and must include many from the north-west of the former USSR. Only very small numbers winter in southern Norway, Sweden, Belgium and Ireland. Birds arrive in North Sea countries from October, but the bulk do not arrive until December or January as intensifying cold pushes them further east. Sometimes peak numbers do not occur in Britain and France until February as intense cold drives them from the Dutch polders. Most leave in March, with only a few stragglers remaining in April and May. Moult gatherings have not been reported from the West Palearctic, but occur in Siberia.

SMEW

The smew (female left, male right) generally ventures south only as far as the nearest ice-free waters.

RED-BREASTED MERGANSER
(Mergus serrator)

THIS is one of the world's most successful species of duck, with a continuous, circumpolar distribution through the northern tundra and boreal zones. But it is also a specialist fish-eater whose taste for salmon and trout has brought it into widespread conflict with man.

History and Conservation

Remains indicate that the merganser was human prey in Britain from the Mesolithic to the Bronze and Iron Ages, and much earlier it occurred at intervals during the Pleistocene, from the Cromerian interglacial to the Devensian. It was recorded breeding in Scotland and north-west Ireland through the nineteenth

Once known as red-breasted shoveler, red-breasted goosander, popping wigeon, tuke, bardrake, rodge, grey diver, lesser toothed diver, sawbill, sawneb, sawbill wigeon, sawyer, spear wigeon, spear drake, sandbill, earl duck, land harlan, herald, herald duck, harle and herle

The species has a long recorded history, going back to the ornithological glossary of Alfred the Grammarian in 998. Many early names are based on the Icelandic *haveld* for duck and the species' French name *Harle*. 'Merganser' itself was created by Gesner in 1555 from the Latin *mergus* for diver and *anser* for goose, and first used as an English word in 1752. Edwards called this species 'red-breasted goosander' in 1747 and Pennant coined 'red-breasted merganser' in 1776. The Latin specific *serrator* derives from *serratus* for toothed like a saw, referring to the bill.

Some 40,000 birds winter in north-west Europe, including an estimated 11,000 in the British Isles, of which perhaps 2,000 occur in Ireland. However, national counts tend to be considerably lower. For example, during 1990–91 the peak for Great Britain was 3,891 (December), with 584 in Northern Ireland (September). Over five years, the top resort was the Inner Moray Firth with an average of 1,450 (October), next best being Tentsmuir with 508 (September). 14 other sites regularly hold over 150. Ireland's top spots are Strangford Lough, with a five-year average of 269 (October) to 1990–91, Dundrum Bay averaging ▶

century and had probably been more or less continuously present since early times. By 1870 it was well established in the Scottish Highlands and islands and achieved major expansion circa 1885–1920 despite tremendous persecution from fishermen. Northern England was colonised in 1950, North Wales in 1953 and Derbyshire in 1973. Ireland, too, has seen considerable southerly range extension since 1900. While increase and range expansion are continuing in Wales and northern England, the population is now stable or increasing only slightly in its Scottish stronghold. There is spread towards the south-east, but persecution by fishermen is depressive in some areas, notably north-east Scotland.

Although the species has been protected in Britain since the passing of the Wildlife and Countryside Act 1981, licensed shooting is still permitted to protect the stock of fish hatcheries and farms. During the 14 months to December 1983 alone 523 were killed under licence in Scotland, and there seems little doubt that the true cull is far higher. There was very strong resistance to the merganser's removal from the quarry list, not because of the bird's modest sporting attraction but because of the significant economic loss it can cause where fish are concentrated. By four weeks old a merganser can take salmon and trout up to 10cm (3.9in) long, and these fish are frequently the main prey of both juvenile and adult on many angling waters. One study on Lake Windermere showed that mergansers hatched there each ate over 20kg (44.1lb) of fish in 100 days.

In 1898 a red-breasted merganser became the first wild duck to carry a leg-ring.

Distribution, Habitat and Population

The species' circumpolar breeding range stretches across Alaska and northern Canada, north to Baffin Island and south to the Great Lakes, around the coast of southern Greenland, much of Iceland, and throughout northern Eurasia from the northern British Isles and Denmark through most of Scandinavia and northern Russia to Siberia and the Bering Straits, south to Manchuria and northern Japan. In its breeding habitat requirements it is more adaptable than many other northerly duck, using tundra as well as forest zones as it is not dependent on trees. Nests are common along rivers with rocky bottoms and on sheltered lakes as well as by salt water, along inlets and estuaries and in shallow bays with sandy rather than muddy beds, especially where spits, islets, projecting banks and rocks are present.

In winter the merganser is predominantly marine yet still prefers enclosed waters in estuaries and sheltered bays. Some populations are only partly migratory but most overwinter well to the south of their breeding grounds. North American birds retreat to the Pacific coasts of Canada and the USA south to Mexico, and from the Gulf Coast north to Nova Scotia. Many also winter around the Great Lakes, even along the south-west coast of Greenland and all around Iceland. They are common around the shores of the British Isles and other North Sea countries as far as the North Cape of Norway. More easterly breeders winter around the Mediterranean, the Black and Caspian Seas, Kamchatka, southern Japan, Korea and China.

The species breeds widely throughout Scandinavia, and there are an estimated 10,000 pairs in Finland. Denmark has a small population, western Germany some 60–70 pairs, eastern Germany about 200–300 pairs, and the Netherlands only a handful of nesting records this century.

Field Characters

This slim bird has a grebe-like shape and noticeable, ragged crest extending from the hind crown. The thin, serrated bill has tooth-like protrusions to grip slippery prey, especially fish. The boldly marked male is easily identified by his red bill, bottle-green head and white neck collar contrasting with his black-spotted red-buff breast. In certain lights he can be confused with the male goosander, but that bird lacks the broad breast-band and ragged crest, has a stouter bill and less pronounced wing-bars. The female is far less striking and has a slightly shorter crest. Her head and upper neck are dull red-brown and, as with the dirty-grey upperparts, are not sharply demarcated from the rest of the body. The sides of her chest are mottled grey-brown, the centre paler. The female goosander is similar but has a crest which slopes noticeably downwards, more uniform grey upperparts and more sharply demarcated upper neck, the white being restricted to the chin. In eclipse, the male resembles the female, but his wing pattern is unchanged and back darker. The juvenile, too, resembles the adult female, but is generally darker grey and has a shorter crest.

The merganser swims and dives easily, using both wings and legs under water. It spends much of the year in moderate-sized flocks. Although poorly adapted for walking, it comes ashore quite frequently and often nests farther from water than most wildfowl. Take-off is laboured, producing a low, humming whistle, but flight is fast with even, powerful wing-beats.

Calls are mainly confined to the breeding season, the male courting with a loud, wheezy purr and the female utters a harsh, rasping *krrr krrr*.

Breeding

The monogamous pair-bond is of seasonal duration, most being formed in late winter or during the spring migration. The male usually deserts during incubation, though some males have been seen with females and ducklings. Polyandry and polygyny are rare. The male's dramatic courtship includes a salute-curtsey sequence, often performed by several birds simultaneously. In salute pose the bill, head and neck are extended diagonally. In curtseying the neck is lowered into the water, the bill opened widely while calling, the rear of the body raised awkwardly above the surface and the tail sharply depressed. But his most frequent display is skating across the surface.

Even during breeding, pairs often gather in large flocks and may nest colonially in areas of high density, especially on islands. There is no clear territory. The nest, never very far from water, is a shallow ground depression which the female lines with nearby grass and leaves, and down. Sites are among scrub and tree roots, in holes and crevices in cliffs, in banks and burrows, or among thick vegetation.

The female's 31/32-day incubation starts on completion of the clutch and hatching is synchronous. The young feed themselves but are cared for by the female and broods sometimes gather in crèches supervised by one mother. Independence is achieved at about 50 days and fledging is at 60–65 days. Age of first breeding is two years.

Diet and Feeding Behaviour

This specialist fish-eater spends much of its time 'snorkelling', with its head under

▶ 153, Cork Harbour and Galway Bay.

The British breeding population is estimated at over 2,200 pairs with some 800 pairs in Ireland. The greatest density is in Scotland, especially around sheltered west-coast waters. It is only thinly distributed over much of the central and eastern highlands. In Ireland it breeds west of a line from Bantry in west Cork to Dundalk in Louth. The only exception is south-east Wexford, where a few pairs nest. The bulk of the small English population is in the north-west, with an outpost in Derbyshire, which is the southerly limit. In Wales most records are from Anglesey and the north-west, with a few from Glamorgan.

The single clutch (replaced after loss) of 8–10 (6–14) blunt ovate, pale-grey to pale-olive eggs, average size 65 × 45mm (2.56 × 1.77in), is laid from late April in Britain, where the main period is May and early June. In Denmark laying commences late May and peaks during the first half of June. In Fenno-Scandia most clutches are laid mid-May to late June, but June is usually the earliest month in Iceland.

water to spot prey before diving. Most submersions are in water only a few metres (feet) deep and last less than 30 seconds, but over two minutes has been recorded. Larger prey is brought to the surface, but smaller items are swallowed underwater, especially at greater depth. Hunting is often co-operative, in pairs, flocks or lines driving prey forward into shallows. Most fish are less than 10cm (3.9in) long and often in shoals. Species include salmon, trout, eel, perch, lampreys, minnow, sticklebacks, pike, grayling, dace, chub, roach, flounder, butterfish, gobies, coalfish, sand-eel, cod, herring, blennies, smelt, sprat, pipefish and hake, from rivers, estuaries and coastal waters. There is no evidence that predation on young salmon has any significant effect on subsequent runs, but where fish are concentrated on farms economic loss may be serious.

Secondary items include crustaceans such as prawns, shrimps and crabs, molluscs, annelids, insects and their larvae, and the leaves, roots and seeds of aquatic plants. Some of these can be seasonally or locally important, especially insects for ducklings.

Movements

It seems likely that the bulk of British and Irish breeders winter around the coast close to their natal areas. However, many mergansers also winter away from any breeding areas, and ringing recoveries suggest that many of these — in England at least — come from Scandinavia, with smaller numbers from further east. Many Icelandic birds winter in northern Britain and Ireland. In exceptionally cold winters large numbers may briefly move inland.

In coastal areas numbers start to build up in July, with the flocking of moulting birds, often in hundreds at some Irish and Scottish sites. But the biggest known moulting flocks in Europe occur in Denmark, where some 8,000 or 12,000 gather at Limfjorden and are probably most fairly local birds.

RED-BREASTED MERGANSER

Although the autumn migration starts in September, some northern breeding grounds are not totally vacated before late October, when there is peak movement through the Baltic. Apparent segregation of the sexes in some areas is due to the tendency for females and young to migrate earlier and further than males, a characteristic of other diving ducks. For example, in the Baltic males often comprise over 50 per cent of flocks but probably under 20 per cent in Switzerland and among winter visitors to Britain. Some north-west European birds do not move far, many from Scandinavia and northern Germany wintering around the Baltic and as far north as the Arctic Circle. But many from the north-west of the former USSR, Finland, Baltic States and Poland migrate south-west or west to the Baltic, some beyond to the Netherlands and Britain. Few reach France, the main north and west European wintering area being Denmark and northern Germany. The spring return may start in late February in a mild year, but the main exodus is in March and more northerly birds may even not reach their breeding grounds before May.

Once known as sawbill, sawneb, sawyer, jacksaw, shell duck, green-headed goosander, gossander, pied wigeon, sparkling fowl, sparling fowl, harle, dun diver, rantock, land cormorant, spear duck, spear wigeon and common merganser

As it shares many of the old local names with the red-breasted merganser, the species is hard to trace in early literature. 'Goosander' is first recorded as 'gossander' in 1622, the current spelling being introduced by Ray in 1678, when the term was probably still used for both species. Origins of the name remain uncertain, one suggestion being derivation from the Scandinavian *gos* for goose and the Old Norse *ond* for drake, alluding to a goose-sized duck. The Latin *Mergus* denotes a diver, while *merganser* combines *mergus* and *anser* for goose.

GOOSANDER
(Mergus merganser)

IN many parts of its range the goosander is regarded as a pest which takes highly valued sport- and food-fish. Indeed, it is even more unpopular than the red-breasted merganser because, unlike its close relative, it favours fresh water and is seen as a serious threat to anglers and fish-farmers.

History and Conservation

Earliest British records are from the last two major glaciations, and it also occurred in Iron Age Somerset. It was probably continuously present throughout the Middle Ages and in good numbers until the advent of reliable guns, when its relative conspicuousness made it an easy target.

The goosander is very unpopular with fishermen because it can take substantial numbers of fish, which are predominant in its diet by the time it is 10 or 12 days old. At the age of four weeks it can take a 10cm (4in) salmon and experiments in captivity suggest that it takes 33kg (72.7lb) of fish to rear one goosander. None the less, it has yet to be shown whether goosander predation on young salmon parr has any significant effect on the number of fish returning to run up the rivers several years on.

The species appears to have become temporarily extinct as a British breeder by the mid-nineteenth century, the first nesting record being from Perthshire in 1871. Sustained colonisation of central Scotland followed a large influx in the winter of 1875–76. Highland counties and the Southern Uplands were claimed by the 1930s, northern England (Northumberland) was colonised in 1941, Ireland in 1969 and the Welsh uplands in 1972, and since 1980 several pairs have nested regularly in Devon. Increase and spread appear to be continuing in many areas despite sustained persecution. The species was not protected by the Protection of Birds Act 1954–67 and under the Wildlife and Countryside Act 1981 licensed shooting is permitted to enable fish hatcheries and farms to protect their stock. During the 14 months to December 1983 alone 347 goosanders were killed in this way in Scotland.

Internationally, the goosander's recent fortunes have been very mixed, with disappearance from some southern parts of the breeding range but increase in others. The effects of climatic amelioration 1850–1950 and subsequent cooling are hard to gauge against sustained habitat degradation and loss and reduction in prey through over-fishing and acidification of waters. One bright spot has been significant provision of nestboxes for this predominantly tree-nesting species, which has contributed to increase in some countries, notably Finland. Further expansion in southern Britain and Ireland seems likely.

Distribution, Habitat and Population

As it is mostly a tree-nester, the goosander avoids the tundra and breeds mainly in the boreal zone of the Old and New Worlds.

In North America it occurs from Alaska right across Canada to Newfoundland, south to the Great Lakes and down the Rockies to California. It is absent from Greenland, but breeds in Iceland and from northern Britain right across Scandinavia, northern Russia and Siberia to Manchuria, Japan and Kamchatka. Southerly outposts are in the Alps from France to southern Germany, and in Denmark, where there has been decline. Further east, there is a very isolated population in the central Asian plateau, where a separate race is recognised. North American birds differ from the main Eurasian population too, being of the subspecies *M.m.americanus*, which has a black bar across the white inner wing.

The Baltic area of the former USSR has some 1,400 pairs and Finland over 4,000 pairs. Sweden's population is apparently stable, while Norway's has declined. Other relatively recent estimates include Switzerland 140 pairs, Germany 150 pairs, France 35 pairs and Denmark 15–20 pairs.

As it is primarily a freshwater bird which cannot make use of relatively ice-free coasts, most goosanders must overwinter well to the south of their breeding areas. North American birds winter in the US but avoid the harsh interior. In Eurasia there are some notable winter concentrations at favoured feeding areas, such as the 15,000 birds on the Volga Delta, but in the main the species is well dispersed. The north-west European winter total is over 100,000. Some populations are largely resident, including that of the British Isles.

Unlike the predominantly coastal red-breasted merganser, the goosander favours the upper basins of rivers; large, clear, inland lakes among forests and mountains, and non-tidal or land-locked seas. Although warm water is avoided, it generally keeps clear of any ice. It also avoids luxuriant aquatic plant growth and, as its main requirement is a rich fish stock, water depth and flow are not usually limiting factors. However, in the breeding season suitable feeding grounds must be within reach of mature trees with hollows or alternative nest-sites. Even in winter, little use is made of marine areas, but then it does favour larger, deeper, more open waters, including reservoirs, canals and ornamental areas, despite widespread persecution. Seasonal abundance of marine fish, such as herring shoals in late summer, is exploited when they come inshore.

In 1977–8 the British breeding population was estimated at 925–1,250 pairs: 735–950 in Scotland, 180–290 in northern England and 10 in Wales. Since then there have been increases in many areas. In 1986 the Welsh population was put at about 100 pairs and throughout the 1980s 1–3 pairs nested in Devon. Ireland's first record was from Donegal in 1969, but since then breeding has been intermittent there with only one or two pairs confirmed nesting in some years, though other birds have been seen.

Field Characters

This is the largest of the sawbilled ducks, with a long, thin, red bill and generally noticeably bigger in head and body than the red-breasted merganser. The cleanly

The length averages 58–66cm (22.8–26in), wing-span 82–97cm (32.3–38.2in), and the average weights are 1,264–2,160g (2.8–4.7lb) for the male and 898–1,770g (1.9–3.9lb) the female.

GOOSANDER

marked male is especially striking, his dark-green head (with slight, rounded crest giving a bulbous appearance) and upper neck and black back contrasting with his white flanks and creamy-white underbody. Altogether, this is a much whiter bird than the male red-breasted merganser. However, more care needs to be taken in separating the females of the two species, the goosander being larger, with a darker chestnut head, ragged crest sloping down towards the back, chestnut foreneck with only the chin white, and generally cleaner-toned plumage. The non-breeding male recalls the female, but is much whiter on the sides and blacker above, with unchanged wing pattern. The juvenile, too, resembles the adult female, but has a shorter crest, weaker head colouring, less distinctively white throat and duller grey upperparts lacking the blue tone.

Gregarious for most of the year, the goosander often gathers in very large flocks on autumn migration or during winter. Its flight silhouette is more like a diver than a typical duck as its long bill, head and neck are balanced by a prominent tail to produce a cigar-shaped body. Take-off is laboured, but flight is fast and direct with powerful, even wing-beats producing a humming whistle. Groups do not adopt any regular flight formation. This bulky bird is buoyant and swims easily. On land, too, it is surprisingly agile.

The voice is used little, except in courtship or when alarmed. The displaying male utters a weak, twanging *uig-a* and a faint, high-pitched, bell-like note. The female's repertoire includes a harsh, threatening *karr karr*, sometimes developing into an excited, cackling *kokokokokok*, and in courtship a snorting *karr-r-r* given in flight. In addition, the half-closed wings produce a hollow, rushing sound when the bird plunges from height.

Breeding

The monogamous pair-bond is of seasonal duration, but occasional polygamy is likely. Pairing starts in November but mostly occurs in late winter and on spring migration. Most males desert during incubation but some have been seen with females accompanying young. Male courtship includes erecting the head feathers, wing-flaps and upward-shakes, ceremonial drinking, circling the female while calling and frequent skating across water with the neck slightly forward.

The goosander is quite gregarious on the breeding grounds and several females may search for a nest-site together, sometimes resulting in 3–4 (exceptionally to 10) nests in the same tree. Holes in banks and among rocks are used less frequently than tree hollows. In addition, nestboxes, holes beneath buildings and roof spaces of houses are readily adopted and sometimes used for many years in succession. Sites are usually close to feeding waters — along deep, fast streams as well as around lakes — but may be up to 1km (about half a mile) away. The female shapes a small hollow and lines it with nearby material and down.

The female's 30/32-day incubation starts on completion of the clutch and hatching is synchronous. After leaving the nest, the young may be taken a considerable distance to the main rearing area and broods may gather at high density. The ducklings feed themselves and become independent at about the same time as fledging, after 60–70 days. Age of first breeding is two years.

Diet and Feeding Behaviour

For their first 10–12 days the chicks depend on insects, but thereafter the diet is

primarily fish, obtained mainly by surface-diving, using only the feet for propulsion, in water to 4m (13ft) deep. The goosander spots most prey through foraging with its head underwater. In shallows fish may be chased and caught without diving but in deeper water the duck always dives — usually for less than 30 seconds, but sometimes for up to two minutes. Most fish are caught in clear water, where they are easily seen, but sometimes in turbid deeps, where they are caught by movement rather than sight. In pursuit the goosander holds its head and neck in front of the body, in a straight line. Prey is brought to the surface for swallowing, but may be consumed below in deep water, especially if small. The bill's backward-pointing 'teeth' make light work of seizing fish across the middle before they are deftly turned and swallowed head-first, and its length facilitates probing among stones. Sometimes birds feed co-operatively, apparently deliberately forming a line to drive fish forward into a confined area where they are caught more easily. Occasionally they up-end and feed opportunistically, for example in taking dead or dying fish caught in nets or turbines, or from gulls.

The variety and quantity of fish taken varies with locality and ease of access, which is something fish-farms should address to avoid the need to kill the birds. Preference for salmonids is apparent in some areas, but may be secondary where other species are abundant. In any event, gamefishermen should note that some predators of salmonids are also taken. Most prey are under 10cm (3.9in) long, the limiting factor being girth rather than length. Freshwater species and maximum recorded lengths taken include: salmon and trout 36cm (14.2in), eel 46cm (18.1in), pike 31cm (12.2in), minnows, perch, grayling, miller's thumb, roach, rudd, dace, carp 31cm (12.2in), barbel 30cm (11.8in) and bleak. Saltwater fish include: cod, gunnel, herring, sand-eel, plaice, blenny and gold-sinny. Secondary foods include insects and their larvae, crustaceans, molluscs, annelids, frogs, water-shrew and birds (unidentified). Plant materials are often found inside birds, but are probably taken accidentally or within prey.

The goosander (this is a female) is seen as a serious threat to anglers. Photo: Dennis Green

GOOSANDER

Movements

It is likely that at least three-quarters of the breeding population of Scotland and northern England, along with their offspring, mainly winter within 150km (90 miles) of their natal areas. No doubt those wintering in southern England and Wales include some northern British birds, especially in cold weather when northern waters are frozen, but ringing recoveries suggest that many are from Scandinavia, Russia and the Continent. Neither is there any evidence that the breeders of southern Scandinavia, north Germany and Poland are very mobile, many moving no further than the western Baltic. It is the breeders from the colder regions of central and northern Scandinavia, Finland, the Baltic States and Russia which must move long distances west to the Baltic, the Netherlands and Britain. Smaller numbers reach west France and north Spain. No Icelandic breeders have been recovered overseas.

Apart from a few hundred gathering on Novaya Zemlya, no marked moult migration or assembly is known in the west Palearctic, though there are many local moult movements. Many moulting and breeding waters are deserted in late August and early September as flocks gather on inland lakes and sheltered estuaries, especially where fish are temporarily concentrated. Most remain until the ice sets in, driving them south and west chiefly in October and early November. North Sea visitors arrive from late October, but the bulk not before December. Intensification of cold drives them ever further west so that Britain's peak count is often not until February. Most return in March and only stragglers remain in non-breeding areas in mid-April. Lingering cold may prevent birds returning to Lapland and northern Russia before May, but generally the goosander returns north earlier than most other wildfowl — even while shores are still icebound.

RUDDY DUCK
(*Oxyura jamaicensis*)

The species' English name comes from the colour of its plumage. The Latin *Oxyura* derives from the Greek *oxus* for sharp or pointed and *oura* for tail, the *Oxyurini* ducks being popularly known as stifftails. The Latin *jamaicensis* means 'belonging to Jamaica' (after Gmelin 1789), though the species is also native to many other countries.

BEFORE the 1950s this duck was found only in the New World. Then a small number escaped from a wildfowl collection in Gloucestershire. Since then the English population has increased dramatically and there are already reports from at least twelve European countries, bringing widespread fears of competition with native species.

History and Conservation

There is no early record of this species occurring naturally in Europe. The current feral population derives entirely from three hand-reared pairs and one drake imported in 1948 from Salt Lake City and Pennsylvania. Having already bred in captivity in North America, they soon settled down at the Wildfowl Trust's Slimbridge centre and started nesting in 1949. Unusually for wildfowl, the ducklings were difficult to rear by hand and it was soon found that better results were obtained through letting the parents take charge. As a result, each year some of the young easily managed to escape being caught and pinioned by the curator and about 70 juveniles flew away between 1956 and 1963.

172

The species has obviously found a vacant ecological niche in Britain. However, its surprising success has also been due to the early development of the ducklings and a prolonged breeding season, the latter factor also having been critical in the collared dove's remarkable world-wide range expansion. Unfortunately, there are well-founded fears of harmful competition with at least two other species. Perhaps less importantly, it competes with the common tufted duck for chironomid larvae in new static waters, but if it does well on the Continent it may displace or hybridise with the related white-headed duck, which is rare in Europe and currently the subject of a reintroduction programme in Hungary and Italy.

In North America the culinary qualities of the ruddy duck were discovered towards the end of the nineteenth century and thereafter huge numbers were shot, mostly for the market, before protective legislation was introduced. However, there have been few signs of recovery as there has been extensive drainage of the preferred shallow-water habitat. Currently the American population is estimated at between 0.5 million and 1 million birds.

Distribution, Habitat and Population

This stifftail's natural breeding range is in western Canada and the USA, with smaller scattered populations in eastern North America, parts of Central America and the West Indies, where there is a separate race; and in a fairly narrow strip right down western South America, where there are two further subspecies. North American birds winter south into Mexico and eastwards across the USA, and their migratory habit has already taken root in Europe.

In North America the natural habitat is more typical of grebes than ducks, chiefly centred on lowland wetlands with lush emergent vegetation and stretches of open water in areas with a temperate continental climate. Flowing fresh water is avoided, but some sluggish rivers are used. Estuaries and sheltered coasts are visited only rarely. As the duck takes most of its food through straining the ooze on lake bottoms, in Britain it has concentrated on shallow waters and impounded reservoirs.

Field Characters

At all times both sexes are distinguished by the dumpy shape, short neck, stiff tail, broad bill and prominent head, which give a top-heavy and weight-forward appearance. In summer the male is very conspicuous with rich-chestnut upperparts, upper breast and flanks contrasting with white cheeks, black cap and nape, bright-blue bill and silvery-white underparts. The breeding female is duller, with red-brown upperparts, but is readily distinguished by her blue-grey bill, dark-brown cap and nape, and pale-buff cheeks bisected by a sometimes faint brown line from the nape to the base of the bill. In winter the male retains his eclipse plumage, his chestnut turning dark-brown and grey, his bill greyer and crown browner. Then he resembles the winter female, but has white cheeks and a paler undertail. The juvenile resembles the adult winter female but is paler and duller, with less flank barring and an ill-defined cheek-line. The related white-headed duck is distinguished by its larger size, swollen bill base, much more white on the head of the male and more clearly defined cheek-stripe in the female.

Gregarious for much of the year, the ruddy duck sometimes forms flocks of thousands at undisturbed sites, but throughout the range parties of fewer than 50 are most common. It swims buoyantly, often with its tail cocked and the male

RUDDY DUCK

First wild breeding was recorded in Somerset in 1960 and by 1972 there were over 25 pairs nesting in the West Midlands. In 1984 there about 1,800 ducks nation-wide, rising to 2,700 in January 1989, including a flock of 1,064 on Chew Valley Reservoir in March, 1987. However, after initial rapid expansion, increase has slowed to some 10 per cent annum.

Northern Ireland was colonised in 1973, when there were four young on Lough Neagh. Scotland's first feral bird was spotted on Unst, Shetland, in 1974 and the country's first nest recorded in 1979, at the Loch of Kinnordy, Angus. Mainland Europe's first sighting came from Sweden in 1965. Now this aggressive duck is often seen on the Continent as birds from the English feral population, and possibly escapees from other collections, disperse and prospect for future nest-sites. Breeding was first recorded in France in 1988 and the species seems set to become a successful west Palearctic colonist.

The length averages 35–43cm (13.8–16.9in), wingspan 53–62cm (20.9–24.4in), and weight 540–795g (1.2–1.7lb) for the male, 310–650g (0.7–1.4lb) the female.

The male ruddy duck is sometimes known as the 'bluebill'. Photo: B. Martin

frequently with his throat and breast puffed out. This is a very aquatic species but when it must visit land it walks reasonably well despite the handicap of legs set well back. It is strong underwater and has the remarkable ability to submerge without actually diving. Like many diving specialists, it is reluctant to take wing, always preferring to sink out of sight or swim away at the approach of danger. The awkwardly placed legs make getting airborne difficult too, yet it flies well enough, with rapid wing-beats, usually close to the surface.

The few calls given are mostly linked with courtship and threat behaviour. Most of the male's sounds are non-vocal, especially in display (see breeding section), but he does utter a *quek* or a frog-like *quok*. The female, too, makes non-vocal sounds, as well as uttering *quaer* in display, a threatening hiss, a high-pitched squeak and a low, grating *raanh*.

Breeding

In Britain the breeding season is prolonged, reflecting the bird's near-tropical origins. The single clutch of 6–10 (up to 20 by more than one female) ovate, dull-white or creamy-white eggs, average size 62 × 46mm (2.44 × 1.81in), is laid any time from mid-April to early October, but mostly in June and July.

The typical extent and duration of the pair-bond remain in doubt. There is evidence of pairing from late winter until late spring and the male may form a series of temporary liaisons with a number of females rather than engage in seasonal monogamy. In Britain some males associate with females throughout in-cubation and even accompany those with broods, but these are not necessarily the pre-laying pairings and the most common pattern remains to be discovered. In his highly ritualised main display the male raises his ear-tufts to form a deep V and, with his tracheal air-sac fully inflated, he repeatedly beats the side of his breast, producing a rattling noise with his open bill and a series of non-vocal, hollow tapping sounds, sometimes ending with a low belch or grunt which may be due to deflation of the air-sac. This is known as a 'bubbling' display because the chest-beating creates many air bubbles on the water around the breast. The male also frequently cocks his stiff tail to flash the white under-feathers.

The ruddy duck (male upper, female lower) is from a group called 'stifftails'.

Nests are usually well scattered and in at least some instances the male and female select the site together. Well-defined territories are not apparent but the male is very aggressive around the nest, which is usually in thick aquatic vegeta-tion well out from the shore but not too near open water. Although both sexes construct resting platforms before breeding, only the female builds the nest — a

174

The main British range is still in England, the chief centres being in Avon, Staffordshire and Cheshire. But there has been relentless infilling and expansion west to Anglesey, east to Leicestershire and north to Scotland. Scottish records have been as far afield as Orkney, Aberdeen, Perth, Lanark, Berwick and Dumfries. In 1984 three broods were reared on the Loch of Strathbeg. In 1986 Ireland had at least eight nests, in Armagh, Donegal, Down and Tyrone. There has been no recent estimate of the British breeding population, but as wintering numbers have risen sharply since the early 1980s the figure must be substantially higher than the 1982 estimate of 200–250 pairs and could easily be double that.

In winter it occurs much more widely, but still chiefly in central England, dispersal of small numbers further afield, including the Continent, depending on the severity of the weather. The 1990–91 peak count for Britain was 3,087 (January), an increase of 9.2 per cent on 1989–90, with a further 34 (October) in Northern Ireland. Britain's main resorts and their average maxima 1986–91 were: Blithfield Reservoir 705, Chew Valley Lake 673, Rutland Water 442, Belvide Reservoir 261, Eyebrook Reservoir 236, Blagdon Lake 213, Woolston Eyes 125, Farmwood Pool 105, Stanford Reservoir 103, Swithland Reservoir 87, Llyn Penrhyn 84 and Llyn Traffwll 84.

platform of reeds, rushes and leaves with a shallow cup (sometimes lined with down) and woven around standing stems. The platform is raised if the water level rises.

The female starts her solo 25/26-day incubation on completion of the clutch and hatching is synchronous. The eggs are large and produce fat, vigorous young which can dive on their first day and often become independent well before fledging at 50–55 days. Because many hatch well into summer they are able to thrive on an abundance of underwater insects when there is little competition. Perhaps it is because of this precocity that the parent-young bond is often loose. Reports of male interest after hatching probably centre around the female only and it is she alone who effectively tends the young, albeit generally for a relatively short period. Age of first breeding is mostly two years, sometimes one.

Diet and Feeding Behaviour

The ruddy feeds like that other spatulate-billed duck, the shoveler, but underwater rather than on the surface. This omnivorous species takes mainly insect larvae and aquatic plant seeds through surface-diving and then straining the ooze on the bottom. It swims over a lake bed sweeping its outstretched head and neck from side to side while opening and closing its bill in a rapid straining action. Sometimes it skims the surface, arching its outstretched head and neck with the bill half immersed. As is common among diving species, which are particularly dependent on light in food location, most feeding is by day. Preferred water depth is about 1m (3ft), thus avoiding competition with up-ending surface-feeders.

In the natural range, the diet varies considerably with seasonal and local abundance, so that either plant or animal foods may predominate. In many samples the chief items are seeds and tubers of aquatic plants or chironomid larvae and pupae. Other foods include leaves and stems of pondweeds, a wide variety of insects, crustaceans, molluscs, annelids and nematodes. Although plant material may provide some three-quarters of the diet by volume, its nutritive value is proportionately low compared with animal items. Thus ducklings may take 100 per cent chironomids to maximise growth rate. Overall, bottom-living invertebrates appear to be the mainstay of the diet in Britain.

Movements

The species is mostly migratory in North America, leaving the bulk of its breeding range to winter in the Atlantic, Gulf and Pacific states of the USA, Mexico and Central America. Most Central and South American birds are resident.

In Britain, the introduced population is resident but, remarkably, has already established a pattern of seasonal movements, which are almost entirely noctural and mostly up to 70km (some 40 miles). After their late-summer moult, most birds start to leave their small breeding pools and marshes and assemble in areas such as the Cheshire and Shropshire meres before leaving to winter on favoured large reservoirs. Flocks generally peak in January and mostly disperse in March and April, but many winter within the breeding range. In hard winters small numbers may disperse more widely in all directions, some reaching the Continent.

Unlike other British wildfowl, this duck has a complete pre-breeding moult, mostly in February and March, when many of the flightless birds remain at the chief winter sites. Others return to their breeding haunts for this feather change.

VAGRANTS AND ESCAPES

In addition to the species described in the preceding main accounts, there are others whose presence in the wild in north-west Europe is very irregular or accidental. Some of these so-called vagrants are Palearctic or Eurasian migrants which wander off course during their annual north-south travels. Others are Nearctic or transatlantic vagrants, which arrive here only after remarkable ocean crossings of up to 5,000km (3,100 miles), though some stop off at Greenland and Iceland along the way. Their arrival often follows exceptional cold or wind and sometimes they get caught up in flocks of other species, which may help pinpoint their origin and thus establish genuine wildness. In some cases identification is very difficult because of great similarity with subspecies which ordinarily reside in north-west Europe (sometimes leading to their being shot by mistake). Even where positive sightings are made, acceptance is often tempered with the proviso that the birds may be escapes as there are so many waterfowl collections in Europe. Most regularly occurring escaped species are listed below but there are others on Britain's feral list, including some 77 bar-headed geese and 21 emperor geese. Not all populations are self-supporting. Many vagrant species appear to be increasing in number, but this may be partly attributable to the growing number of expert bird-watchers. But whatever the case, it is great fun to watch for these birds.

NOTE: Details of vagrants which are races of species otherwise regularly occurring in north-west Europe are given under main accounts. Notes on accidentals outside north-west Europe are not given unless relevant.

AMERICAN WIGEON
(Anas americana)

This North American breeder is accidental in the British Isles, Iceland, Germany and Norway. In 1990 there were 17 records for the British Isles, mostly in Scotland (first 1907) and northern England, bringing the total to 234. In Ireland there were three to 1966 and 26 1966–88. Some records are of escapes. The male is readily distinguished from the European wigeon (*A.penelope*) by his white forehead and crown, wide bottle-green eye-stripe, black-speckled grey lower head and mainly pink-brown rather than grey body. The females are much more difficult to distinguish, but the head of the European wigeon is brown whereas the American species' is greyer and more boldly marked, as are her wing-coverts.

BAIKAL TEAL
(Anas formosa)

This north-east Siberian breeder is accidental in Finland, Sweden, Germany, the Netherlands, Belgium, Britain and Ireland (6 accepted records from 1954 (first) to 1990), France and Switzerland. Many records are suspect as the species is commonly kept in waterfowl collections. The beautiful male has a distinctive harlequin head pattern of green, yellow, black and white, soft-grey flanks, a pink-brown breast and buff-and-brown plumes cascading from the back. The female is much more sombre, with generally brown upperparts and pale underparts, but is distinguished by a circular white patch at the front of the cheek and dark-brown lines almost forming a cross through the eye.

BLACK DUCK
(Anser rubripes)

This North American breeder is accidental in the British Isles and Scandinavia. Within the British Isles there were 18 records from the first in 1954 to the end of 1990. Both sexes resemble a very dark-brown female mallard, from which they are best distinguished by the contrasting silvery-white underwings, more contrasting head and near absence of white on the upperwings and tail. There are escapes and mallard hybrids to confound the observer.

BLUE-WINGED TEAL
(Anas discors)

This North American breeder is accidental in Britain, Ireland, France, Belgium, the Netherlands, Denmark, Sweden and Germany. Many records are believed to be of escapes, especially in Britain and Ireland, where there are only a few in most years. To 1990 there were 167 accepted records for the British Isles. In 1988 a female paired with a male shoveler in Cambridgeshire and reared three young. The male is readily distinguished by his blue-purple head with a large white crescent in front of the eye, pale-blue forewing and boldly brown-spotted body. The female resembles the female garganey but she too has the blue forewing.

BUFFLEHEAD
(Bucephala albeola)

This North American breeder is accidental in the British Isles (only 7 records to the end of 1990) and Iceland. The male is like a small goldeneye, from which it is separated by a broad band of white around the back of the head. The female's best field mark is the oblong white patch across the cheek on a dark grey-brown head.

FERRUGINOUS DUCK
(Aythya nyroca)

This species breeds widely through central Eurasia but only patchily in southern and eastern Europe, with unstable outposts in southern France, Iberia and Italy. There are a few records of breeding in the Netherlands (11 1856–1969), Belgium and western Germany, some involving escapes. It is accidental in Britain and Ireland (though only annual, in small numbers, in England), Norway, Denmark, Sweden, Finland and Belgium. The sexes are similar and best distinguished by the

Bufflehead ♀ ♂

Ferruginous duck ♂

Lesser scaup ♀ ♂

Hooded merganser ♀ ♂

Ring-necked duck ♀ ♂

White-headed duck ♀ ♂

Wood duck
(also known as Carolina) ♀ ♂

Spectacled eider ♀ ♂

female's lack of the white eye, which earned the old name 'white-eyed pochard'. Both are a warm chestnut on the head, neck, breast and flanks, with a brownish-black back and distinctive white undertail (beware confusion with female tufted duck, which is separated by its rounded crown).

HOODED MERGANSER
(Mergus cucullatus)

This North American breeder is accidental in the British Isles (only 6 accepted records to the end of 1990) and continental north-west Europe. The handsome male is unmistakable with his erectile, fan-shaped, black-tipped, white crest; white breast edged with two vertical black stripes, red-brown flanks and black back. The female slightly resembles the female goosander and red-breasted merganser, which are separated by their longer, reddish bills and flatter, more ragged crests.

LESSER SCAUP
(Aythya affinis)

This North American freshwater species was first recorded in the British Isles in 1987. To the end of 1990 only three individuals had been recorded, in Northern Ireland and Nottinghamshire. It is difficult to distinguish from the greater scaup (*Aythya marila*), but the crown of the lesser is almost crest-like and peaks at the rear whereas the greater has the peak well forward and a downward sloping hind crown. The greater's bill is proportionately larger. In flight both sexes may be separated by the wing-bar, which is white right across in the greater but grey-brown on the outer wing of the lesser, giving the impression of a white speculum.

RED-BREASTED GOOSE
(Branta ruficollis)

A north-central Siberian breeder which winters in south-east Europe and is accidental in Britain, the Netherlands, Norway, Finland, Sweden, Germany and Austria. This is Europe's rarest goose. To the end of 1990 there were 39 accepted records for Britain, mostly in England (first bred in captivity at Woburn in 1926). There are also many escapes from wildfowl collections. The sexes are similar.

RING-NECKED DUCK
(Aythya collaris)

This North American breeder is accidental in Britain (first reliable European record 1955), Ireland (first record 1959), France, Belgium, the Netherlands, Iceland, Norway, Germany and Switzerland. Many records are thought to involve escapes. To the end of 1990 there were 297 well-dispersed records for the British Isles. Superficially like the tufted duck, the male is black, with a peaked, triangular purple-black head, clearly demarcated grey flanks and white belly and a mainly grey bill which is banded white and tipped black. The generally brown female is best recognised by her 'spectacles' which form a distinct white eye-ring and narrow line behind.

RUDDY SHELDUCK
(Tadorna ferruginea)

This bird breeds widely in Eurasia, from south-east Europe east to China, and in North Africa. It is accidental in Britain, Ireland, Iceland, France, Belgium, the Netherlands, Denmark, Germany, Norway, Sweden, Finland, Switzerland and Austria. In the British Isles all the recent records are considered to be of captive origin (it is often kept in wildfowl collections) and it was last recorded in an apparently wild state in 1946 (Ireland). Both sexes are easy to identify with their goose-like shape, orange-chestnut body, paler head and white wing-coverts.

SNOW GOOSE
(Anser caerulescens)

A breeder of north-east Siberia, arctic North America and north-west Greenland which is accidental in the British Isles, Iceland, the Faeroes, the Netherlands, Norway, Finland, Denmark, France, Belgium and Germany. Escapes from British and European wildfowl collections are common so it is almost impossible to establish its true status. The all-white western race (the lesser snow goose — *A.c.caerulescens*) is among the most unmistakable of wildfowl, though may be confused with Ross's goose (distinguished by much smaller size and triangular blue-based bill), which also frequently escapes from wildfowl collections. The eastern race (the greater snow goose — *A.c.atlanticus*) is like *caerulescens* but has a bulkier body, longer legs and longer and heavier bill. The dark morph, known as the blue snow goose, has most of the hindneck and all of the upperparts grey, marked black and tinged blue on the mantle and scapulars, contrasting with white head, foreneck and upper tail-coverts, dark-grey tail with white rim and grey/ white underparts. There are also many hybrids between the morphs. The sexes are alike, though the male is a little larger. It is almost annual in Scotland and Ireland, but less often in England. Both races occur in the British Isles in a feral population of 150.

SPECTACLED EIDER
(Somateria fischeri)

This north-east Siberian and Alaskan breeder is accidental in Norway and north-west Russia. There are no accepted records for the British Isles. It is the ugliest of the eiders, both sexes having distinctive, goggle-like eye-patches and a massive frontal shield above the bill. The male is further distinguished from the considerably larger common eider by his orange bill and green hind crown and nape. The female's general colouring is very similar to that of the female common eider, but with less distinct barring and buff eye-patches.

SURF SCOTER
(Melanitta perspicillata)

A North American breeder which is accidental in Britain, Ireland, France, Finland, Sweden, Norway, Denmark, the Faeroes, Iceland, the Netherlands and Belgium. Most records are in autumn and winter, but in Finland and Sweden mostly May and June, indicating that they may arrive with velvet scoters, with which they commonly associate. In the British Isles it is virtually annual (14 being recorded in 1990, bringing the total to 363) and widespread, but chiefly in Orkney and Shetland. There has been marked recent increase in Ireland. At close range the adult male is easily separated from the other scoters by the bill pattern and the white patches on the forehead and nape. If the female's lack of a white wing-patch cannot be established, she may still be distinguished from the velvet scoter by her bill shape and pale nape-patch. The smaller common scoter has faster wing-beats. As these birds are not kept in waterfowl collections there is no reason to suppose that they are not genuinely wild. See painting on page 147.

WHITE-HEADED DUCK
(Oxyura leucocephala)

The species has a much-fragmented breeding range around the Mediterranean (including Spain) and in central Eurasia. It has bred in Italy, Greece and Rumania. Now accidental in the Netherlands, Germany, Austria, Portugal, Belgium and Switzerland. It is being reintroduced to Hungary and Italy using eggs laid in England, through a scheme organised by the Wildfowl and Wetlands Trust. Both sexes are easily recognised by the large, predominantly white head and deep-based bill (pale blue in male) contrasting with the rufous/brown body.

WOOD DUCK
(Aix sponsa)

A numerous North American breeder, commonly kept in captivity in Europe, where most records almost certainly involve escapes. Britain has small feral populations in the Lake District, East Anglia and south-east England, though these may not be self-supporting. The attractive male has a bright, orange-red bill and eye, black head patterned with lines of white, a large green crest, white-spotted chestnut breast, lemon-coloured flanks and a bottle-green back. The duller, brown-grey female has spotted underparts and a white eye-patch. She is easily confused with the female mandarin, but is darker and glossier above and has more white around the eye.

Red-breasted goose ♂♀

Snow goose ♂♀

Ruddy shelduck

Snow goose, blue phase ♂♀

American wigeon

Baikal teal

Black duck

Blue-winged teal

FLIGHT SILHOUETTES

Familiarity with flight silhouettes is always useful to help identify birds at long distance and in poor light, but especially so with wildfowl because they tend to be very active in the half-light of dawn and dusk. Therefore, it is well worth studying their profiles shown here, especially in conjunction with the text notes on flight characteristics, calls and behaviour. To help further, closely-related species are pictured together to allow comparison of size as well as profile. Armed with this information, positive identification of that fleeting shadow or distant skein crossing the sunset will be made much easier.

Long-tailed duck

Velvet Scoter

Harlequin

Surf scoter

Common scoter

Pochard

Red-crested pochard

Tufted duck

Scaup

Eider

Ruddy duck

Steller's eider

Goosander

King eider

Red-breasted merganser

Smew

Barrow's goldeneye

Goldeneye

Whooper swan

Mute swan

Bean goose

Bewick's swan

Pink-footed goose

White-fronted goose

Lesser white-fronted goose

Greylag goose

Brent goose

Canada goose

Barnacle goose

Shelduck

Egyptian goose

Mandarin

Teal

Garganey

Gadwall

Shoveler

Mallard

Wigeon

Pintail

FURTHER READING AND MAIN REFERENCES

Albin, E. *A Natural History of Birds*, London 1731–58.

Atkinson-Willes, G.L. *Wildfowl in Great Britain* (HMSO, 1963).

Batten, L.A., Bibby, C.J., Clement, P., Elliot, G.D., and Porter, R.F. (editors) *Red Data Birds in Britain* (Poyser, 1990).

Bewick, T. *A History of British Birds* (Walker, 1799 and 1821).

Bewick, T. *Supplement of Rarer Species to the History of British Birds* (Walker, 1821).

Bird Study, the journal of the British Trust for Ornithology, The Nunnery, Nunnery Place, Thetford, Norfolk IP24 2PU.

Birds, quarterly journal of the Royal Society for the Protection of Birds, The Lodge, Sandy, Beds.

Birdwatching, a popular monthly magazine, published by EMAP, Bretton Court, Bretton, Peterborough PE3 8DZ. Includes regular regional bird reports.

Birkhead, M. & Perrins, C. *The Mute Swan* (Croom Helm, 1986).

British Birds, Fountains, Park Lane, Blunham, Bedford MK44 3NJ. This excellent independent monthly magazine often includes detailed papers and notes on wildfowl and reports of rare birds.

Campbell, Bruce, and Lack, Elizabeth (eds) *A Dictionary of Birds* (Poyser, 1985).

Cramp, Stanley (chief editor) *Handbook of the Birds of Europe, the Middle East and North Africa* vol 1 (Oxford University Press 1977, reprinted 1988).

Delacour, J. *The Waterfowl of the World*, (Country Life, 1954).

Gesner, Conrad *Historiae Animalium* (1555).

Gooders, John *Ducks of Britain and the Northern Hemisphere* (Dragon's World, 1986).

Gotch, A.F. *Birds — Their Latin Names Explained* (Blandford Press, 1981).

Greenoak, Francesca *All the Birds of the Air* (André Deutsch, 1979).

Harrison, Colin *The History of the Birds of Britain* (Collins/Witherby, 1988).

Hutchinson, Clive *Birds In Ireland* (Poyser, 1989).

Ibis, the quarterly journal of the British Ornithologists' Union, c/o British Museum (Natural History), Sub Dept of Ornithology, Tring, Herts HP23 6AP.

Kear, Janet *Man and Wildfowl* (Poyser, 1990).

Kirby, J.S., Ferns, J.R., Waters, R.J. and Prys-Jones, R.P. *Wildfowl and Wader Counts 1990–91* (Wildfowl & Wetlands Trust, 1991).

Knox, A.G. (compiler) *Checklist of Birds of Britain and Ireland*, (British Ornithologists' Union, 1992).

Lack, Peter (compiler) *The Atlas of Wintering Birds in Britain and Ireland* (Poyser, 1986).

Lever, Christopher *Naturalized Birds of the World* (Longman, 1987).

Lever, Christopher *The Mandarin Duck* (Shire Publications, 1990).

Lockwood, W.B. *The Oxford Book of British Bird Names* (OUP, 1984).

Long, J.L. *Introduced Birds of the World* (Sydney: Reed, 1981).

Marchant, J.H., Hudson, R., Carter, S.P., Whittington, P. *Population Trends in British Breeding Birds* (BTO/NCC, 1990).

Martin, B.P. *Sporting Birds of the British Isles* (David & Charles, 1984; revised and reissued as *Sporting Birds of Britain and Ireland*, 1992).

Martin, B.P. *World Birds* (Guinness, 1987).

Morris, Rev F.O. *A History of British Birds* (Groombridge, 1850).

Ogilvie, M.A. *Wild Geese* (Poyser, 1978).

Owen, Myrfyn *Wild Geese of the World* (Batsford, 1980).

Owen, Myrfyn *The Barnacle Goose* (Shire Publications, 1990).

Owen, Myrfyn and Black, J.M. *Waterfowl Ecology* (Blackie, 1990).

Pennant, Thomas *British Zoology, 1768*.

Ray, John *The Ornithology of Francis Willughby, translated into English and enlarged, 1678*.

Sharrock, J.T.R (compiler) *The Atlas of Breeding Birds in Britain and Ireland* (Poyser, 1977).

Swinton, W.E., *Fossil Birds* (British Museum, 1958).

Thom, Valerie *Birds in Scotland* (Poyser, 1986).

Wildfowl, annual publication of the Wildfowl & Wetlands Trust, Slimbridge, Glos. Contains a good selection of scientific papers.

Wildfowl & Wetlands, biannual magazine of the Wildfowl & Wetlands Trust.

ACKNOWLEDGEMENTS

My very special thanks to Alastair Proud for producing such an accurate, yet wonderfully evocative set of main paintings, as well as the studies of vagrants and helpful flight silhouettes. My thanks also to all the photographers credited. Few people realise just how good an ornithologist you have to be to get pictures of this quality. Finally, my thanks to David & Charles editor Tim Jaycock, and once again to my wife Carol for her help and encouragement in so many directions.

INDEX

Numbers in *italics* indicate illustrations